Toward A Federal Policy On Education And Work

By Barry E. Stern
Office of Deputy Assistant Secretary for
Education/Policy Development

March 1977

U.S. DEPARTMENT OF HEALTH, EDUCATION, AND WELFARE

Joseph Califano, Jr., Secretary
Education Division

Mary F. Berry, Assistant Secretary for Education

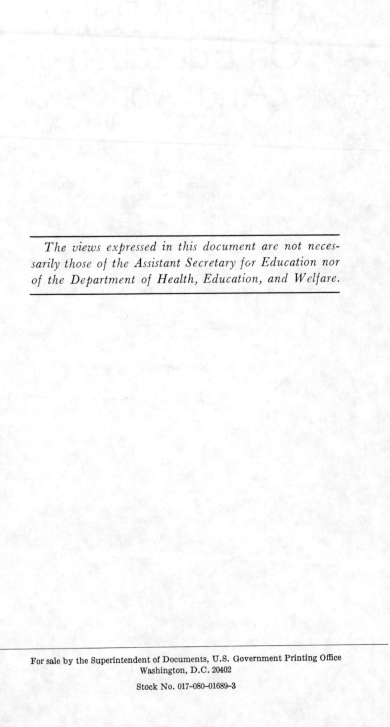

The views expressed in this document are not necessarily those of the Assistant Secretary for Education nor of the Department of Health, Education, and Welfare.

For sale by the Superintendent of Documents, U.S. Government Printing Office
Washington, D.C. 20402

Stock No. 017–080–01689–3

Foreword

One of the prominent themes in American education today is the relationship between education and work. This volume describes various aspects of the relationship for both youths and adults, identifies problems, and points the direction for future Federal policy in this area. Though the document is directed to Federal concerns, it is useful, also, to policymakers at the State and local levels who must cope with the same problems. In addition, it provides researchers with broad hints about new kinds of data and analysis which are needed for more refined policy formulation.

Too often, discussions of this controversial subject are polemical rather than informative, lack clarity because of the use of imprecise nomenclature, and lack comprehensiveness and cohesion among the various parts. Happily, this document avoids these pitfalls. Instead, it objectively marshals data to help us describe problems and estimate the consequences of alternative solutions. Moreover, it attempts to integrate specific proposals into a theoretically consistent framework of change. Though few would disagree that a reasoned overall philosophy should guide change, such philosophies often are not based on a rigorous examination of data which indicate what people want and how well they are served by what has been provided already. This volume is significant in that it is an exception to this rule.

"Toward a Federal Policy on Education and Work" examines the nexus of these two important facets of life from a data-rich perspective. It is a well-written, organized, and coherent document which provides a much-needed philosophical buttressing to the concept we have come to call "transitioning." There is considerable documentation about the extent and effectiveness of Federal activity in this area which will be useful to other analysts with similar concerns. Also appreciated is the clear statement of problems and issues, various alternatives for problem resolution, and several directly presented recommendations.

This volume is intended to provoke discussion and stimulate debate about what the Federal role should be in improving the articulation of education and work. Such a dialog is particularly appropriate at a time when the Federal Government is examining such management reforms as zero-based budgeting to make the delivery of services more effective and efficient. The application of new management practices without an informed discussion of the issues could have undesirable results, for these practices tend to focus on what already exists and not on what could be. Management reform, then, should proceed concurrently with policy planning and analysis for optimal results. We hope this document by Barry Stern will be among those that encourage movement in this direction.

PHILIP E. AUSTIN,
Deputy Assistant Secretary for Education,
U.S. Department of Health, Education, and Welfare.

Preface

Since the early 1970's the absence of a systematic and fruitful relationship between education and work has been identified as a problem by the Federal Government. Evidence of this concern is seen in the passage and implementation of career education legislation, a Presidential speech on the subject, and the establishment of the Interagency Task Force on Education and Work, involving the U.S. Departments of Health, Education, and Welfare; Commerce; and Labor. Generally, these activities were intended to: (1) Make education more experiential, so that students would have greater awareness of and involvements with work and workplaces; (2) encourage communities, especially business and labor, to take greater responsibility for the education of the young by cooperating and collaborating with the schools; and (3) make employers and workers more receptive to what they could learn from the education community in facing the problems of production and the quality of life.

Under the banner of *career education* or *education and work*, a considerable amount of activity has been undertaken by both the public and private sectors. Now that the movement is well underway, it is timely to assess progress toward achieving goals and whether action so far is pointed in the right direction. This document attempts to identify current issues in the area of education and work and then determine whether and to what extent current Federal, State, and local programs are addressing these issues.

After a brief introduction, the monograph is divided into two parts: (I) Youths and (II) Adults. Part I concerns the problems that youths face in making a successful transition from school to work. After the problems are identified, an attempt is made to assess the effectiveness of current programs, especially Federal programs, in addressing these problems. Then program options are set forth by problem area along a continuum from minimal to considerable Federal involvement and support. Finally, some very general considerations for implementation are stated.

Part II concerns the problems which adults face in finding opportunities to change their career or life directions if they should so desire. The section focuses on the job-shortage problem and how it is related to the access of educational and leisure opportunities throughout life. A suggestion is made to achieve greater flexibility in working life through a more equitable distribution of work, leisure, and education between the younger, middle-aged, and older population groups. In this regard, some policy recommendations of modest magnitude are made which would provide the kinds of information needed before contemplating more dramatic steps.

Three caveats are in order in the consideration of this monograph for Federal policy planning. First, the document should be viewed as a pointer or direction finder, not a plan. Detailed planning with respect to implementing any of the program options or recommendations is a step which would follow decisions by policymakers to select among the options. Second, it is acknowledged that preparation for employment is not the sole purpose of education. The intention here is not to suggest that this particular goal should receive greater priority than other legitimate educational goals, but that certain policies be adopted which would allow it to finally attain a place among the most important. Third, and finally, this monograph presents judgments about spending priorities within the context of the education and work budget in the Department of Health, Education, and Welfare. It attempts to determine the most effective use of resources that are normally committed to this area. This document does not attempt to make tradeoffs or establish priorities among the various parts of the education budget, nor does it put the Department of Health, Education, and Welfare (HEW) in budget competition with other Federal agencies which also commit resources to improve the relationship between education and work. It is merely a planning tool (not a plan) for HEW in this particular area. It identifies problems, estimates the aggregate effectiveness programs to resolve these problems, and suggests what else might be done to improve the situation. As such, the document focuses on the what should be done and why, while leaving, for the most part, the issue of organizational location of new programs to policymakers.

The writer is indebted to a number of people both within and outside of the Department of Health, Education, and Welfare (HEW) who reviewed and commented upon portions of the draft or provided valuable data and research evidence which were incorporated into the paper. A labored recital of all the particular contributions of these individuals would fill many pages. Let it suffice to mention their names in alphabetical order and their respective organizational affiliations.

Paul Andrisani, Temple University
Deborah Ashford, Bureau of Occupational and Adult Education, U.S.
    Office of Education

Philip Austin, Deputy Assistant Secretary for Education, U.S. Department of Health, Education, and Welfare
Paul Barton, National Manpower Institute
Fred Best, Consultant to the Office of the Assistant Secretary for Education
Ronald Bucknan, National Institute of Education
Robert Calvert, National Center for Education Statistics
Marjorie Chandler, National Center for Education Statistics
Thomas Corcoran, Fund for the Improvement of Postsecondary Education
Salvatore Corrallo, Office of Planning, U.S. Office of Education
Leroy Cornelsen, Bureau of Occupational and Adult Education, U.S. Office of Education
Lois-ellin Datta, National Institute of Education
Paul Delker, Bureau of Occupational and Adult Education
Richard Devlin, Office of the Secretary of Labor
Marguerite Follett, Women's Program Staff, U.S. Office of Education
Marcia Freedman, Columbia University
Joseph Froomkin, Consultant to the Office of the Assistant Secretary for Education
Evelyn Ganzglass, Employment and Training Administration, Department of Labor
Mary Golladay, National Center for Education Statistics
John Grasso, West Virginia University
Howard Hjelm, Bureau of Occupational and Adult Education
Ken Hoyt, Director, Office of Career Education, U.S. Office of Education
Robert Maroney, Office of Planning, U.S. Office of Education
Arthur Melmud, National Institute of Education
Jean Miller, National Institute of Education
David O'Neill, Center for Naval Analysis
Richard Pesqueira, Office of the Secretary of Labor
Beatrice Reubens, Columbia University
Corinne Rieder, National Institute of Education
Justine Rodriguez, Office of the Secrteary of Health, Education, and Welfare
Alice Scates, Office of Planning, U.S. Office of Education
Arthur Sheekey, Office of the Assistant Secretary for Education
Dorothy Shuler, Office of Planning, U.S. Office of Education
Gregory Smith, National Manpower Institute
Marshall Smith, National Institute of Education
Robert Stump, National Institute of Education

Of this group, special thanks are extended to Paul Barton, Leroy Cornelsen, Joseph Froomkin, John Grasso, Beatrice Reubens, Justine Rodriguez, Gregory Smith, and Robert Stump for their careful reading of early drafts and suggestions which helped shape the final product.

BARRY E. STERN, Ph.D.,
Office of the Assistant Secretary
for Education.

March 1977.

Contents

Charts

EXECUTIVE SUMMARY: ARTICULATION OF EDUCATION AND WORK

BACKGROUND

Beginning with the original Land-Grant Colleges Act (First Morrill Act) of 1862, the Federal Government has attempted to legislate a closer relationship between education and work. The purpose of the Land-Grant Colleges Act and associated legislation passed later was to develop a new kind of collegiate institution that would be responsive to the economic and social needs of individual States and communities. Moreover, the legislation sought to blend a liberal education with scientific-technical education by encouraging research and experimentation to resolve problems of local agricultural and industrial production.

The Smith-Hughes Act of 1917 carried the spirit of the land-grants colleges' legislation to the Nation's secondary schools by establishing vocational education programs with training authorized in agriculture, home economics, and trade and industrial occupations. The National Defense Acts passed in 1941–43 and the subsequent George-Barden Act of 1946 expanded the eligible fields of instruction and supported the training of war workers and returning veterans. In 1962, the Manpower Development and Training Act (MDTA) and then the Vocational Education Act (VEA) of 1963 greatly enlarged the Federal role in supporting vocational education programs, with special attention to groups which had not been served adequately. Based on analyses of the effects of the 1963 act, Congress passed the 1968 amendments to it which required States to set aside portions of their grants to serve the disadvantaged, handicapped, and postsecondary school populations. The amendments also established other categorical programs under special authorization (e.g., home economics and consumer education, cooperative education, research and exemplary projects, etc.), but these are consolidated somewhat under the Education Amendments of 1976.

In 1974 the Federal Government supplemented its vocational education programs with demonstration career education programs which intended to give all students a better understanding of work. Unlike the specific occupational training typical of vocational education and appropriate only for some students, career education programs attempt to provide information and experience to all youths on a wide selection of work options so that their choices will be more consistent with personal values, goals, and capabilities.

Current Federal expenditures on education and work total about $700 million per year with almost all allocated to vocational education. With the help of these Federal dollars, the 1965–75 decade has witnessed a steady increase in the number of vocational education students—to the point that in 1976, more than one-third of the Nation's high school students were enrolled in such programs.

Despite steadily increasing financial support for vocational, career, and adult education programs and the high public expectations regarding the contribution of education to success in worklife, evidence is accumulating that young people leaving school are still not well prepared for the adult world and that there is little incentive provided by the labor market for many youths to become well prepared. Along with appropriate skills and a sufficient number and variety of occupational opportunities to reward their evident interest in work, youths need factual information about the realities of the labor market so that they may be able to make personally satisfying career-entry decisions. For adults, the problems are more complex and involve finding more opportunities to change their career or life directions if they should so desire. A more detailed analysis of the problems of youth and adults with policy recommendations follow.

YOUTH: THE SCHOOL-TO-WORK TRANSITION

Behavioral and attitudinal data suggest that young people are seriously interested in work. The labor force participation rates of teenagers continue to increase (except during the recent recession when the rates declined for males, especially black males). Teenage unemployment rates, which also serve as an indicator of desire to work, have remained high despite a rapidly expanding number of youth jobs and a slightly higher number of jobs per capita for the 16- to 19-year-old cohort. High school students overwhelmingly rate being successful in work as their most important life goal, and they want more work-relevant curriculums and help from the school in obtaining work experience. Other attitudinal studies have shown that not only are work values strong (and possibly getting stronger) among both college and noncollege youth, but also that young people today are concerned less about money and more about whether the work they do is socially useful.

Problem

Having been socialized successfully to accept work, a significantly large minority of youths are denied access to it or have difficulty in obtaining the financial and psychological rewards from work that society and their parents have led them to expect. The inability of youths, especially older youths, to find work, or work that a person would enjoy or respect, can result in their being negatively labeled, which, in turn, can result in feelings of alienation and withdrawal from basic societal institutions. Youths who no longer feel they have a "stake" in society are more likely to commit deviant acts.

There is little solid evidence, however, that not being able to find suitable work is related to such symptoms of youth discontent as higher rates of delinquency, drug abuse and alcoholism, and suicide. The limited evidence available suggests that for youths 17 years of age and under, access to occupational roles is of no significance as a determinant of juvenile delinquency. If anything, juvenile delinquency (age 10 to 17) fluctuates with the level of economic activity; i.e., it rises during periods of economic growth and slackens off during recessions. Though occupational identity is thought to become important around ages 18 to 22, there are no national time series data with which to test (for this cohort) the relationship between delinquency and fluctuations in employment opportunity. Drawing policy conclusions from the myriad of available studies is hampered further by inadequate measures of crime and juvenile delinquency, and of the quality of the work experience itself.

Not being able to find suitable work is a problem having both quantitative and qualitative aspects. Not being able to find any work is a problem for minority youths in cities, where their unemployment rates are fully twice that of whites. Reasons for their excessively high unemployment rates include: (1) The flight of business and industry from the central cities into the suburbs or to other regions of the country; (2) the higher turnover associated with the peripheral jobs that minority youths hold in disproportionate numbers and the elimination of such low-skill jobs; and (3) the discriminatory hiring practices which put all youth (teenagers), but especially minority youths, at the end of a hypothetical hiring queue.

While obtaining work is a problem for some youths, finding career-related work which has advancement potential and access to further training is a problem for others. The series of youth jobs en route to age 21 or 22 are frequently casual jobs which count little toward career employment opportunities; they are fine for 16- to 17-year-olds but are labeled disparagingly as "jive jobs" by older youths who expect some advancement after having paid their dues at the bottom of the job market.

Among those who leave school, finding work offering advancement possibilities is much more of a problem for female and minority youths than for young white males. The latter do tend to progress—albeit slowly—from low-paying, unskilled jobs into career-type jobs as they enter their mid-twenties. Although educational attainment is related to the likelihood of entering career-type work [1] (in one's first job) among both white and minority youths, this relationship is stronger among white youths. The relationship, however, between educational attainment and hourly wage rates and annual earnings is equally strong among white and minority youths. Among youths who hold non-career-type or unskilled jobs, returning to school is likely to help white but not minority youths break out of this (secondary) labor market and into career-type work. Regardless of ethnic background or level of education, youths who are fortunate enough to obtain career-type work are likely to do well and are unlikely to regress to unskilled work that offers little advancement potential. In other words, the best predictor of subsequent occupational success is previous occupational success.

Youths who remain in school and work part time are much less likely than out-of-school youths to obtain career-related work. While many youths decide to sacrifice career-type work for further school, students who are able to get career-type work have a distinct early labor market advantage over those who cannot. Whether in or out of school, getting career-related work soon after entering the labor market, especially if on a full-time basis, is the best predictor of subsequent success there.

Barriers or factors which adversely affect jobholding by the young, particularly career-type jobs, include:

1. *An inadequate supply of jobs.*—If youths are to obtain a greater share of existing of existing jobs, they are likely (under the current structure of work) to displace adult workers from their jobs.

2. *Laws and regulations that make employment for young people difficult.*

3. *Employer and union discrimination against young workers.*

Although schools can do little to influence these realities, they can perform other functions which will increase the likelihood that the young will find and prepare themselves adequately for jobs that they like or, at least, find acceptable. Helping students become employable is a worthy educational goal regardless of the particular economic conditions. Unfortunately, there is little evidence that schools help young people make a successful transition to work. Instead:

1. Students do not know much about working and lack information about the nature and requirements of different occupations, about employment prospects, and about the educational and experience requirements for career entry and progression.

---

[1] Career-related work is that type of work that offers advancement potential and access to skill development opportunities. This type of work is more likely to be skilled than unskilled, and it pays better than non-career-related work.

2. Students do not know much about their own abilities and aptitudes which might be useful in selecting an appropriate career or in considering further educational experiences.

3. The early socialization of young people into occupational roles is unduly limited by sex, ethnicity, and social class; and the schools contribute to this problem.

4. Competencies learned in school are not certified in a way useful to their continued education or to entry and progression in various occupations.

5. Students possess few jobseeking skills and receive little assistance from any institution in finding work.

In addition to these deficiencies or problems, many would hold that young people lack the work habits and basic skills needed to learn on their own. There is little evidence, however, that this problem is now more serious than in the past. Although it is true that today's high school students manifest deterioration in skills which are the most rote or mechanical (computation and writing) or timebound (vocabulary), less deterioration (science achievement) or outright improvement is observed among abilities relevant to problem solving (abstract reasoning and creativity). Possibly, the latter are just as important as the more mechanical skills to succeed at work.

Another frequent criticism of schools charges that they do not equip sufficient numbers of students with specific vocational skills which are suitable for career entry. No doubt the argument about which skills are marketable skills will persist for some time. A substantial amount of research evidence on the subject suggests that vocational education overall is no better and no worse than other curriculums in creating labor market advantages for its graduates. In view of the negligible private benefits of vocational training and an economy characterized more by shortages of jobs than of skills, the fact of more or fewer youths engaged in vocational training does not now appear to concern the national interest.

Federal Role

Federal assistance to help localities improve the school-to-work transition can be justified on several grounds:

1. The problems are of sufficient magnitude and are sufficiently widespread.

2. Efforts to resolve the problems by the private sector or by State or local governments are not adequate and have little likelihood of becoming so in the near future.

3. For most of the problems there are solutions already tried and tested.

4. The Federal Government has a sufficient degree of expertise in the problem areas to be able to help most localities and States.
5. The benefits of the proposed Federal activities or programs are likely to justify the cost.

Despite the justification for Federal involvement, this question can still be raised: Why can't the States and communities do it? Answer: They can, and some are; but the process of bringing the worlds of education and work closer together will probably move along faster if the Federal Government plays a catalytic role.

A more fundamental question, perhaps, is: Why has the Nation permitted education and work to become so isolated from each other? There are several reasons. First and foremost, education has been viewed uncritically for so long as a way to get ahead that few people thought it important to relate education systemtically to the world of work. In the *sellers* market which existed during the quarter century following World War II, employers could do little else than accept the products of the schools; no other supply sector was doing any better and industry needed educated or, at least, literate people. In the *buyers market* of the 1970's, however, when skill surpluses rather than shortages prevail, employers have become more selective and schools feel pressure from parents to teach their children the competencies needed to become employable.

Other reasons for the progressive isolation of the worlds of education and work especially for high school students, have been the following:

1. The post-Sputnik emphasis on recruiting more high school graduates for professional careers requiring college preparation with correspondingly less emphasis on placing the non-college-bound graduates into jobs (although Federal vocational education legislation did attempt to redress this imbalance).
2. The focus on *equality of educational opportunity* which similarly stressed movement (of the disadvantaged and minorities) into further education, while assuming that this would improve access to jobs (economic opportunity).
3. The rise of a number of school trends such as pass-fail grading, grade inflation, automatic promotion, and open enrollment—all of which were intended to motivate students to learn, yet they made it more difficult for students to become sufficiently aware of their abilities and aptitudes to be able to match them with the requirements of different occupations.
4. The rapid growth of community colleges and proprietary vocational schools, which enabled many more students to obtain specific occupational skills and placement assistance, thereby making it less necessary for high schools to concern themselves with the transition to work.

5. The progressive reluctance of school officials to hire professional personnel who lack teacher certification or who offer extensive experience in noneducational work. The latter situation has evolved chiefly from the increasing power of teacher organizations to influence school employment practices and, in part, from the declining growth rates of school budgets.

To a considerable extent, the progressive isolation of the worlds of work and education grew out of well-intended national policy to increase the Nation's supply of highly trained manpower while achieving a greater degree of social justice by making postsecondary education more accessible and attractive to more people. This policy has largely succeeded, though somewhat at the expense of youths' preparation to enter the world of work, whether or not they go to college. Perhaps it is time to evaluate and reemphasize this *preparation-for-working-life* function of education—not to give it to more priority than other legitimate educational functions, but merely to allow it to finally attain a place among the most important.

Federal Policy Options

To increase the supply and quality of jobs available to youths is perhaps the most effective way to assure their successful transition from school to work. If young people are reasonably confident that hard work in school will be rewarded by suitable job opportunities, they are more likely to strive to acquire in school the skills and knowledges which will enhance their employability. Improving youth job opportunities is easier said than done, however. There is little consensus on which macroeconomic or manpower policies ought to be followed. Alternative strategies which are currently being discussed and debated include: (1) Policies to promote general economic expansion, (2) financial incentives to employers for hiring youths, such as tax credits, (3) public works and public service employment, including required public service for the young, and (4) job sharing or redistribution of work. The major unresolved problem is how to create useful and productive employment for youths without taking jobs away from adult workers.

Although some time may elapse before consensus is rallied around a plan to improve the youth employment situation, there are a few actions which the schools can take to help young people make their job search more efficient and their subsequent work more personally satisfying. In general, the options put forth here are intended to help young people approach career decisionmaking with a greater sense of realism about themselves and about the labor market. In addition, they call for more direct assistance from the school in helping young people make contact with both employers and workers. These school-based activities will not have any major effect on the youth employment situation. To the extent, however, that they decrease job search time (because of knowing what one wants and getting assistance to obtain it) and quit rates (because of wanting to keep satisfying work), youth unemployment rates would be reduced also.

On the assumption of relatively constant Federal expenditures for education and work,[2] a strategy to effect a more successful transition from school to work would gradually shift the Federal funds used to support school-based vocational training to other activities which appear at this time to be more strongly associated with a successful transition. Possible Federal actions classified by problem area are identified as follows.

Problem A. Inadequate Knowledge of the Labor Market

Of the various ways to improve secondary school students' knowledge of the world of work, affording them career-type work experience (i.e., work offering advancement potential and training for further skill development) and providing them direct access to occupational data (especially realistic job outlook forecasts) through information systems or guidance-placement programs are the most effective. While some classroom-based career education programs have expanded the career awareness of students, evaluation evidence accumulated thus far suggests that incorporation of occupational information into secondary school curriculums is generally not effective, unless students are actively involved in using the information in *learning by doing* contexts. Public policy should emphasize the expansion and qualitative improvement of both paid and unpaid work experience programs for secondary students, as well as the development and dissemination of comprehensive, high-quality occupational and educational information.

Option 1: Provide Secondary School Students With More and Better Work Experience Opportunities (see chart 1).

Supervised and planned experience in the workplace can help some students acquire academic knowledge as well as help them learn about work. Many successful work experience models exist. Minimally, a Federal effort should be made to classify and evaluate these models by type of school setting and then to disseminate the result. In addi-

---

[2] Of course, the education and work budget ought to compete with other educational areas for Federal funding. No attempt is made here, however, to make such tradeoffs or establish priorities within the overall Federal education budget. Similarly, no attempt is made to put HEW in budget competition with other Federal agencies which also commit resources to the education and work area.

Chart 1.—Options to Provide Work Experience to Students

Problem	Program objectives	Range of options (from little to considerable Federal involvement and support)				
		Little support		Considerable support		
		I Demonstration of local education and work councils	II Federal technical assistance and training	III Expansion of demonstration programs	IV Federal student volunteers program	V Federal student work experience program
Inadequate knowledge of the labor market.	To encourage communities to provide more and better work experience opportunities which will allow students to learn about work by participating in it.	Bring trade associations, service organizations, unions, public and private employers together to generate more work experience slots for students.	Identify and package effective models of paid and unpaid work experience, classify and rate these by type of school setting. In collaboration with interest groups and associations, disseminate information about these models and develop a public information program to persuade local authorities and employers to increase the number and quality of work experience slots for students. Sponsor conferences, workshops, etc. for work-study coordinators ($1,000,000 to $2,000,000 per year).	Fund more demonstrations of EBCE program through VEA exemplary projects and NIE laboratories ($4,000,000). Fund demonstration program to encourage youth entrepreneurship along lines of Canadian youth opportunities program. National Commission on Resources for Youth might be willing to develop and administer some models ($4,000,000 to $6,000,000). Fund NIE to demonstrate feasibility of exploratory work experience programs for junior high school students ($400,000). Expand DOL/USOE WECEP. Extend best of NIE-developed career exploration models for postsecondary students to more institutions ($800,000).	New legislation to provide students in high-youth unemployment areas with paid community service opportunities ($300,000,000).	Legislation to give schools financial incentives to increase the number of work experience slots. (On the assumption that the cost of creating one new slot is $500 per year, and that it is desirable to give work experience to 10 pct (2.4 million) more high school students, the annual cost would be $1.2 billion).

KEY TO ABBREVIATIONS

EBCE=Experience-based career education.
VEA=Vocational Education Act.
NIE=National Institute of Education.

DOL=U.S. Department of Labor.
USOE=U.S. Office of Education.
WECEP=Work experience and career exploration program.

tion to this technical assistance effort, the U.S. Department of Health, Education, and Welfare (HEW) might wish to invest more of its discretionary funds in a wider demonstration of the more successful work experience examples, like the experience-based career education (EBCE) and the executive high school internships programs (which use the workplace as a setting for learning) and the Canadian youth opportunities program (which pays students to create their own public service jobs). Those programs which encourage youth entrepreneurship in the private sector might be demonstrated, as well. If more Federal funds were to become available to increase substantially the number of work slots for students, priority ought to be given to youths in high unemployment areas, and care should be taken to assure that their work experience has some educational value. Work experience programs which segregate younger workers should be avoided, because they tend to end in transfers of income and not in the accomplishment of real work with defensible performance standards (e.g., Neighborhood Youth Corps). Young workers need to interact with older workers for the experience to have either productive or educational value.

Option 2: Provide Students With More and Better Career Information (see chart 2). Students are not getting the information they need for intelligent job choices. Yet knowledge of occupations (duties, requirements, wages, and employment prospects) is associated with early labor market success. Lack of Federal initiative in this area will perpetuate a situation where much misinformation about the labor market is disseminated to students.

A range of Federal activities to provide students with accurate, up-to-date, and locally relevant career information ought to be considered. Modest amounts of Federal dollars would support a variety of technical assistance and training activities, including the development of short courses and materials in the *Interpretation and Utilization of Labor Market Information*, and the dissemination of effective models of occupational and educational information systems, career education, vocational guidance, and career exploration. More money would enable HEW to demonstrate on a larger scale some of the more successful models for providing career information. For example, HEW could help the U.S. Department of Labor extend its eight-State demonstration to three or four more States and could provide funds and guidance to improve the educational information contained in the systems. In addition, HEW could extend to more areas the best projects which help students understand and use career information materials.

Moving beyond technical assistance and demonstration programs, HEW and DOL should jointly consider establishing career information systems in all parts of the country. Their involvement might be in the form of "seed money" to persuade States to develop their own systems which would become self-supporting within a few years, or a full-fledged federally supervised and funded system might be instituted. At present, the country is moving in the direction of State-operated rather than federally run career information systems, witness the DOL eight-State domonstration program which utilizes the seed money approach. Regardless of which strategy is employed, DOL would be concerned mostly with the quality of the occupational information in the system, while HEW would be responsible for the quality of the educational information.

Problem B: Inadequate Knowledge of Own Abilities and Aptitudes

Several recent school phenomena in combination have made it more difficult for students to know where they stand in relation to their ability to enter work or pursue further education. These include pass-fail grading, grade inflation, automatic promotion, open enrollment in courses of study and educational institutions, and the lowering of academic standards and entrance requirements to assure full enrollments in many postsecondary institutions. On the other hand, the Family Educational Rights and Privacy Act of 1974, which guarantees students and parents access to the school's information about them, is likely to help students learn about their abilities and aptitudes. Given the fact that few schools have enough personnel who can help students understand and intelligently use such information, this act needs to be supplemented by activities which will help students become more knowledgeable about themselves. Examples of such Federal initiatives might include (see chart 3):

1. Development and testing of a new course or module in *Consuming Postsecondary Education* which would help high school students learn how to ascertain the veracity and usefulness of information obtained from schools and colleges.
2. Development of easily understood materials that would help students interpret their performance on standardized achievement, aptitude, and interest tests.
3. Development of a series of State-specific booklets or course modules in conjunction with the States themselves which inform dropouts about the alternatives available to them if they do not return to the regular high school.
4. Expansion of industry-based research on how test scores predict successful job performance in different occupations.
5. Development of experimental educational brokering services which would remove some aspects of counseling from the high school and put them directly at the service of the student and

Chart 2.—Options to Provide Career Information to Students

Problem	Program objective	Range of options (from little to considerable Federal involvement and support)				
		Little support			Considerable support	
		I Local education and work councils	II Federal technical assistance and training	III Expansion of demonstration programs	IV States grants program to establish career information systems	V Federal career information system
Inadequate knowledge of the labor market Students don't know much about working and lack information about the nature and different occupations, about employment prospects, and about the educational and experience requirements for career entry and progression.	To provide students with more and better career information (i.e., occupational and educational information).	Small grants to 15 to 30 communities to establish councils, which would disseminate local occupational data and information to schools and encourage visits, field trips, etc. to bring students into greater contact with employers and workers. **$1,000,000 to $2,000,000.**	Through HEW-DOL-Occupational Information Coordinating Committee: Sponsor short courses in **Interpretation and Utilization of Labor Market Information** for State and local manpower and education planning staff, vocational counselors, work experience coordinators, etc. Develop LMI dictionary and users manual (**$300,000 per year**). Identify and package effective models of occupational and educational information systems, career education, vocational counseling and exploration, etc. Collaborate with associations and interest groups to identify such models and disseminate information about them (**$2,000,000 per year**). In 8 States having DOL, OIS program, fund a State vocational education board	Extend DOL 8-State demonstration of Occupational Information Systems to 3 to four States with HEW participation (**$1,000,000 per year**). Extend best of FIPSE educational information projects to more areas (**$1,000,000 per year**). Extend to more areas best of projects which help students understand and use career information materials (**$1,000,000 per year**).	New legislation to expand DOL, OIS program to all States with HEW participation. DOL responsible for quality of occupational information. HEW responsible for quality of educational information. Local user agency assumes delivery or equipment costs. State systems to become self-supporting within 4 years. (DOL and HEW each contribute **$5,000,000 per year for 5 yr**).	Legislation to establish federally supervised and funded system to to provide career information to students and adults. DOL and HEW share cost and responsibility for demonstration and delivery of occupational and educational information, respectively (each agency contributes **$15,000,000 to $20,000,000 per year**).

staff member to work with OIS staff and serve as program's "extension agent" to manpower and vocational education planning bodies ($200,000 per year).

Require all public, proprietary, and home study schools receiving Federal aid to report program completions by appropriate OE education course codes and DOL **Dictionary of Occupational Titles** codes.

KEY TO ABBREVIATIONS

HEW = U.S. Department of Health, Education, and Welfare.
DOL = U.S. Department of Labor.

LMI = Labor market information.
OIS = Occupational information system.
FIPSE = Fund for the improvement of postsecondary education.

his/her family. (Different methods of financing such brokering services ought to be tried, including counseling vouchers given directly to the student.)

6. Help to reform counseling in schools to reflect a consumer advocacy approach by providing counselors with inservice and preservice training in: (*a*) How to consume postsecondary education, (*b*) how to interpret student scores on standardized tests, (*c*) how to interpret and use occupational information in career decisionmaking, and (*d*) juvenile law and children's rights.

The aforementioned options are not mutually exclusive. All are low-cost and could be implemented singly or in various combinations.

Problem C: Restricted Occupational Socialization

Despite some progress in reducing occupational stereotyping in schools, the great majority still use materials which perpetuate the problem by showing women in subordinate roles and primarily as teachers and nurses. State legislation, such as the California regulation prohibiting the use of public funds to purchase school texts that reinforce such stereotypes, can be supplemented by Federal efforts to develop films, TV and radio programs, counselor and teacher guides, etc., which characterize occupations in a sex- and race-fair manner.

HEW's Education Division has rapidly expanded its activities in this area during the last 2 to 3 years and the Education Amendments of 1976 authorize even more vigorous activity (e.g., the $2.6 million authorized under the vocational education provision to fund in each State staff responsible for this area). During fiscal year 1976, the Education Division spent some $6 to $8 million on projects to reduce sex-role stereotyping compared to about half that sum during the previous year. In the absence of performance standards or criteria which indicate success, however, it is difficult to determine how much Federal initiative is enough. As HEW continues and expands its research and development (R. & D.) and dissemination activities to reduce occupational stereotyping, the department should develop appropriate goals and performance criteria to permit more coherent planning. Moreover, the various agencies within HEW which are concerned about this area should coordinate their activities in order to avoid needless duplication of effort while assuring dissemination of the most promising projects or practices.

Problem D: Nonfunctional Ways of Certifying Competencies

Given the current temper of the courts and the absence of any pending conceptual breakthrough which is generic to the measurement and assessment of occupational competencies, the Federal role with respect

Chart 3.—Options To Help Students Get Accurate Feedback About Their Academic Performance and Aptitudes

Problem	Program objective	Options (not mutually exclusive)		
		I Develop materials to help students learn about themselves in relation to future educational and occupational choices	II Research, development, and demonstration	III Federal technical assistance and training
Students have inadequate knowledge about their own abilities and aptitudes which might be useful in selecting an appropriate career or further education.	Reform counseling in schools to reflect a consumer advocacy approach, which focuses on helping students get accurate feedback and information about their academic achievement and aptitudes.	Develop and test materials for new course or module in Consuming Postsecondary Education which would help high school students learn how to ascertain the veracity and usefulness of information obtained from schools and colleges ($250,000). Have each State develop within Federal guidelines a booklet and/or a short debriefing module or course which informs dropouts about alternatives if they do not return to the regular high school ($20,000 per State=$1,000,000). Develop easily understood materials that would help students interpret their scores on standardized achievement, aptitude, and interest tests ($300,000).	Supplement industry-based research on how test scores predict successful job performance in different occupations ($1.5 million). Develop experimental educational brokering services which remove some aspects of counseling from the high school and put them directly at the service of the student and his/her family. Include counseling vouchers for students as one way of paying for such a service ($1.5 million). Develop experimental student advocacy service in high school where students would participate along with school authorities in selecting counselors and structuring their tasks ($1.5 million).	In collaboration with interest groups and associations, provide in-service and pre-service training to counselors in: (a) How to consume postsecondary education and training. (b) How to interpret student scores on standardized achievement, aptitude, and occupational interest tests. (c) How to interpret and use occupational information in career decisionmaking. (d) Juvenile law and children's rights ($3,000,000 per year). Furnish local education agencies with foot-locker of best materials on how to help students with self-appraisal. Continually update this package ($2,000,000).

to competency-based education ought to be catalytic and not programmatic. Federal R. & D. activity in this rapidly expanding area should continue, not only to capture and disseminate rich experience having widespread utility, but also to bring employers and educators together around a common problem (certification) and to persuade educational institutions to be more forthright and explicit about what they are teaching or certifying.

In addition to developing and evaluating innovative competency-based education and assessment techniques which help people earn occupational licenses and educational credentials, the Federal Government should closely monitor and evaluate State and local efforts to award competency-based high school diplomas (e.g., Oregon and California).

Problem E: Inadequate Assistance to Students To Find Work and Develop Jobseeking Skills

Thousands of public dollars are invested in providing one young person with years of preparatory higher education, but very little is put into seeing what can be done about another's moving directly from high school to work. School guidance personnel, for example, help many graduates proceed to college yet they seldom help work-bound students find jobs.

Though there are several successful school placement models, most schools still do not routinely provide such services; and the U.S. Employment Service (ES) serves only a minute percentage of students (ES does serve many out-of-school youth, however). On the optimistic side, a recent national survey of school districts indicates that this situation is improving rapidly—over half of the school-based placement programs now in existence were begun during the last 5 years. Expanding local interest in school-based placement services suggests that the propitious time has come for the Federal Government to infuse some guidance and support to help assure that high quality services are provided.

On a spectrum of little to considerable involvement and support, four Federal strategies which would stimulate schools and other local agencies to provide students, recent graduates, and dropouts with job placement assistance ought to be considered: (1) Establish local education and work councils; (2) provide technical assistance and training; (3) conduct a large demonstration and comparative evaluation of alternative placement models; and (4) provide grants to local areas to establish high school placement programs. These can be considered either as mutually reinforcing or competing (mutually exclusive) strategies (see chart 4).

The least costly option would be to demonstrate the feasibility of local education and work councils (EWC), which would bring several community agencies and interest groups together in order to provide services, including job placement, that would help students make more successful transition from school to work. Although the Federal Government could earmark some council funds for placement, most resources for this purpose would come from the local institutions themselves.

Another low-cost way to divert local resources for job placement assistance would be to provide Federal technical assistance and training. Under this strategy, the Federal Government could: (a) Disseminate information about successful school placement models through conferences, workshops, public information programs, and the like; (b) designate employment service personnel to lend technical assistance to school-designated placement coordinators, and (c) comparatively evaluate the various courses or modules in *Job Search Techniques and Achievement Motivation for Youth* which have been developed under the auspices of career education, and disseminate information about best practices to schools, perhaps with the help of national business and trade associations.

A somewhat more ambitious and expensive Federal strategy, though still within the framework of existing legislation and appropriation levels, would be to conduct and evaluate large demonstrations of two or three successful school placement models in each State (see chart 4). This would require considerable planning and coordination between HEW and DOL. A related demonstration activity would be to fund several local education agencies (LEA's) with high youth unemployment to stagger summer vacations or use the quarter system so that large numbers of students are not entering the labor market at the same time.

A fourth strategy to provide students and recent school leavers with job placement assistance would establish high school placement services on a widespread basis with the help of Federal grants. The Federal cost of $50 to $150 million per year could be reduced by requiring school districts to match funds or gradually take over the financing of the program.

Integrative Options

In addition to Federal categorical assistance where new programs are developed to address specific problems, forms of Federal assistance which address problems through building local capacity should be considered. Demonstration of the feasibility of local education and work councils consisting of representatives from the schools, manpower agencies, and business and industry has been mentioned as an example of such an approach. Through better coordination and utilization of resources these councils attempt to improve the effectiveness of

Chart 4.—Options To Provide Placement Assistance to Students and School Leavers

Problem	Program objective	Range of options (from little to considerable Federal involvement and support)			
		Little support		Considerable support	
		I	II	III	IV
		Demonstration of local education and work councils	Federal technical assistance and training	Large demonstration and comparative evaluation of successful models	Grants to LEA's to establish high school placement programs
Students and school leavers conduct job search in a haphazard and ineffective manner. The great majority of students expect their school to help them find jobs, but few schools do.	Provide more job placement services that help students, graduates, and drop-outs find part-time, full-time, and summer jobs.	In addition to other activities to improve the school-to-work transition, bring together schools, local employment service, trade and service organizations, unions, etc. to develop appropriate type of job placement service for students ($1,000,000 to establish 15 to 20 councils). Earmark special funds for placement services in cities having an education-work council ($100,000 per city or $1.5 million total).	Identify and package effective school placement models. In collaboration with interest groups and associations, disseminate information about these models through regional conferences, workshops, etc. and develop public information program to persuade local authorities to adopt a suitable placement model, if not already in place ($2,000,000). Employment Service would designate 1 placement specialist to lend technical assistance to school-designated placement coordinators in each of 200 major school districts ($4,000,000). Comparatively evaluate courses or modules in Job Search Techniques and Achievement Motivation for Youths,	Fund each State to establish and comparatively evaluate 2 to 3 delivery systems for school placement services: (1) Outstationing of Employment Service personnel in schools. (2) Hiring of placement staff by LEA. (3) Hiring and supervision of placement staff by education-work council, industry-education council, local CETA planning council, and the like ($15,000,000 per year for 3 yr). Fund 20 LEA's in areas with	Program would provide 1 placement specialist for every 1,500 students in grades 10 to 12. Such personnel would take and list job orders, refer students or school leavers to job openings, solicit jobs from employers, provide job counseling and instruction in job search techniques, conduct followup studies, and seek assistance from community volunteers. School may choose a variety of delivery systems (see strategy III). Cost: Assuming unit cost of $20,000 per specialist:

which have been developed under auspices of career education. Identify best practices and disseminate materials and hold regional conferences, workshops, etc. ($4,000,000).

high youth unemployment to experiment with the quarter system or staggered vacations so that large numbers of students are not entering labor market simultaneously ($5,000,000 per year for 2 yr).

Coverage of ⅓ of high school students—$50,000,000.

Coverage of ⅔ of high school students—$100,000,000.

Coverage of all high schools $150,000,000.

Note.—Federal costs could be reduced by requiring school district to match funds or gradually take over financing of program. School districts already having a placement service would get funds anyway.

KEY TO ABBREVIATIONS

CETA = Comprehensive Employment and Training Act.

LEA = Local education agency.

local institutions in helping people integrate their education with their work. In so doing, the councils may opt to address one or several of the problems described previously. Aside from achieving better coordination among local institutions, the councils might wish to institutionalize reform by offering new program alternatives to students in their last years of high school and support these with innovative financing mechanisms.

Implementation

With the exception of programs to increase the number of work slots for students, it is unlikely that the total cost of vigorous Federal activity in all five of the problem areas would exceed $200 million per year over a period of 4 to 5 years. The Vocational Education Act or the Comprehensive Employment and Training Act (CETA) would have to be amended to effect the two most important changes, namely, the provision of school-based placement services and the establishment of State career information systems. Federal activities in three of the five problem areas—certification of competencies, occupational socialization, and self-knowledge of abilities and aptitudes—fall entirely within the categories of R. & D. or technical assistance and training and could be funded under current discretionary authority and budget levels.

ADULTS: CAREER AND LIFE REDIRECTION AND RENEWAL

Problem

The basic human resource problem among adults in the United States is not a shortage of skilled individuals, but a shortage of jobs—unskilled or skilled. The problem is larger than our current economic difficulties. For the last half century, this Nation has not been able to provide jobs during peacetime for everyone able and willing to work.

This undercapacity to provide jobs has given rise, in part, to a variety of social ills—a large, expensive, inefficient and degrading welfare system, crime, mental illness, etc. These ills have been borne disproportionately by minority groups, women, youths, and older persons. Though employment discrimination against these people remains a problem, some progress has been made in eliminating it for minority group members and women. Not so for youth and older people, whose position in the job market has deteriorated steadily during the last several decades.

Although the compression of work, especially highly skilled work, into the middle period of the lifecycle merely confirms a long historical trend which has had basically healthy features (e.g., child labor laws and the possibility of retirement with a pension) there is evidence that the trend has gone too far. As work, especially career-type work, has become monopolized more and more by the middle-aged cohort of the population, the entry of many young people into career-type work has been deferred for an unnecessarily long period; meanwhile the age of compulsory retirement has been lowered to the point where retirement for many has become a predicament rather than a welcome rest from a life of work.

The progressively inequitable distribution of career-type work among the three large age cohorts has led to a rigid sequence—from school during youth to work during midlife to leisure during old age. The lockstep is especially frustrating for youths and retirees, who both want more work, independence, and responsibility. There is also evidence that a significantly large minority of prime-age workers want more leisure without having to sacrifice too much in the way of economic security and job status to get it.

A combination of social and demographic forces will soon exacerbate the inequities in the distribution of work, leisure, and education. Younger and older people will experience greater difficulties than before in getting or keeping career-type work. Youths will compete directly with middle-aged women who are reentering the labor force for the entry-level career-type jobs. Prime-age workers will find it more difficult to get career-type work if they do not have it; and if they do, they will find it more difficult to get promoted or to change into some other occupation providing similar job status and pay. This job stagnation or reduced occupational mobility will occur precisely at a time when other social forces will act to increase the desire for both vertical and horizontal occupational mobility. The resulting dissatisfaction with career progression could well result in diminished worker productivity.

What, then, are these social and demographic forces which are likely to inhibit occupational mobility while other forces increase the desire for it? First is the imminence of a "promotion squeeze" or a lesser amount of vertical career mobility within the middle-aged cohort—as the large, well-educated baby-boom generation atempts to move past the lower echelons of the occupational ladder, as the younger better educated members of minority groups seek the job opportunities denied their parents, and as more women became full-time career workers. More people will compete for the relatively limited share of *preferred* jobs, and because of the higher occupational expectations resulting from higher levels of educational attainment, a higher proportion of middle-aged workers than in the past, particularly white males, will become unhappy with their progress. Further, this state of affairs will work to the disadvantage of younger workers, who will not be able to dislodge experienced workers who are "stuck" above them, and it will bring additional pressure for even earlier compulsory retirement.

As demographic trends make promotions more problematic, the ever-present job shortage situation will make it more difficult to change jobs and careers. Public employment programs *might* increase the number of jobs, but they are unlikely to satisfy the demand for career-type jobs, if our experience with these programs is any indication. Holders of preferred jobs are less likely to give them up in a slack labor market—witness the greatly decreased turnover in the teaching profession during the last few years.

While our present economic situation discourages occupational mobility, the desire to change careers is heightened by: (1) The increased awareness of different kinds of work, due to a more highly educated work force and increased coverage by the mass media; and (2) increased willingness to risk leaving one's job or occupation as larger proportions of adults are free of dependents for greater portions of their lives.

These decreasing dependency ratios are due to increasing propensities of Americans toward later marriages, smaller families, nuclear families (two generations in residence), double-income households (both spouses working), more frequent divorce, and financial self-reliance during old age.

Despite the factors which increase the desire for career change and improvement, economic and demographic factors for the rest of this century are probably too strong to permit a degree of occupational mobility which will satisfy the desire for it. Unless some effort is made by society to restructure or redistribute work, we can expect continued high unemployment along with increasing amounts of job stagnation, boredom, and the underemployment of skills and knowledge provided by formal education. A negative aspect of redistributing work is that higher aggregate wage costs for an industry might be associated with constant output, thereby reducing productivity.

If the job shortage problem (especially career-type jobs) is unlikely to be resolved by public employment programs, it is even less likely to be resolved by manpower training and adult education programs. From what is known at this time, the number of adults who participate in such programs has no particular bearing on the national interest. Aside from failure of past Federal investments in education or training programs to pay off in an expanded national supply of jobs, new Federal incentives for adults to continue their education would not seem to be necessary or merit priority for two additional reasons:

1. Too many workers (between one-fourth and one-third) feel overqualified for their jobs, as they are unable to utilize skills obtained during their formal schooling in their present work. Promoting further education among adults might exacerbate such feelings by raising occupational expectations which are not likely to be fulfilled. At the same time, it might accelerate un-

employment among high school graduates and dropouts as many jobs suitable for them are taken by persons with college training or degrees.

2. Adult education is flourishing and growing without significant increments in Federal assistance. Furthermore, millions of workers do not take advantage of company-provided education or training when it is made available. Among the additional fringe benefits desired by American workers, education benefits are given very low priority.

Even if it were assumed that having more adults enrolled in education or training programs is in the national interest, such increments in enrollments are as likely to result from a more equitable distribution of work and leisure as from increased availability of educational programs per se. Evidence suggests that once a person advances in age beyond his/her mid-twenties, participation in educational activiites for the purpose of improving or maintaining career status is as likely to result from the kind of work that one does as to lead to such work.

Recommendations for Federal Policy

The (aggregate) job shortage problem is not going to be improved by a mere expansion of education or training opportunities. The problem is more likely to be resolved by a strategy which promotes macroeconomic expansion as well as greater flexibility in working life through a more equitable distribution of work, leisure, and education between the younger, middle-aged, and older cohorts of the population. Although a policy to provide more career-related work to younger and older people while providing more leisure and educational opportunities to midcareer people is appealing, there is little likelihood that the Nation will make a major effort in the near future to restructure or redistribute work. It is recommended, nonetheless, that a variety of Federal activities be pursued which would contribute in a modest way toward making working life more flexible while providing valuable information which would be needed before contemplating more dramatic steps. In order of progressing degrees of involvement, the Federal Government could:

1. *Expand research to assess the kinds of life scheduling patterns which appeal to people as well as serve the collective public interest.*—While Americans appear to want a more equitable distribution of work, leisure, and education, there is considerable confusion and controversy over how this should be done. Various redistribution plans should be compared and contrasted in terms of their likely impact on the economy and political structure. Such plans might include the shortened work week or work year, public employment, required public service for the young, job sharing, work sabbaticals, extended vacations as reward for

length of service, guaranteed leave of absence without pay, and age-neutral educational entitlement plans which might take the place of some of the present Federal student aid programs. Following up on such a study, the Federal Government might support some of these innovations on an experimental basis; furthemore, the Government should carefully evaluate and monitor such programs when they are initiated by State and local governments or by business and industry.

2. *Help States establish occupational and educational information systems as well as (education consumer) brokering services which would help individuals of all ages make more intelligent choices about careers and educational and leisure activities.*— The development of career information systems make as much sense for adults as for youths. Several experimental and demonstration programs indicate the feasibility and desirability of establishing such systems while providing early Federal guidance (see youth section).

3. *Develop a public information program that would encourage labor and management in both the public and private sectors to negotiate plans and collective bargaining agreements that allow individual employees to choose among varying amounts of and ways of scheduling work and time off.*—To facilitate a wider public discussion of time-income tradeoff and work scheduling options, the Federal Government would convene meetings, conferences, and the like, as well as disseminate information about the outcomes of such plans which have already been implemented.

4. *Consider legislation which would enable more workers to take a temporary leave of absence from their jobs in order to participate in activities which might facilitate career or life improvement, renewal, or redirection.*—Such legislation would help neutralize economic and demographic forces which inhibit risk-taking with respect to changing jobs or preparing oneself in school to qualify for another or a better job. It would also provide people the time to "do the things they've always wanted to do" before their retirement years. Finally, it would provide preretirees the opportunity to prepare for retirement or to experience it somewhat before it is actually upon them.

A range of options along a spectrum of minimal to considerable amounts of Federal involvement or regulation should be evaluated. One type of option would provide financial or tax incentives for employers who agree to allow employees to take leaves of absence. A more activist option would involve consideration of legislation to enable more wage and salary employees, whether full time or part time, to obtain a certain number of weeks of release time after having worked for the same employer for a specified length of time. In both cases, the amount of leave would likely depend on the length of service with the employer. If, indeed, national consensus could be rallied around some plan, a plausible next step would be to find ways to maintain income during the leave of absence. Short of a plan to provide Federal support, labor and management might work out payroll savings or flexible pension plans and the like which could supply some income during this period.

Implementation

An expanded research effort to assess the issues of redistributing work and facilitating career and life redirection and renewal would require additional research funds, especially if some actual experimentation with incentive structures were contemplated. NIE should remain as the focus for this type of research within the Education Division. Because of the many sectors of society which would be influenced by such research, other Federal agencies ought to be involved as well, including the Departments of Commerce and Labor, and other agencies of HEW.

The establishment of a nationwide network of career information systems in the 50 States and other eligible areas would cost about $10 million per year over a 5-year period, assuming a gradual phasing in of the program to about 15 States a year. DOL and HEW ought to share in the funding and administration of the State grants. All of the State systems would be expected to become self-supporting after an initial 3- to 4-year Federal grant. In addition, relatively small planning grants might be given to States to establish educational brokering services for adults.

A Federal public information program to encourage a nationwide discussion of time-income tradeoff and work scheduling options would be carried out ideally by a multi-agency task force or consortium (principally the Departments of Commerce, Labor, and HEW) ; or the project could be housed in a private non-profit organization and draw its resources from the relevant Federal agencies. The cost of a public information program depends, obviously, on the magnitude of the effort and the extent of participation by various groups.

Legislation to enable more employees to take a temporary leave of absence following a minimum length of service with an employer would be administered by the Department of Labor. The costs of such a program would depend on whether and to what extent financial incentives (in the case of voluntary collaboration by employers) or compensation (in the case of mandatory cooperation) were used to implement the law. A way to determine costs as well as program effects would be to try out different plans in different parts of the country on an experimental basis.

Conclusion

The job shortage problem might persist for virtually all of the rest of this century. The traditional remedies of macroeconomic expansion and public jobs might not be enough, given the fact that women, youths, and minorities want—indeed, are demanding—a greater share of available jobs, especially the preferred jobs. The presence of these "new workers" with serious vocational aspirations suggests that work sharing be considered as a third alternative for coping with the job shortage problem. One advantage of this approach is that it can be structured to deal with a number of other social problems at the same time, particularly inadequate access to leisure and education throughout life, and the need to ease the lockstep progression from school to work to retirement. The goal of making work more accessible, while making education and leisure more accessible as well, merits high priority on the Nation's policy research agenda.

TOWARD A
FEDERAL POLICY ON
EDUCATION AND WORK

Introduction

Beginning with the original Land-Grant Colleges Act (First Morrill Act) of 1862, the Federal Government has attempted to legislate a closer relationship between education and work. The purpose of the Land-Grant Colleges Act and associated legislation passed later was to develop a new kind of collegiate institution that would be responsive to the economic and social needs of individual States and communities. Moreover, the legislation sought to blend a liberal education with scientific-technical education by encouraging research and experimentation to resolve problems of local agricultural and industrial production.

The Smith-Hughes Act of 1917 carried the spirit of the land-grants colleges' legislation to the Nation's secondary schools by establishing vocational education programs with training authorized in agriculture, home economics, and trade and industrial occupations. The George-Barden Act of 1936 and subsequent National Defense Acts passed in 1940, 1941, and 1943 expanded the eligible fields of instruction and supported the training of warworkers and returning veterans. In 1962, the Manpower Development and Training Act (MDTA) and then the Vocational Education Act (VEA) of 1963 greatly enlarged the Federal role in supporting vocational education programs, with special attention to groups which had not been served adequately. Based on analyses of the effects of the 1963 act, Congress passed the 1968 amendments to it which required States to set aside portions of their grants to serve the disadvantaged, handicapped, and postsecondary school populations. The amendments also established other categorical programs under special authorization (e.g., home economics and consumer education, cooperative education, research and exemplary projects, etc.), but these are consolidated somewhat under the Education Amendments of 1976.

In 1974 the Federal Government supplemented its vocational education activities with demonstration career education programs in-

---

Note.—Footnotes follow the text, listed in numerical order.

tended to give all students a better understanding of work. Unlike the specific occupational training typical of vocational education and appropriate only for some students, career education programs attempt to provide information and experience to all youths on a wide selection of work options so that their choices will be more consistent with personal values, goals, and capabilities.

Current Federal expenditures on education and work sum to about $700 million per year with the great bulk allocated to vocational education. With the help of these Federal dollars, the 1965–75 decade has witnessed a steady increase in the number of vocational education students—to the point that in 1976 more than one-third of the Nation's high school students were enrolled in such programs.

Despite steadily increasing financial support for vocational, career, and adult education programs and the high public expectations regarding the contribution of education to occupational success, evidence is accumulating that young people leaving school are still not well prepared for the adult world, and that there is little incentive provided by the labor market for many youths to become well prepared. In addition, adults are frustrated at not being able to alter their career or life direction or to engage in a variety of renewal activities (education or leisure pursuits) which would facilitate such change.

Along with appropriate skills and a sufficient number and variety of occupational opportunities to reward their evident interest in work, youths need factual information about the realities of the labor market so that they are able to make personally satisfying career-entry decisions. For adults, the problems are more complex and involve finding more opportunities to change their career or life directions if they should so desire.

The consequences of failure to prepare youths and adults for career choice, entry, and progression are believed to be costly and far reaching. Among the problems cited by proponents of career-related educational reform are the stress-induced illnesses and reduced productivity associated with work dissatisfaction; the use of real jobs for career exploration that might more effectively take place outside paid employment; the wasteage of millions of dollars in providing schooling for youths who lack interest because their courses seem unrelated to the kind of work they do care about; the use of postsecondary education as an "aging vat" where young people contemplate what they are going to do with their lives, rather than work toward previously thought-out goals; and the inequities in income and opportunity among women and minorities due to their early socialization into delimited occupational groups, a condition which is perpetuated by the schools themselves. A more detailed analysis of these problems follow. Inasmuch as the problems for youth and adults differ, the policy analysis for each cohort is performed separately.

Youth:
The School-to-Work
Transition

DESIRE TO WORK AMONG YOUTHS

Behavioral and attitudinal data confirm that young people are seriously interested in work. The labor force participation rates of teenagers continued to increase (except during the recent recession when the rates declined for males, especially black males).[1] Teenage unemployment rates, which also serve as an indicator of desire to work, have remained high (between 12 and 20 percent since 1969) despite a rapidly expanding number of youth jobs (from 4.1 million teenagers employed in 1961 to 7.4 million in 1974)[2] and a slightly higher number of jobs per capita for the 16- to 19-year-old cohort (from 0.39 jobs per capita in 1961 to 0.45 jobs per capita in 1974).[3] High school students overwhelmingly rate being successful in work as their most important life goal, and they want more work relevant curriculums and help from the school in obtaining work experience.[4] Other attitudinal studies have shown that not only are work values strong (and possibly getting stronger) among both college and non-college youths, but also that young people today are concerned less about money and more about whether the work they do is socially useful.[5]

ACCESS TO WORK AND SOCIALIZATION CONSEQUENCES

Having been socialized successfully to accept work, a significantly large minority of youths are denied access to it or have difficulty in obtaining the financial and psychological rewards from work that society and their parents have led them to expect.[6] Not being able to find any work is a serious problem for minority youths in cities,[7] where their unemployment rates are fully twice that of whites.[8] Reasons for their excessively high unemployment rates include: (1)

5

The flight of business and industry from the central cities into the suburbs or to other regions of the country; (2) the increasing numbers of mature women workers who frequently compete with youths for the same entry level jobs; (3) the higher turnover associated with the peripheral jobs that minority youths hold in disproportionate numbers and the elimination of such low-skill jobs; (4) the decline in industries which traditionally employed youths or those with low academic ability; (5) the narrowing wage differentials which make young workers more expensive to hire; and (6) the discriminatory hiring practices which put all youths, but especially minority youths, at the end of a hypothetical hiring queue. [9] Because of higher birth rates among minority groups, the unemployment problem among minority youths will remain difficult to resolve. For example, the Department of Labor (DOL) estimates that between 1970 and 1985 the number of black teenagers in the labor force will increase by 34 percent compared to a decline of 17 percent in the number of white teenage workers. [10]

While obtaining any work is a problem for some youths, finding career-related work which has advancement potential and access to in-company training is a problem for others. The series of youth jobs en route to age 21 or 22 are frequently casual jobs which count little toward career employment opportunities; they are accepted by 16- to 17-year-olds but are labeled disparagingly as "jive jobs" by older youths who expect some advancement after having paid their dues at the bottom of the job market. [11]

There are some indications that the quality of jobs available to youths has deteriorated as their portion of the total labor force increased. Cross sectional data on occupation and age from the 1960 and 1970 "Census Public Use Samples," for example, demonstrate that young people during that decade became more concentrated in those occupations and industries where young workers traditionally have been overrepresented. Table 1 shows that among the 21 occupation-industry categories (from a matrix of 270 such categories) in which there were at least 100,000 workers under age 25 in 1970 and in which young workers were overrepresented (in comparison to their share of the total labor force), the percent of youth overrepresentation increased in 17 categories from 1960 to 1970 while it decreased in only four categories. [12] Freedman further confirms the notion that young people have become more concentrated in deadend, low-skilled jobs by showing that young workers (and mature women) were more heavily overrepresented in jobs falling in the lower third of the earnings distribution in 1970 than in 1960 (see table 2). [13] Moreover, some of the greatest increases in the number of young workers occurred in those categories having the least promotion potential; e.g., service jobs in restaurants and hotels and clerical jobs in several industries.

Table 1.—Youth Labor Market, 1960 and 1970 [1]

Occupation industry	1970 Employees (in thousands)	1970 Percent of labor force	1960 Employees (in thousands)	1960 Percent of labor force	Percent of change 1960–70 employees (in thousands)	Percent of change 1960–70
Laborers: retail nondurable	352	70.0	147	73.1	145	−3.1
Sales workers: printing, publishing	140	65.4	153	68.3	−13	−2.9
Nonoffice clerical: retail nondurable	409	43.2	236	37.2	173	6.0
Nonoffice clerical: communications	149	41.2	90	23.9	59	17.3
Nonoffice clerical: education	194	41.1	71	40.6	123	.5
Operative retail: nondurable	330	40.6	261	39.7	69	.9
Office clericals: finance, insurance, real estate	382	38.7	285	45.0	97	−6.3
Service: restaurants, hotels and motels	813	37.3	364	21.1	449	16.2
Nonoffice clericals: finance, insurance, real estate	219	35.3	166	28.9	53	6.4
Office clericals: education	265	34.0	88	27.2	177	6.8
Office clericals: producer services	189	31.5	95	28.4	94	3.1
Laborers: agriculture, forestry, fisheries	308	31.4	416	32.0	−108	−.6
Office clericals: health services	129	29.7	59	27.7	70	.2
Office clericals: wholesale	107	29.5	59	24.3	48	5.2
Sales workers: retail nondurable	613	27.9	462	23.8	151	4.1
Office clericals: retail nondurable	102	26.8	49	25.4	53	1.4
Service workers: health services	424	26.2	124	15.9	300	10.3
Office clericals: public administration	150	25.8	74	20.9	76	4.9
Laborers: construction	162	24.9	143	19.3	19	5.6
Service workers: other consumer services	398	22.1	442	19.0	44	3.1
Service workers: education	246	21.2	93	13.9	153	7.3
Proportion of total civilian employed labor force		19.7		15.1		4.6

[1] Criteria for inclusion: (1) at least 100,000 workers less than age 25 in 1970; (2) young workers (less than age 25) constituted greater share of cell employment than of total (employed) labor force.

Source: Unpublished data provided by Marcia Freedman, who developed the occupation-industry classification scheme in her book, **Labor Markets: Segments and Shelters,** Allanheld, Osmun & Co., Montclair, N.J., 1976, app. D.

Table 2.—Labor Market Stratification by Age and Sex, 1960 and 1970

Population group	Job category according to earnings distribution 1960 (percent distribution) High	Medium	Low	1970 (percent distribution) High	Medium	Low
Total labor force	22.0	42.0	36.0	21.0	33.3	46.0
Mature males	32.0	43.8	24.1	32.8	41.0	26.2
Young males	12.0	42.0	46.0	12.9	32.0	55.1
Mature females	8.4	36.9	57.4	7.7	23.4	69.4
Young females	3.3	38.1	58.4	4.7	19.0	77.0

Source: Marcia Freedman, **Labor Markets: Segments and Shelters,** Allanheld, Osman & Co., Montclair, N.J., 1976, table 4.2, p. 75.

Whether or not the increasing overrepresentation of youths in jobs lacking career potential constitutes a problem depends on what the job means to the jobholder and how long he/she has to remain in such a job after qualifying to begin career-type employment; i.e., work having advancement potential and access to skill development opportunities. This type of work is more likely to be skilled than unskilled, and it pays better than non-career-related work. To a great extent, advancement to this kind of work depends on whether or not the jobholder is a student. Students are willing to put up with lesser skilled, low-paying work because their identity as students tends to be more important to them than their identity as workers. Frequently, these low-skilled jobs help finance the student's education. Career-related work becomes much more important after he/she leaves school.

Unfortunately, the type of work that youths obtain has not been disaggregated by school enrollment status. Nonetheless, analysis of youth employment and unemployment data can help us infer that students are less likely than out-of-school youths to get career-related work. First, much of the increase in youth employment over the last 15 years has resulted from the influx of students into the youth labor force. The students were willing to accept work on a part-time basis to support their studies. This is suggested by the fact that the labor force participation rates for students increased much faster than the rates for nonstudents of the same age (see table 3). [14] Student jobs are more likely to be temporary than jobs held by out-of-school youths. Witness the slightly higher unemployment rates of students (see table 4), their lesser amount of long-term unemployment (see table 5), and their greater propensity to say that they are between temporary jobs when asked why they are looking for work (see table 6). The more unstable work experience of students is further reflected by the fact that they tend less than nonstudents to believe their work

Table 3.—Labor Force Participation Rates of Youths by Sex and Enrollment Status, 1963–73

	In percentages		
	1963	1968	1973
Enrolled men, age:			
16 to 17	33.7	39.4	44.2
18 to 19	36.7	42.9	45.5
20 to 24	49.9	51.2	54.7
Not enrolled men, age:			
16 to 17	78.2	71.1	77.4
18 to 19	93.5	87.8	90.0
20 to 24	95.9	94.2	94.5
Enrolled women, age:			
16 to 17	23.8	28.5	38.0
18 to 19	28.7	31.8	38.1
20 to 24	38.4	43.6	50.3
Not enrolled women, age:			
16 to 17	43.8	38.9	48.8
18 to 19	61.3	62.9	66.4
20 to 24	49.3	57.1	64.5

Source: Unpublished data provided by Bureau of Labor Statistics.

has career potential. Out-of-school graduates of the high school class of 1972, for example, were more likely than graduates who were both working and studying to believe that their present job provided opportunities for: (a) promotion and (b) further skill development, both 1⅓ and 2⅓ years after graduation (see table 7). Both groups of graduates, however, were more likely than nongraduates to find jobs having these career-related characteristics as they grew older.[15]

Athough out-of-school youths are more likely than students to find jobs offering career potential, progression into this kind of work is not easy for them, either. Using cross sectional data on occupation and age from the 1960 and 1970 censuses and longitudinal data on the labor force behavior of a national sample of young men between 1976 and 1971, Freedman [16] and Andrisani,[17] respectively, observed that among those who had left school, finding work with advancement possibilities was much more of a problem for female and minority

Table 4.—Unemployment Rates by School Status and for High School Graduates and Dropouts, by Age, Sex, and Race, October 1974

Sex and age	Enrolled in school		Not enrolled in school (percent)					
			Total		Graduates [1]		Dropouts [1]	
	White	Black	White	Black	White	Black	White	Black
Both sexes:								
16 to 24	11.5	28.0	9.3	21.0	14.6	38.5	16.2	31.6
16 and 17	14.9	36.8	20.8	(2)	NA	NA	NA	NA
18 to 19	10.1	31.1	14.0	31.4	NA	NA	NA	NA
20 to 24	7.2	16.5	7.1	16.9	NA	NA	NA	NA
					Both races		Both races	
Men: 16 to 24	11.0	24.1	8.8	19.4	15.3		24.5	
Women: 16 to 24	12.0	33.9	9.9	22.8	18.6		36.2	

[1] Graduating or dropping out during the academic year 1973–74.
[2] Percent not shown where base is less than 75,000.

Source: Bureau of Labor Statistics, **Students, Graduates, and Dropouts,** Special Labor Force Report, No. 180 (1975).

Table 5.—Duration of Unemployment by Enrollment Status

Age range and enrollment status	Percent distribution			
	1 to 4 weeks	5 to 14 weeks	15 to 26 weeks	27 plus weeks
Students 16 to 24	54.6	37.3	6.1	2.1
16 to 19	55.0	36.8	6.7	1.5
20 to 24	53.1	39.0	3.4	4.5
Not enrolled graduates 16 to 24	50.1	33.7	11.9	4.3
Not enrolled dropouts 16 to 24	55.9	31.0	10.1	3.0

Source: Bureau of Labor Statistics, **Students, Graduates, and Dropouts,** Special Labor Force Report, No. 180 (1975).

Table 6.—Reasons for Looking for Work Among Unemployed Youths Age 16 to 21 Years, by Enrollment Status, 1974

Enrollment status	Percent distribution			
	Want temporary jobs	Quits	Layoffs or lost job	Other
Enrolled_____	50.4	10.3	8.8	30.4
Not enrolled:				
Graduates_____	3.7	26.3	27.8	20.4
Dropouts_____	8.7	20.6	32.7	20.4

Source: Bureau of Labor Statistics, **Students, Graduates, and Dropouts,** Special Labor Force Report, No. 180 (1975).

Table 7.—Perceptions of Opportunities for Promotion and Skill Development by Labor Force Status

Year and perception of present job	Labor force status (percent)		
	Working, or working and studying	Working only	Working and studying
1973:			
Opportunity for promotion_____	59.6	63.1	53.1
Opportunity for developing new skills_____	64.4	68.3	57.1
1974:			
Opportunity for promotion_____	63.7	66.6	56.5
Opportunity for developing new skills_____	69.1	72.0	62.3

Source: Unpublished data from the 1st and 2d followups of the "National Longitudinal Study of the High School Class of 1972," which were administered in October 1973 and October 1974, respectively.

youths than for white males. The latter did tend to progress—albeit slowly—from low-paying, unskilled jobs into higher paying career-type jobs as they entered their mid-20's. Andrisani found further that while educational attainment is related to the likelihood of entering career-type work among both white and minority young men, the relationship is stronger for whites.[18] The relationship, however, between educational attainment and hourly and annual earnings is equally strong among white and minority youths. Among out-of-school young men who held non-career-type or unskilled jobs during the first year of the (longitudinal) study, returning to school was likely to help white but not minority youths break out of this (secondary) labor market and into career-type work.[19] Regardless of ethnic background or level of education, young men who obtained career-type work were likely to improve their hourly wages and unlikely to slide back into unskilled or dead end work.[20]

While many youths decide to sacrifice career-type work for further school, students who are able to get career-type work have a distinct early labor market advantage over those who cannot.[21] Whether in or out of school, then, getting career-related work soon after entering the labor market is the best predictor of subsequent labor market success; i.e., the best predictor of occupational success is previous success.

Barriers or factors which adversely affect jobholding by the young, particularly career-type jobs, include:

1. *An inadequate supply of jobs.*—For the last half century American society has not been able to provide jobs during peacetime for everyone able and willing to work. The need to lay off workers is met by a last-in-first-out policy that puts the particular brunt of it on the youngest members of the work force. Similarly, programs which attempt to combine education and work (e.g., work-study, cooperative education, etc.) run into the sobering fact that employers are reluctant to provide experiential learning slots for students when former employees who had seniority are on the unemployment rolls. To provide youths with a greater share of existing jobs, particularly career-type jobs (under the current structure of work), they would have to displace adult workers from their jobs, a situation not likely to be tolerated by the older population.

2. *Laws and regulations that make employment for young people difficult.*—The scarcity and insecurity of the 1930's is still reflected in overlapping State and Federal child labor laws—often misunderstood and misapplied by employers.[22]

3. *Employer and union discrimination against young workers.*—Employers, especially, are prone to generalize from the high quit rates among youths that all young people are irresponsible or that they will not respond to incentives to remain with the firm. Such employers are unable frequently to distinguish applicants with only a casual attachment to employment from those who are ready to get on with their careers.

4. *Public generosity and familial affluence which reduces the economic need of many youths for jobs.*—Failure of society to provide an adequate opportunity structure for a significant number of youths raises the issue of whether or not their socialization into adult roles will be impeded. Several blue-ribbon panels and commissions which studied the problems of adolescents and schools have argued that the inability to find appropriate work has unnecessarily prolonged the period of schooling for many young people.[23] This increase in the average amount of schooling for young people, they contend, exacerbates the social segregation of adults and youths and prolongs the latters' dependence. They assume that prolonged dependence alienates youths and impairs their abilities to assume adult responsibilities, that age segregation increases peer group influence, and that these factors together cause greater intergenerational hostilities and an unstable, "diconnected" youth culture. Such assumptions about the problems

11

of youth socialization frequently lead to recommendations which would facilitate greater interaction between students and adults, such as lowering the age of compulsory school attendance, making high schools smaller, and greater community and student participation in school governance.

Premises of the youth socialization argument already described have been questioned by a recent Rand Corp. study conducted for HEW.[24] The study suggests that while age segregation is almost certainly greater today than in the 19th century in terms of day-to-day contact among age groups in the home and workplace, many youths are in contact with adults in workplaces, in other homes, in schools, in military service, in recreational and social service organizations, and— vicariously—through television and radio. The net effect of these several trends on the quality of relationships among age groups is not known. While greater peer influence can lead youths with poor family relationships into further difficulty, peer relationships for most adolescents seem instrumental to their growth. According to the Rand study the existence of an unstable, "disconnected" youth culture is difficult to document if values, rather than manners and taste, are used as the criteria. The study suggests further that fears of this Nation's being separated by age-specific alien groups do not seem well founded.

The difference in opinion on whether or not there is a youth socialization problem is largely a matter of degree. The blue-ribbon commissions and panels obviously believe that there is a large and growing "youth problem"; Rand does not. While it is difficult to determine whether young people today are any less integrated into American society than youths of previous generations, there is evidence of a needlessly large group of present-day teenagers who are unhappy, discouraged, alienated, and apathetic. Youth crime and school vandalism statistics are the most depressing.[25] Further evidences of a "youth problem" are the rates of running away, suicide, drug abuse, and alcoholism among youths. Their political apathy is demonstrated by their low voting record.

HEW's Office of Human Development takes a middle ground position on the youth socialization question. It concludes that the policies and practices of our institutions operate so that most youths have access to roles which are personally gratifying and socially acceptable. However, a significantly large minority of youths are denied access to positive roles, like appropriate work, and are therefore negatively labeled with resultant feelings of alienation and withdrawal from basic societal institutions. These youth no longer feel they have a "stake" in society, and are more likely to commit deviant acts.[26]

Of the many activities which would give youths the feeling of having a stake in society, work appears to be one of the most important.

Indeed, there is some evidence that symptoms of youth discontent are related to their inability to obtain work. Of the young offender population participating in 26 rehabilitation projects sponsored by the Department of Labor (DOL), for example, more than half had been unemployed or underemployed at the time of arrest, and more than two-thirds had been unemployed during 1 or 2 months of their last year of freedom. Frequently, those who were employed had low-paying, high-turnover, unskilled or semiskilled, dead end jobs.[27]

Despite these examples, evidence is inconclusive on whether or not the inability to find a job is related to such manifestations of youth discontent as delinquency, drug abuse, alcoholism, and suicide.[28] In fact, for youths 17 years of age and under, most evidence suggests that access to occupational roles is of no significance as a determinant of juvenile delinquency. If anything, juvenile delinquency (ages 10 to 17) fluctuates with the level of economic activity; i.e., it rises during periods of economic growth and slackens off during recessions.[29] Though occupational identity is thought to become important around ages 18 to 22, there are no national time series data with which to test (for this cohort) the relationship between delinquency and fluctuations in employment opportunity. Drawing policy conclusions from the myriad of available studies is hampered further by inadequate measures of crime and juvenile delinquency and of the quality of the work experience itself.[30]

Inattention to the quality of the work experience in government youth programs may explain their apparent ineffectiveness in preventing delinquency. The jobs provided generally contribute little to a participant's subsequent employability—that is, they afford little training and infrequently lead to higher level jobs—and for many youths they offer less attractive economic and psychological rewards than criminal activity. Ghetto youths call them "jive jobs." Oddly enough, the influence of the provision of *career-related* work (i.e., jobs having advancement potential and training) on juvenile delinquency has rarely been investigated.[31] This is a ripe area for future research.

PERFORMANCE OF SCHOOLS IN FACILITATING TRANSITION FROM SCHOOL TO WORK

Schools can do little directly to influence economic conditions, the structure of the labor market, policies and practices regarding recruiting, selection, and promotions, the nature of the workplace, and technological changes affecting the demand for certain skills. Nevertheless, the schools can perform other functions which will increase the likelihood that the young will find and prepare themselves adequately for jobs that they like or, at least, consider acceptable. Moreover, whatever the economic conditions, schools can and should help people: [32]

—become more aware of the role of work in their lives and in our Nation's economy,

—become better informed about the nature and requirements of different occupations, and the education and experience needed to enter and progress in these,

—acquire self-knowledge in relation to different occupational futures,

—avoid socializing the next generation into delimited occupations and overcome self-imposed limitations on career choice due to socialization by others,

—improve their ability to make career decisions and to develop career plans that will help them reach their occupational goals insofar as possible.

—develop some of the skills, abilities, and attitudes needed to enter and progress in careers,

—acquire certification of skills and abilities obtained through formal and nonformal learning experiences,

—find appropriate work by putting them in contact with those who provide it.

Unfortunately, there is evidence that schools generally do not do these things well enough to help enough young people make a successful transition to work. In particular:

1. *Students don't know much about working and lack information about the nature and requirements of different occupations, about occupational prospects, and about the educational and experience requirements for career progression as well as career entry.*—For example, 61 percent of a sample of 32,000 11th graders believe that persons never change jobs throughout their adult life; 43 percent believe that unemployment rates are lower for youths than adults; 46 percent believe women never work after marriage. The facts are that most people change their occupations three to five times during the course of worklife; youth unemployment rates are almost four times as great as those for adults; and 42 percent of married women work—a percentage projected to increase in the future.[33] Several American studies indicate that a majority of young people are not satisfied that they possess enough information about the occupational world, whatever its source.[34] Data from two national surveys of teenagers conducted in 1964 and 1970 suggest that teenagers are becoming less content: only 25 percent of the high school seniors in 1964 felt that they got as much job information as they needed; in 1970 15 percent of the seniors felt that way.[35]

14

2. *Students don't know much about their own abilities and aptitudes which might be useful in selecting an appropriate career or further educational experiences.*—Several recent school trends in combination have made it more difficult for students to know where they stand in relation to being able to enter work or pursue further education. These include pass-fail grading, grade inflation, automatic promotion, open enrollment in courses of study and educational institutions, and the lowering of academic standards and entrance requirements to assure full enrollments in many postsecondary institutions. In addition, many teachers are reluctant to apprise students about poor performance. For example, Massey, Scott, and Dornbusch,[36] found that economically disadvantaged minority high school students in San Francisco had highly inaccurate appraisals of how they fared on standardized achievement tests, how well they were learning compared to other students in the courses they were taking, and how appropriate their study habits were to obtain good grades. The students, for the most part, perceived their teachers to be warm and friendly, but the teachers did little to feed back to these students the fact about how well or poorly they were doing. Appropriately, the investigators titled their study, "Racism without Racists."

3. *The early socialization of young people into occupational roles is unduly limited by sex, ethnicity, and social class, and schools contribute to this problem.*—For example, boys say they fail math because "I didn't try hard enough"; girls say they fail because "I'm not good in math." [37] Evidence that a considerable amount sex role stereotyping still exists among the young comes from a followup of 18,000 class of 1972 high school seniors a year and a third after graduation.[38] Among those who pursued postsecondary education, choices of subject fields by men and women differed markedly and followed the lines of traditional sex roles. Men tended to choose business, engineering and mechanics, and the physical sciences, while females chose education, the humanities, fine arts, home economics, nursing, and office and clerical fields. Among the 65 percent of the cohort who were working full time or part time, most women were employed in traditional female occupations such as clerical and sales jobs, while working males held mainly blue collar jobs.

4. *Competencies learned in school are not certified in a way useful to continuing one's education or to entry and progression in various occupations.*—Employers are handicapped because high school diplomas or completed courses which appear in transcripts may not reflect the competencies needed on the job. College admissions counselors have difficulty in determining whether individuals who have been out of school for some time have

learned enough in the interim to be able to succeed in college-level courses. To a certain extent the latter problem is minimized by the administration of standardized achievement and aptitude tests.

5. *Students possess few jobseeking skills and receive little assistance from any institution in finding work.*—Students are normally at a loss about whom to see if they want a job, and three-quarters of the time they must depend on parents or friends for this information.[39] That students are not happy with this situation is suggested by a national longitudinal study finding that while 77 percent of the Nation's high school seniors in 1972 felt schools should help students find jobs when they leave school, only 29 percent thought their school placement services were good or excellent.[40]

In addition to these deficiencies or problems, many would hold that young people lack the work habits and basic skills needed to learn on their own. There is little evidence, however, that this problem is now more serious than in the past. Although it is true that today's high school students manifest deterioration in skills which are the most rote or mechanical (computation and writing) or time-bound (vocabulary), less deterioration (science achievement) or outright improvement is observed among abilities relevant to problem solving (abstract reasoning and creativity). Possibly, the latter are just as important as the more mechanical skills to succeed in work.

Another frequent criticism of schools charges that they do not equip sufficient numbers of graduates with specific vocational skills which are suitable for career entry. If this allegation were so, graduates with specific vocational skills ought to fare better in the job market than graduates who lack such skills. This is not the case, however. A substantial amount of research evidence on the subject suggests that vocational education overall is no better and no worse than other curriculums in creating labor market advantages for its graduates. The U.S. economy is characterized more by a shortage of jobs than by a shortage of skills.*

EXTENT AND EFFECTIVENESS OF ACTIVITIES DESIGNED TO IMPROVE SCHOOL-TO-WORK TRANSITION

The successful transition of too many young people from school to work has been impeded by: (1) Their lack of knowledge of the world of work; (2) their lack of knowledge of their own abilities which might be useful in selecting an appropriate career; (3) their

---

*The issue of whether or not the schools are equipping American youth with sufficient basic skills and vocational skills, is discussed more fully in the section on marketable skills.

early socialization into delimited occupational roles because of sex, race, or social class; (4) the nonnegotiability of certificates or diplomas received in school to use when applying for a job or entrance into postsecondary education; (5) their lack of jobseeking skills and help from institutions in finding work; and (6) their lack of marketable skills; i.e., specific occupational skills and/or the work habits and basic skills needed to learn on one's own. Some of these are bigger problems than others, and some are being addressed more vigorously than others. This section attempts to determine how well and to what extent local, State, and Federal programs address these particular deficiencies.

Knowledge of Work

Recognition of American students' naivete about the world of work, as well as recent evidence that young people who are knowledgeable about occupations fare better in the labor market than those who are less knowledgeable,[41] has given impetus to a variety of Federal programs designed to acquaint students with work. Three general strategies are currently being employed: (1) To provide occupational information directly to students, normally through the school's guidance program; (2) to incorporate information about work into school curriculums; and (3) to provide students with a greater variety of school-supervised or coordinated-work opportunities, both paid and unpaid. Each of these strategies will be explained, including a capsule history of how and why they emerged as they have.

Occupational Information. Dissemination of information about the job market to students has been traditionally a function of school guidance. This function was performed better in the early days of school guidance than it is now, though it never has been done particularly well. Early counseling emphasized vocational counseling and placement, whereas today's guidance programs tend to be more concerned with developmental problems and future college concerns. A national survey of over 1,000 counselors conducted along with the "National Longitudinal Study of the High School Class of 1972," for example, indicated that only 16 percent of a high school counselor's time was spent on vocational guidance and job placement or referral, compared to 31 percent of the time spent on entrance to postsecondary education, 26 percent on attendance, discipline, and personal problems, and 28 percent on academic problems and program scheduling.[42] A study in the San Francisco Bay Area in 1968 revealed that only 18 percent of the counselors' time was spent on assistance in planning job futures.[43]

The decreasing interest in vocational counseling in the schools was helped along by five phenomena: (1) The information explosion, which made it all but impossible for a counselor having many duties and counselees to keep up with the rapid changes in the world of work; (2) the emergence of a large and aggressive employment security system, which theoretically at least, was supposed to relieve schools of the need to provide students with occupation information and placement assistance; (3) the National Defense Education Act which, in reaction to the Russian "Sputnik," stressed the early identification and guidance of talented youth toward advanced educational preparation (particularly in mathematics and the sciences), and resulted in a much larger proportion of young people going to college and the need for more counselors to assist them, and (4) the consuming demands of the Federal financial aid to students and other grant/loan programs over the years which have reduced time available for counseling. Whatever the reasons for the change in orientation, the extent of the change has been unfortunate in that the school counselors' prior link with the institutions of work was the primary contact that the schools had.[44] The disappearance of this linkage has had the most disastrous effect on the noncollege bound who are often left to flounder on their own without any direct assistance in making a next step.

Today's students rarely seek or obtain occupational information from counselors, most of whom have little experience with noneducational work, and infrequently consult with them in making career or job decisions.[45] Teachers are not consulted much either, unless they happen to be vocational teachers who teach courses that are related to the students' vocational plans.[46] Like the rest of the population, students usually get occupational information and advice from friends and relatives. Only 19 percent of 18,000 high school seniors surveyed in 1972 indicated that a teacher or counselor had "a great deal of influence" on their own post-high-school plans.[47] No doubt teachers and counselors would have greater influence on students' post-high-school plans if they knew more about the world of work.

Largely through the impetus on the Federal Government's emphasis on vocational and career education, hundreds of experimental or demonstration programs have been launched to incorporate occupational information into school guidance programs. These projects have involved variously local school districts, State employment services and educational agencies, universities, and agencies of the Federal Government. Frequently, funding for these projects comes from the Federal Government, either directly through discretionary research and development (R. & D.) funds or indirectly through formula grants made to States and local areas.[48] The projects are quite dissimilar from one another in terms of their underlying assumptions about what students need to support intelligent career exploration and job choice. Some projects attempt to develop idealized career guidance systems which identify the key components of career exploration and decisionmaking. These systems have used the full gamut of information media such as computers, microfilm and microfiche, films, filmstrips, video-tapes, and printed materials. A few of the systems emphasize the mere retrieval of information, but most focus on the complex processes which attempt to match personal and occupational characteristics. Such systems typically include data about occupations, colleges, technical and specialized schools, military programs, job placement, and about the user himself.[49]

The quality of the career information disseminated by these systems is very uneven. Most of the systems deliver national information selected from such reputable sources as the *Occupational Outlook Handbook* or the *Dictionary of Occupational Titles* or some commercial re-write of the Labor Department publications, but no localized information is delivered. Although the systems, as such, help many students explore occupations, they fail to temper vocational preferences with outlook information about the prospects for finding certain kinds of jobs in or near the community where the students live. Inasmuch as most early career decisions appear to be based on impressions of the local and not the national occupational structure, the provision of local information would seem essential. Besides, even the verified national information that reaches students is usually out of date by the time it is published.

Career guidance systems which provide localized occupational information typically do little to assure the accuracy and currency of the information. What passes as a "system" is more often a career resource center which includes any and all occupational material which can be thrown together, whether verified or not. System staff members usually have little training in how to develop the update occupational information from existing data sources. Frequently, these people make needlessly expensive attempts to collect their own data, and continually pester employers and labor unions with questionnaires and telephone surveys. School authorities ordinarily do not know how to judge the quality of the information disseminated by these systems and base their decisions to "buy" or not on the appeal of the delivery media—computers, microforms, and the like.[50]

Federal guidance is likely to be needed soon before these "ad hoc" systems become thoroughly entrenched. While one cannot blame local authorities for attempting to meet their own needs, Federal assistance and expertise in this complex area might well be required to assure that such needs are met.

HEW involvement in the systematic dissemination of career information began in the late 1960's with the sponsorship of experimental career guidance and information systems which used computers or various microforms as the delivery vehicle. Though some valuable experience resulted from these activities, it is questionable whether the subsequent benefits justified the cost. The computerized systems attempted to model complex career guidance processes and were too expensive for schools to adopt.[51] The microfilm systems were far less costly, but shared with the computerized systems the common problem of poor quality or unverified occupational information. Indeed, many of the "systems" were misinforming students about the nature of work in their respective communities.

HEW's Education Division continues to fund experimental programs to disseminate career information, including information about opportunities in postsecondary education and training. Some programs pay attention to the quality of the information; but most do not, preferring instead to focus on the manner of delivery or the subsequent use of the information for career decisionmaking. In fiscal year 1975, almost $5 million from the U.S. Office of Education (OE), the National Institute of Education (NIE), and the Fund to Improve Postsecondary Education (FIPSE) supported such projects. OE's Bureau of Occupational and Adult Education spent about $2.5 million of its VEA-part C research funds on projects which used occupational information for career guidance and/or vocational education planning. Also, in fiscal year 1975 NIE spent almost $1 million (or a cumulative amount of $4 million from 1973 to 1976) on two career guidance projects—one designed and tested career counseling materials to help students explore careers by guiding their access to personally relevant occupational materials; the other developed telephone counseling procedures to help adults choose careers, learn about education and training opportunities, and develop better jobseeking skills. Finally, in fiscal year 1975 FIPSE spent about $1.3 million on some 27 projects which were attempting to develop and/or disseminate information about the programs and characteristics of postsecondary institutions and to link this information to the education and training requirements of several occupations.

The Department of Labor (DOL) has been impressed, also, by the magnitude of the problem of uninformed career choice and has recently begun a demonstration program which provides grants to eight States to develop occupational information systems, which will compile, appraise, and disseminate existing occupational data to a wide range of potential users, especially students in secondary schools and community colleges.[52] The DOL program emphasizes the accuracy, currency, and local relevance of the occupational educational information which is disseminated. The grants totaled $3 million in both fiscal years 1975 and 1976, or an average of $370,000 per State per year.[53]

The proliferation of Federal R. & D. in the information systems field during the last few years has had a catalytic effect. Several States and local areas have recognized the same needs and problems addressed by these Federal programs and have tried to develop such systems on their own, frequently with the help of their Federal block grant funds; e.g., VEA and Comprehensive Employment and Training Act (CETA) funds. [54] Unfortunately, many of these efforts, like some of the federally supervised activities, have been expensive while not providing occupational information that was particularly useful to career decisionmakers.

Despite the fact that a decade of federally sponsored research in this area has yielded many valuable lessons about what is desirable and feasible, most students around the country remain woefully uninformed about work and their prospects for obtaining jobs in certain occupations. Perhaps the time has come to consolidate and pull together the scattered research, development, and demonstration activities of HEW and DOL which attempt to deliver career information to students and begin a more operational, national-in-scope program.

As policymakers consider the merits of allowing the career information systems field to emerge from R. & D. status, it is important that DOL and HEW work together on any new and more widely targeted program. With some notable exceptions (like the joint HEW/DOL effort to translate OE vocational program codes into *Dictionary of Occupational Titles* occupation codes), [55] failure to coordinate occupational information efforts in the past has led to needless duplication of effort, poorly focused programs, poor information, and an unduly heavy freight of public costs.

Curriculum. The incorporation of occupational information into school curriculums is perhaps more widely practiced than its incorporation into school guidance programs. The curricular approach in career education typically provides teachers with methods and instructional materials to help them make their courses more related to the world of work. Most of the Office of Education's 81 exemplary projects in career education reflect this approach as do some of NIE's research projects. [56]

Efforts to infuse career education into schools' instructional programs have been accelerating. [57] The initiative for this curricular reform is coming largely from the State and local education agencies with only modest financial assistance from the Federal Government ($10 million from OE in fiscal year 1975 and $3 million from NIE between fiscal years 1973 and 1975). A study conducted by the Council of Chief State School Officers indicates, for example, that of the 5,000 local school districts across the country which have initiated career education programs only 500 have received Federal funding. The study also reports that 25 State legislatures have appropriated line-item funds earmarked for career education; 42 States and other eligible areas have assigned an official to serve as a State coordinator of career education; 5 State legislatures have enacted specific career education laws; and at least 6 others have such legislation under consideration. [58] While efforts to implement career education were occurring long before Federal programs were initiated in this area, the Federal attention and publicity given to it probably has had some catalytic effect in spreading the idea around the country.

It is difficult to assess what positive achievements have resulted from the flurry of activity in career education. A recent General Accounting Office (GAO) study attempted to evaluate 14 of the 111 OE career education projects which were operative during the fall of 1973.[59] The resultant report describes career education as a potpouri of programs and projects with varied and vaguely defined objectives and little systematic evaluation. The only "tangible" finding reported was that career education is taking hold the fastest in the elementary schools. A more recent survey conducted by the American Institutes for Research (AIR) in June 1975, however, reports greater activity at the secondary level.[60] The explanation for this contradiction probably lies in the facts that: (a) The GAO study concentrated on innovative activities while the AIR survey covered all activities, both innovative and traditional; (b) the AIR study was more national in scope but less in depth than the more geographically limited GAO study; and (c) possibly secondary schools became more active in implementing career education in the 2½ years intervening between the two studies. Regardless of which conclusion is to be believed, the utility of both studies is diminished by the lack of data about program outcomes. In the absence of such data, the recommendations of both studies almost had to be fairly innocuous: "to analyze the problems in implementing career education, to provide inservice and preservice training of teachers, to develop evaluation criteria and use these in conducting evaluations," and so forth.

Possibly, the reason why innovative attempts to infuse career information concepts into curriculums have succeeded at the elementary but not at the secondary school level is that these elements tend to make learning much more experiential in the former while they do not have a similar effect in the latter. One could hypothesize that to the extent that learning by doing is promoted by career education, career education concepts will become adopted by teachers and produce the desired effects on students. The career education projects singled out by GAO as the most promising lend support to this hypothesis. Many of the most popular projects in the secondary schools, for example, helped students interact directly with employers, either through direct or simulated work experience. (Much work, of course, requires learning by doing.) Other exemplary secondary school projects cited by GAO led directly to work, such as those which incorporated career counseling and/or placement assistance. Though followup studies of program completers to determine the impact of the program on early labor market experience were not included in the evaluation designs of most of the secondary school career education projects, the ones which had the most intuitive appeal and which appeared to be most popular among teachers and students were those that enabled students to learn by doing; i.e., to experience real or simulated work or to plan their own next steps in preparing for or entering a career. On the other hand, courses or projects which merely attempted to introduce occupational information into traditional courses did not appear to catch on.[61]

An example of a classroom project which has successfully used learn-by-doing techniques in acquainting secondary school students with the world of work is a program begun in Houston, Tex., with a DOL grant and was extended later to more school districts by the Texas Education Agency. By means of various group processes, including such techniques as business development games, management games, and role playing, students are exposed to national and local labor market information and manpower trends, learn and implement techniques for employment and career planning, and become adept at jobseeking techniques. These techniques and processes are incorporated into the regular school curriculum and are taught by classroom teachers with the help of appropriate inservice training and instructional materials. This group guidance project, originally targeted on high schools having large numbers of disadvantaged students, significantly increased the students' knowledge of the world of work, increased the job placement rate among participants when compared to other noncollege-bound students who did not participate, and elicited extremely favorable student attitudes toward the program itself. The program probably exposes students to more accurate and interesting occupational information than do most other programs due to its emphasis on involving local firms, business and trade associations, and organized labor offices with the project staff and participating students.[62]

Experience with classroom-based career education suggests that new Federal research or demonstration efforts to incorporate career information or concepts into traditional classroom subjects ought to be limited to those which reflect the learning by doing approach. Curriculum projects which merely expect students to passively absorb information about the world of work tend to be ineffective and unpopular.

As research and demonstration projects develop classroom applications of career education which lead to improved educational and labor market outcomes, these techniques should be made known to teachers through inservice and preservice training. Given the fact, however, that so few career education curriculum projects clearl ' lead to such positive outcomes, massive programs to train or retrai ι teachers in this field (as suggested by the GAO and National Advisor ɣ Council on Career Education reports) are not warranted yet. Th:s would appear to be especially true at the secondary level, where very few programs to infuse career information and concepts into traditional courses have yielded positive outcomes. Despite notable exceptions like the group guidance project in Texas, evidence of positive outcomes would appear to be insufficient to persuade teachers of traditional high school courses to welcome the intrusion of career education on their subject matter. In the absence of reasons to train most high school teachers in career education techniques, an equally plausible suggestion would be to allow them to engage in noneducational work from time to time (with the option to return to teaching).[63] Maybe teachers need experience outside of the schools as much as students do; and maybe exposure to noneducational work is the best kind of inservice training in career education. At this point, we just do not know.

The promotion of teacher training in career education, in the absence of evidence on the relative effectiveness and costs in achieving specific educational or labor market goals, is likely to do a disservice to career education in the long run. A more appropriate strategy for that type of career education which intends to influence instruction in classrooms (school-based career education) would be to "separate the wheat from the chaff" in career education classroom practices through a continued and vigorous research, evaluation, demonstration, and dissemination effort. A modest acceleration of these kinds of activities might well be proposed. A more costly proposal to have the Federal Government widely promote classroom-based career education all over the country is clearly without empirical foundation at this time.

The preceding discussion of classroom-based career education does not imply that this should be the dominant form of career education. In fact, it is the dominant form. Although there are career education programs conducted in the workplace itself (described in the next section) and which are integrated with school guidance and placement programs, these are far less numerous than classroom-based programs. An issue which can be raised in the light of evidence accumulated thus far is whether or not classroom-based career education should be the dominant mode, especially at the high school level. Federal career education funds for high school programs might well be redirected from classroom programs to support the more promising work experience-based programs. NIE's funding of career education already reflects this strategy. OE's wider demonstration of the NIE-developed *Experience-Based Career Education* (described in next section) indicates that it, too, is receptive to career education approaches in the high schools which emphasize learning in the workplace and in the community at large.

A related issue is whether some age groups ought to receive priority for Federal career education fundings. At present the Federal effort to stimulate career education is fully a kindergarten through grade

12 (K–12) program. Though an article of faith in the education community is that curriculums reform must be a K–12 venture, we may wonder whether the great problems being faced by the Nation's high schools warrant the equal concentration of Federal career education funds at all grade levels. Clearly, the most troubled part of our educational system is the high school—if such indicators as test scores, vandalism, absenteeism, drug abuse, alcoholism, and the like are used as criteria. Midadolescence is,also the time when most young people begin to make career decisions. The suggestion to concentrate scarce career education funds at the high school level is not intended to disparage efforts to introduce career information and concepts to elementary school children. But does the fact that occupational socialization begins early mean that the Federal Government ought to give priority to influencing it at an early age when so many adolescents now leave high school with little appreciation for the realities of the job market? Perhaps early occupational socialization matters little when a person has to make a career decision based on current labor market realities. Perhaps the only aspect of occupational socialization worth influencing at an early age, because of its probable long-term effect, is sex and race stereotyping.[64] Certainly, what is known about occupational socialization ought to bear on the Federal strategy to fund career education. But the clear and present dangers inherent in disintegrating high schools should affect Federal funding priorities as well.

Work Experience. Almost every commission on the reform of secondary and postsecondary education and on ways to improve the relationship between education and work recommends expansion of work-experience programs in which students learn about the adult world and the range of alternative careers.[65] Though most students 16 to 19 years old work at some point during the year and 42 percent of them either work or are looking for work at any one time, the opportunities for students to explore work having career potential are very limited. Only 2 percent of postsecondary students and 6 percent of secondary students are currently enrolled in cooperative education, which does attempt to provide students with work experience related to their career plans.[66] The kind of jobs students get is usually dead end work with little advancement potential and in-company training, and as the labor force participation rates of students increased, this situation worsened. Of those employed students in the high school class of 1972, just over one-third worked at jobs they felt they would like to do in the future. In addition, only 13.5 percent of them were engaged in work which was related to their studies. This was apparently of concern to the students in the sample because even though over 76 percent were involved in some type of paid or unpaid work experience, 59 percent of them felt their schools should have provided more practical work experience.[67] These data seem to suggest, therefore, that a vast majority of students work primarily to earn money or credit but feel this is not sufficient and would prefer that their work experience also be related to their educational program.

Despite the fact that students are convinced that the best way to learn about work is to participate in it, there are only sparse data which corroborate or reject that view. One of the difficulties is that no study of the factors contributing to occupational knowledge has attempted to determine whether or not the work experience is career-related. One study, however, indirectly suggests that career-related work experience is significantly related to occupational knowledge while noncareer-type experience is not. Specifically, when Grasso [68] put factors which might predict a male high school student's score on an occupational knowledge test into a multiple regression analysis, work experience (i.e., having worked) was a significant predictor for blacks but not for whites, whereas among high school graduates the opposite was true—years of work experience was a significant predictor of occupational knowledge for whites but not for blacks. White high school students were probably less likely than blacks to have had jobs which were like the ones they would get following high school. If black high school students, in fact, had more career-related work than whites, it seems reasonable to assume that such experience would help them learn more about the labor force. On the other hand, because of discrimination and the lack of opportunity, black high school graduates were probably more likely than white graduates to remain in the types of jobs they had while white graduates were more likely to advance up the occupational ladder and get career-type jobs. Hence the number of years worked among white graduates would be a determinant of occupational knowledge, whereas it would not for blacks. Though this interpretation is conjectural, the data exist to test such a hypothesis.

There is currently a wide variety of work experience programs at both the secondary and postsecondary levels. Many of these receive Federal support. They range from strictly student assistance programs to those in which students are paid for employment which is directly related to their occupational choice. Among the OE-sponsored programs which involve work experience for students are: [69]

1. Cooperative vocational education programs (VEA-pt. G), costing $19.5 million in fiscal year 1975, and serving an estimated 196,000 secondary and postsecondary students. In addition, States fund cooperative education under the part B basic grant programs. During fiscal year 1974, for example, 605,140 cooperative enrollees were reported, including 145,342 who were funded under part G. Work experience in these programs is related to the school instructional program in vocational education.

2. Vocational education—work-study programs (VEA-pt. H), costing $9.8 million in fiscal year 1975 and serving 29,000 secondary and 10,000 postsecondary students. Work is not necessarily related to the instructional program. Compensation cannot exceed $45 per month or $360 per year.
3. College work-study program, costing $300.2 million in fiscal year 1975 and enabling about 500,000 students in 3,154 postsecondary institutions to obtain part-time work.
4. College cooperative education, costing $10.7 million in fiscal year 1975 and enabling 371 institutions to strengthen their programs and administration, train their cooperative education coordinators, or conduct research.

The National Institute of Education has sponsored, also, some experimental work experience programs including:

1. The experience-based career education (EBCE) program, costing $12 million between 1972 and 1975, which enables high school students to obtain unpaid work experience in several occupations and in a variety of work or community settings. An unusual aspect of this program is that experience in work settings is used to develop academic knowledge as well as knowledge of the world of work. In other words, the EBCE program does not develop world-of-work awareness at the expense of more conventional academic knowledge. A wider demonstration of EBCE will be facilitated by its inclusion in the Office of Education's vocational education exemplary projects program (VEA-pt. D). At least 1 school system in each of about 40 States is implementing the EBCE model under this fiscal year 1976 program. Recipients are expected to receive funding for 3 years, on an annually renewable basis. In addition to these projects receiving VEA-part D funds, another 50 school districts are implementing the EBCE model without Federal funding but with a certain amount of technical assistance and training from NIE's developer laboratories.
2. The career intern program, which cost $1.3 million in fiscal year 1974 and which provides 11th and 12th graders who are not doing well in school with a closely supervised and combined academic and career-entry program. This experimental program has been completed.
3. The executive high school internship program initiated in New York City and now being operated in 20 cities, though not sponsored by NIE, will be evaluated by NIE. This innovative program is helping students explore managerial and executive level positions.
4. The career education occupational exploration program, costing $1.1 million in fiscal years 1974–76 and which helps eighth and ninth grade students learn about careers by acquiring work ex-

perience under controlled or simulated work conditions and relating such experience to personal attitudes, interests, and aptitudes.

The Department of Labor provides youths with work opportunities under four programs: [70]

1. Employment development programs under CETA-title I which provide classroom and on-the-job skill training.
2. Youth work experience programs, including: (a) CETA-title III's summer youth employment program, which help youths under age 21 find summer or part-time jobs, (b) the vocational exploration program in the private sector (VEPS) in which the National Alliance of Businessmen and the AFL–CIO's Human Resources Development Institute attempt to find each year some 200,000 unsubsidized jobs for youths in the private sector, and (c) a public employment service effort to find 300,000 summer jobs in the private sector for youths.
3. Public service employment under titles I, II, and VI of CETA, which provides full-time jobs in the public sector.
4. Work experience and career exploration program (WECEP), which suspends certain child labor regulations to permit low-income 14- and 15-year olds to take part in closely supervised work.

Of these only the youth work experience and WECEP programs serve students predominantly. This can be inferred from the fact that almost three-fourths of those served by the youth work experience program (excluding unsubsidized jobs in the private sector) are under 18 years of age, compared to 3 percent of the manpower training (i.e., employment development) participants. Again, counting only publicly subsidized jobs and training, youths between the ages of 18 and 21 make up about 30 percent of the youth work experience participants, 26 percent of the manpower trainees, and 2 percent of the public service employment participants. Most of these 18- to 21-year-old youths are high school graduates. [71]

The only DOL activity, then, which provides a large number of subsidized work opportunities to students is the youth work experience program, which is called different things by different CETA prime sponsors. Many have kept the program title of its MDTA predecessor, the Neighborhood Youth Corps (NYC). In fiscal year 1975, approximately 75 percent of the 1.2 million participants were high school students, and about two-thirds of all the participants got their jobs during the summer. Like NYC the vast majority of the jobs under these CETA youth programs are unskilled jobs which effectively redistribute income to the poor but do little to improve participants' subsequent employability. [72]

The programs are more concerned with providing needy youths with jobs than they are with providing youths with high-quality work experience which will enhance career awareness, exploration, and decisionmaking. Little is known about the career utility or educational value of the half million unsubsidized jobs in the private sector which are obtained under the auspices of the VEPS and summer employment service programs.

Although many approaches to provide career exploration and knowledge through work experience have been tried, the tradeoffs among them in terms of costs, acceptability in the local situation, feasibility, and payoffs for learners are not known. Educational policymakers have been reluctant to expand work experience programs without this information, and some key groups have been opposed or skeptical due to concerns that may or may not be justified in practice, such as the fear that work programs for students would mean a loss of jobs for teachers or adult employees in firms which provide students with work experience.

A further complication for policymakers contemplating an expansion of work experience programs, or the expansion of one kind of work program at the expense of another, is the problem of self-selection. That is, it is almost impossible to conclude that one work experience program is better than another because students want and expect different things from the different programs. An analysis of two studies which attempted to evaluate cooperative education in high schools illustrates the phenomenon of self-selection. One is Stromsdorffer and Fackler study [73] of the cooperative education program in Dayton, Ohio, and the other is System Development Corp.'s (SDC) .study [74] of a national sample of 50 work-education programs. Despite very different research designs and methodologies, the two studies show remarkably similar characteristics among "coop" students, whose work experience is related to their schooling, and among working students whose work is not related to their schooling.

The primary message from both the Stromsdorffer-Fackler and Frankel (SDC) studies is that students who enroll in cooperative education have different expectations from their schooling than students who do not. The results do not suggest that one form of schooling (Stromsdorffer) or work experience (Frankel) is "better" than another.[75] Instead they suggest that students who enroll in coop education have more specific career goals than those who do not and that coop students are less interested in aspects of school which do not contribute directly to the attainment of these career goals.[76] An early career orientation is more likely to be the reason for selecting a coop experience than an outcome or result of such an experience.

In view of the problem of self-selection and the fact that most studies show no clear value of one kind of school-arranged work experience over another, the search for the perfect work experience package for students is bound to be as pointless as seeking the perfect curriculum. Students should be offered diverse work experience programs just as they are offered choices among curriculums or academic majors. Federal policy ought to be oriented toward helping school districts provide such diversity.

How to help school districts provide students with a variety of work experience alternatives is a particularly challenging issue for Federal policy. Some observers would like to see some school-supervised work required for all high school students and would provide Federal incentive grants to bring this about.[77] In support of such a policy, they would cite the tremendous and frequently unfulfilled desire of high school youths for work having career advancement or learning potential, as well as evidence that not getting it is associated with antisocial behavior and feelings of alienation and apathy among some youths. They would say, further, that an essentially R. & D. approach to expand school-related work experience would not be sufficient to meet the need.

Much as expanded work opportunities for students are desirable, the direct subsidy of work experience slots by the Federal Government is not likely during the late 1970's and early 1980's, except perhaps in areas having unusually high rates of youth unemployment. In the first place, the amount of money required to significantly expand the number of work experience slots for students would be too large a burden for the Federal Government to assume, especially inasmuch as the educational share of the Federal budget is expected to remain about the same. Unfortunately, there are no data on the number of students who now participate in school-arranged work experience. If it were considered advantageous to have 10 percent more of our 18.8 million secondary school students participate in school-arranged work experience, and if the cost of persuading local education agencies (LEA's) to do this were $500 per student, almost $1 billion of Federal funds would be required. A second reason for reluctance to use the incentive grant approach is that many States and local education authorities would probably object to such Federal intrusion on their prerogative to determine school curriculums. A third reason is that it would be extremely difficult to prepare and enact any legislation to specify the minimal standards for work experience that would be appropriate for all or most local situations. Though Federal legislation could well increase the number of students participating in school-arranged work experience, as the current Vocational Education Act has helped to expand the number of students taking vocational training, it could not assure either quality or diversity without such minimal standards.

Perhaps the most viable strategy for the Federal Government to pursue, then, in persuading communities to offer their secondary school students additional and more varied work opportunities would be the technical assistance and dissemination route, which is closely integrated with R. & D., as opposed to the traditional categorical program approach. A technical assistance and dissemination strategy would affirm the following principles:

1. That the Federal Government would attempt to persuade local communities to provide practical work experience, paid or unpaid, to secondary students who want it. Accumulating evidence suggests that school-arranged work experience programs (e.g., cooperative education, distributive education, experience-based career education, etc.) do not do students any harm in terms of their acquisition of basic skills and early labor market success and are as worthwhile as any other kind of school-arranged experience. Public information programs and the establishment of local education and work councils, 25 of which are being supported on a demonstration basis by DOL, are examples of ways to catalyze local action through Federal support.

2. That a much greater effort be made by HEW's Education Division to develop information which can be used by local school authorities and students in deciding to offer or participate in one work experience program or another. Much of the Division's R. & D. machinery would have to be reoriented to effect this. Rather than put the major effort into the development and testing of shiny new work experience programs, emphasis would be placed on evaluating and classifying the various programs and experiments which already exist and possibly on modifying these to fit new situations or environments. Tremendous diversity already prevails in work experience programs. Knowledge of how, how well, and to what extent current work experience programs can be implemented in different kinds of communities would appear to be more crucial to expanding the number of work opportunities available to students than continually developing new models.

3. That more emphasis should be placed on determining the community saturation level for a given work experience program. Contrived or natural experiments would attempt to determine the maximal number of slots which can be made available for the program before: (a) Additional numbers of students no longer elect it, (b) teachers organize in opposition to the program, (c) employers feel overloaded with students, and (d) unions feel threatened because school-age workers are expropriating jobs formerly held by older workers.

4. That following a concerted effort to develop disseminable information about work experience programs, the Education Division should organize resources to disseminate it and lend technical assistance to communities that wish to expand or improve their work experience programs. Federal technical assistance should be coordinated with efforts made by community groups, to improve the school to work transition; e.g., industry-education councils, education and work councils, CETA planning councils, etc. Ultimately, the Federal Government recognizes that each community itself must determine the appropriate amount and mix of school-arranged work experience.

In order for the Federal Government to help school districts improve, expand, or diversify their work experience programs, it is essential as a first step to systematize and bring together the scattered research and demonstration activities in this area. OE, NIE, ACTION, and the Departments of Labor, Agriculture, Commerce, and Interior all sponsor research or operational programs which provide students with work experience. So do countless trade, professional, and civic organizations, such as the National Alliance of Businessmen, chambers of commerce, public service internship programs, Boy Scouts and Girl Scouts, etc., as well as local and State governments. As Federal research programs and local and State agencies develop and test new work experience programs, a concurrent effort should be made to identify and classify what is already going on and record what good has come from these programs. Once a comprehensive data base for work experience programs is developed, more efficient dissemination of successful practices can be inaugurated and a more systematic agenda for research in this area can be developed.[78] One promising vehicle for accomplishing such program coordination is the multiagency Education and Work Task Force established by President Ford in the fall of 1974. This task force has helped achieve much better coordination in the work experience area between the Departments of HEW and Labor. Another organization around which to rally interagency cooperation and program coordination is the Interagency Panel for Research and Development on Adolescence. Regardless of which organization coordinates research on work experience programs, the need to systematize and disseminate what is known about the field remains.

The National Institute of Education has made a promising start in this direction in its fiscal year 1977 program plan.[79] Its basis strategy is to determine the costs, feasibility, and effectiveness of selected ways to expand career exploration opportunities for junior and senior high school students, and postsecondary students. For junior high school students, NIE intends to test career exploration programs through voluntary organizations such as the Boy Scouts, Girl Scouts, and Junior Achievers. For senior high school students, NIE will: (1)

Continue to field test its community-based career exporation program (experience-based career education), with particular emphasis on how to facilitate the transition from an experimental to an operational program; (2) evaluate briefer internship experiences (such as the executive high school internship program and the public service internship program); (3) expand work experiences and career exploration within schools, including simulated and real production unit experiences in the school itself; (4) expand and/or evaluate career exploration through youth organizations and through the initiative of the business, industry, and labor communities; (5) expand the career exploration component of work-study programs; and (6) develop summer career exploration programs, including the possibility of providing direct grants to students who would develop their own work experience (e.g., like the Canadian youth opportunity program). Finally, for postsecondary students, NIE intends to evaluate and systematically classify the various work-study and career exploration programs already available to postsecondary students. In the future, NIE might attempt to try out some of its secondary school approaches on the postsecondary population.

While OE and NIE research programs have begun to provide information on the costs and benefits of different work experience programs, no research at all is being conducted on community saturation issues. Such research should be initiated as soon as possible. The New Education Division Task Force on Dissemination is the logical group to determine how the division might organize the technical assistance effort for work experience programs that is recommended here.

Summary. Of the three ways of improving secondary school students' knowledge of the world of work, the provision of career-type work experience (i.e., work having advancement potential and training for further skill development) and the direct provision of occupational information to students through information systems or guidance-placement programs are the most effective. Evaluation evidence accumulated thus far suggests that incorporation of occupational information into secondary school curriculums is generally not effective, unless students are actively involved in using the information in learning by doing contexts. Public policy should emphasize the expansion and qualitative improvement of work experience programs for secondary school students through a strategy of technical assistance and the vigorous dissemination of what is known about school-arranged work experience. As for the direct provision of comprehensive, high-quality occupational information, the Federal Government should consolidate its scattered research and demonstration activities into a more operational program which is national in scope and which provides for considerable Federal-State cooperation.

Knowledge of Self in Relation to Career Development

Largely due to the launching of Sputnik by the Soviet Union and the subsequent National Defense Education Act (NDEA) and its amendments which stressed the early identification and guidance of talented youth toward advanced educational preparation, measurement of students' abilities, aptitudes, and occupational interests has received considerable national attention and priority. The number of standardized tests administered to public school students increased four times between 1958 and 1967 (the number of public school students increased by 33 percent, or 1.3 times), whereas for the private schools the increase was 2.5 times (the number of private school students increased by 18 percent, or 1.2 times). During the same period, the number of full-time equivalent counselors serving public secondary school students increased almost threefold—from 13,000 in 1958 to 38,000 in 1967 (compared to only a 64-percent increase in public secondary school students).[80] To a great extent the increase in counselors and tests was made possible by NDEA title V funds, which constitute by far the largest infusion of Federal funds ever to support the training and activities of counselors. Most of the counselors in schools today were trained during this period.[81]

Resources devoted to counseling and testing have leveled off in the 1970's, but they remain high. Despite the continued significance of these activities in the Nation's secondary schools, and the fact that school guidance programs have achieved the goal of getting the most talented youth into college, there is little evidence that guidance plays a decisive role in the career plans and outcomes of most students.[82] Yet students overwhelmingly express a need for help in career planning, including self-assessment in relation to careers.[83]

Improving the quality of career guidance is a major goal of HEW career education activities. Research has begun or is contemplated in such areas as: (1) Involving parents in the school-sponsored career counseling programs; (2) identifying crucial occupational and educational decision points in an individual's lifetime and the major factors (economic, family, peer relationships, etc.) which influence these decisions; (3) the role of self-perceived interests and abilities in making career decisions; and (4) determining the kinds of information about occupations and educational requirements which are likely to influence career decisions. In addition, the Education Division is holding career workshops and seminars for counselors and is developing materials that will assist them in the field.

Valuable as these research, technical assistance, and dissemination activities are, the fact still remains that students, especially non-college-bound students, have not benefited much from an enormous and federally aided expansion of school guidance and testing services. A recent study of guidance and counseling by the New York State Education Department demonstrated the low esteem in which counselors were held by both students and parents.[84]

Some new circumstances in high schools and colleges are making it more difficult for counselors to provide effective career guidance and for students to learn about themselves in relation to their future career development. These circumstances include the emergence of pass-fail grading, grade inflation, open enrollment in courses of study and educational institutions, and the lowering of academic standards and entrance requirements to facilitate full enrollments in many post-secondary institutions. Pass-fail grading and grade inflation (teachers giving higher grades on the average than in the past) do not discriminate much between high- and low-achieving students and therefore do not enable a student to know how well he is doing compared to others who take the same courses. Open enrollment or the reduction of entrance requirements to take certain courses of study (e.g., elimination of tracking and fulfilling prerequisites in order to be able to enroll in certain courses) or to matriculate in certain postsecondary institutions can interfere with accurate feedback about one's true academic performance.

Another emerging factor which makes it difficult for a student to get accurate feedback about himself is the reluctance of public schools to refuse to promote the poorest students and the reluctance of a growing number of financially strapped postsecondary institutions to deny places to students who do not meet entrance requirements or maintain the academic standards required for continued enrollment. Such institutional behavior is usually self-serving. Keeping enrollments high and preventing dropouts help justify bigger educational budgets and the continued employment of faculty and other educational personnel. In fact, faculty members of several institutions which are facing or experiencing a decline in enrollment are getting pressure from administrators to ease up on their grading requirements so that fewer students will "flunk out."

The move away from strict grading, promotion, and enrollment practices is not totally without reason. On the positive side, many students—especially disadvantaged and minority students—are getting the opportunity to enroll in courses and institutions which in the past had all but been closed to them. On the negative side, well-meaning instructors not wanting to offend nor contribute to a poor self-concept on the part of the low-achieving students, do not provide these students with accurate feedback about their performance or level of effort.[85] Such students often have a rude awakening when their subsequent employers fire them for not possessing the skill or knowledge that their teachers certified they had.

The response of many educational institutions and employers to problems associated with grade inflation, pass-fail grading, and open enrollment policies has been to open a whole new round of standardized testing and criterion-referenced tests. The evils of using such achievement and aptitude tests to assign students to certain academic tracks or experiences are well known. Another response has been to establish high school graduation requirements which assure that a graduate has at least minimal survival skills. The State of Oregon, especially, has moved in this direction.[86] OE's Adult Education Division has sponsored an experimental attempt to identify and measure such "survival" skills in adults.[87]

The appropriate Federal response to the problem of high school and college students getting inadequate feedback about their academic performance is not clear. Some reject any Federal responsibility and say that schools and colleges should reinstitute strict grading, promotion, and degree-granting practices and believe that this would provide students with the best feedback possible. Others, especially representatives from minority and economically disadvantaged groups, say that a return to the old system would discriminate anew against these groups and deny them access to good jobs or postsecondary education. Spokespersons for the latter point of view normally advocate additional support services—remedial courses, additional guidance and counseling, etc.—for "marginal" students and say that the Federal Government should pay for them.

A national concensus is emerging for a return to academic standards and the return of meaning and significance to academic diplomas and certificates. What is less clear is how to accomplish this swing of the pendulum without the reintroduction of the old abuses of that system. While the Federal Government might continue to fund and evaluate the worth of such programs as upward bound, talent search, and special services which provide additional support benefits including counseling to marginal secondary and postsecondary students,[88] it might also wish to explore a consumer advocacy approach which focuses on helping students get accurate information about themselves and the probable consequences of their educational decisions. Such an approach would: (1) Guarantee students access to records of their performance on all school-arranged or administered tests; (2) help students interpret the results of such tests so they know what they mean and don't mean, including the preparation and dissemination of easily read manuals which can aid such interpretations; (3) help students relate test scores to skills and knowledge required to perform successfully in certain occupations, when such verified information becomes available; (4) help students become more intelligent consumers of different kinds of secondary (vocational, academic, general, cooperative, etc.) and postsecondary education by providing them with results of studies which demonstrate the probable outcomes, especially labor-market-related outcomes, of participating in different educational programs.

Though many of the aforementioned features of consumer or student advocacy remind us of tasks which counselors are supposed to perform, the focus is a bit different. Counselors who normally perform under the constraints of a single institution, have traditionally used information about students to guide them into one educational program or another. The consumer approach does not do this. Instead, it attempts to guarantee students information about themselves so that they know where they stand academically in relation to where they want to go in their career choices. It would also attempt to provide students with information about the probable career consequences of certain educational decisions. Student advocates, who may or may not be counselors, would attempt to get such infromation to students on demand. Students would make their own interpretations based on materials that would be provided to them, or they might wish to seek help from the advocate or other school personnel about how to interpret and use this information.[89]

The Federal Government would contribute to the development of the consumer advocacy approach in several ways. First, it might develop and test a new course or module in *Consuming Postsecondary Education* which would help high school students learn how to ascertain the veracity of information (about courses, degrees, admissions, and financial aid) obtained from schools and colleges, as well as identify and answer questions which they would want to have answered before deciding to enroll in a particular course or postsecondary institution. An important part of such an activity would be to identify and evaluate the effectiveness of methods and materials which already have been designed to equip students with decisionmaking and information processing skills.[90] Second, the Federal Government might develop for high school students simply written and appealing materials that would help them evaluate their current educational performance, including their performance on standardized achievement and aptitude tests. Third, the Government might develop a series of State-specific booklets in conjunction with the States themselves which inform dropouts about the alternatives available to them if they do not return to the regular high school; e.g., job opportunities, information about the general education development (GED) test and external degree programs, etc. Fourth, the Federal Government might provide inservice training to guidance and other school personnel in how to be a consumer advocate for students ("telling it like it is"). Fifth, it might expand its research on how and to what extent test scores predict successful job performance in different occupations. Sixth, it might adapt the development of educational brokering services which presently serve postsecondary students, like the Regional Learning Service of Central New York, to serve secondary school students as well. In effect, this would remove some aspects of counseling from the school system and put them directly at the service of the consumer. Seventh, the Federal Government should vigorously enforce its new "truth-in-advertising" regulations for schools and colleges which make claims for preparing and then placing people to work in certain occupations. The Federal Trade Commission has had such regulations for proprietary vocational schools for over a year. Section 133 of the more recent Education Amendments of 1976 (or sec. 497a of the Higher Education Act as amended) authorizes the Commissioner of Education to remove from eligibility status (eligible to receive Federal education grants or loans) those institutions guilty of misrepresenting their educational offerings, record of placing graduates, or information about fees and costs or programs of financial assistance. Regulations for implementing this legislation will be released (by law) by June 1977.

Restricted Occupational Socialization

Schools and other institutions do many things to limit people's career options, but not all limitations are due to overt discrimination. Some are self-imposed restrictions derived from differential socialization, other's expectations, misinformation, and lack of awareness. The result of this for girls and some ethnic minorities is lower and narrower career aspirations. For example, as early as elementary school approximately 66 percent of all girls limit their career aspirations to teaching or nursing. At the same age, boys select up to three times as many different occupations as girls. The effect on minority group children takes place a little later—around 12 years of age—but the result is the same: lower career aspirations (than their Caucasian counterparts).[91] The restriction of career options for girls and minority group members continues throughout adolescence and adulthood, as can be seen from a 1972 study which found over half of the high school girls sampled selected occupations in only 3 out of a possible 25 job categories.[92] These data suggest the importance of beginning early to expand awareness of career options.

Federal support of ways to improve career awareness for primary school age children has included: (a) Demonstration program grants funded through OE's Office of Career Education (between 1970 and 1974 through pt. D of the Vocational Education Act (VEA)) including programs for kindergarten through grade 12 (K–12) children, (b) VEA support for 16 career awareness "spots" in the Captain Kangaroo program (now available commercially through the *Encyclopedia Britannica*), and (c) development of prototype materials for K–12 to infuse career information into school curriculums and guidance programs funded through the National Institute of Education.

In addition to promoting general career awareness among elementary school children, there have been some governmental efforts to decrease early occupational stereotyping with respect to sex and race. For example, some States (California, for one) have issued regulations prohibiting the use of public funds to purchase school texts which reinforce such stereotypes. Within the Federal Government, NIE has been the most active. For example, NIE funded Abt Associates to develop a learning kit for counselors to promote sex-fair counseling and guidelines for sex-fair publications, and in its third study of career education materials for NIE, the Educational Products Information Exchange Institute recommended guidelines on how to select sex- and race-fair career education materials. Also, NIE has funded the first few films in a series on *The Role of Women in American Society*. The largest of the current NIE projects is a 3-year, $3.2 million effort to produce a series of 26 half-hour television programs for grades four to six presenting women and men in a variety of life and occupational roles. These will be aired on public broadcasting to schools and homes and will be supplemented by teacher and parent guides and community outreach activities to help the programs reach their intended audiences. Another current NIE project will attempt to find out why girls do not elect to take mathematics and subsequently choose careers requiring very little mathematical ability.[93]

At the secondary school level, sex stereotyping is most evident in vocational education programs, except for distributive education where male and female enrollments are about equal.[94] Although in some instances this is largely cultural and not the result of intentional discrimination, other school districts openly discourage girls from enrolling in shop courses, while boys are not encouraged to enroll in home economics. Title IX of the Education Amendments of 1972 makes it illegal for school districts receiving Federal funds to continue such practices.

An analysis of 1972 and 1975 (national) enrollment data in vocational education suggests that gradual progress is being made in eliminating sex-role stereotyping from several occupational programs. The progress is greater for males, however. In the female dominant occupational programs; i.e., health, consumer and homemaking, occupational home economics, and office occupations, there was a significant increase in male enrollments. In health occupations the percentage of male enrollment increased from 15.3 to 28.3 percent; in occupational home economics from 13.9 to 26.8 percent; in consumer and homemaking from 7.9 to 18.1 percent; and in office occupations from 13.6 to 30.7 percent. By contrast, the increase of females enrolled in male dominant occupational programs between 1972 and 1975 was much more modest. In agriculture the percentage of female enrollments increased from 5.4 to 9.2 percent; in trades and industry, from 11.7 to 12.6 percent; and in technical occupations, from 9.8 to 10.7 percent.[95]

Dissatisfaction with the progress being made in eliminating sex-role stereotyping in vocational programs has prompted OE to place continued priority on it. For example, OE has given priority to research in the area of sex bias and will continue to provide technical assistance to help State and local programs comply with title IX. Also, new vocational education legislation in the Education Amendments of 1976 contains provisions which require stronger efforts to eliminate sex-role stereotyping from vocational programs.

Beginning in fiscal year 1976, HEW's efforts in this area were supplemented considerably by OE's Women's Program Staff (WPS) which awarded approximately $2.4 million in grants (authorized under the Women's Educational Equity Act) to support activities which would help teachers, counselors, administrators, and parents combat problems of sex-role stereotyping.[96] These activities included the development, evaluation, and dissemination of methods and materials (or modules), inservice and preservice training for school and college personnel, and the development of model programs to encourage female students to enter scientific and technical careers. Another $2.3 million in grants was awarded by the WPS to support activities which help female students and professionals gain access to all educational programs and leadership positions. In addition, WPS has awarded $1.7 million in contracts to evaluate their projects, to facilitate communication between them, to develop a clearinghouse on all programs or research related to educational equity for women, and to provide technical assistance (design materials and conduct workshops)' to help educational institutions receiving Federal funds to comply with title IX of Public Law 92–318 which prohibits them from discriminating on the basis of sex.

In recent years, the Education Division has become more and more active in sponsoring research, developing projects, and implementing legislation which is intended to reduce occupational stereotyping. In fiscal year 1976, the division spent $6 to $8 million on such activities, compared to about half that during the previous year. Whether or not these efforts are sufficient is largely a value judgment. Whether they are effective is a matter for further research and evaluation.

Federal policy in this area is hampered by the absence of performance standards or criteria which would have to be met in order to claim success in eliminating occupational stereotyping. The lack of national consensus on how fast this kind of cultural change should proceed, obviously, makes it difficult to develop such standards. But unless standards and criteria are developed, it will be impossible to determine the extent to which the problem exists and the extent to which government activities to combat it are effective. In the absence of measurable goals and standards, the best policy, perhaps, is to continue relevant research and development and disseminate successful practices. Furthermore, the various agencies and staffs within HEW which are concerned about this area should coordinate their activities in order to avoid needless duplication of effort while assuring dissemination of the most promising projects or practices.[97]

Certification of Competencies

That we require certificates as a qualification to learn how to do certain things, to do them, and to keep on doing them is not inherently bad. However, problems surface when such pieces of paper are used to discriminate unnecessarily or unfairly.

In the United States today, certification has become a multifaceted problem. One aspect of the problem has been labeled "credentialism," which is the imposition of excessive or irrelevant educational requirements to be able to enter or remain in certain occupational fields. The opposite facet of the problem emerges when inadequate licensing or educational requirements certify minimal competence in a certain field. A third part of the problem is inaccessibility of credentials, whereby some individuals are unable to obtain required credentials for occupational entry because of either insufficient or inconvenient training facilities and program segments. Despite some successes in resolving these problems, and some court cases which point the way for future action, much remains to be done before we can say that the United States has a fair and equitable system for allocating the credentials which influence opportunities for career entry and progression. Discussion of each of these three dimensions of the problem along with suggested Federal strategies in dealing with them follow.

Excessive or Irrelevant Credentials. The judicial history of the *Griggs* vs. *Duke Power Company* case and related court decisions is testimony to the limitations of presently available ways of assessing competencies essential to adequate or superior performance on a job. [98] The Griggs and related decisions have ruled that test scores or educational credentials cannot be used to select employees in situations where the results of such use is discriminatory and where the relevance of the selection criteria to occupational performance has not been demonstrated. [99] Pending cases include challenges to the U.S. Civil Service Commission examinations as well as to the measures used by certain businesses and industries and professional associations (e.g., the District of Columbia Bar examination and the national teacher examination administered by the Educational Testing Service which have been alleged to be discriminatory and irrelevant to performance as a lawyer or a teacher, respectively).

These court actions may slow a growing tendency of employers to use formal educational attainment as a screening device in selecting employees. However, it must be noted that use of attainment as a screening criterion is a direct consequence of two phenomena : (1) The rising level of education within the labor force and (2) a surplus of workers, especially when the economy is stagnant. As a result of these factors, employers have been able to impose arbitrary educational requirements and find job applicants who meet them. Since the rates of educational attainment among workers are expected to continue to rise through 1980 and 1990, [100] job prospects of persons with limited educational background thus may be bleak in spite of court actions.

Parallel to the imposition of excessive or irrelevant educational qualifications for occupational certification is the requirement of excessive or irrelevant academic preparation for entry into colleges and universities. Several States and educational institutions have resolved this problem by introducing open enrollment whereby entrance to college is guaranteed to all high school graduates or at least to all high school graduates who complete the requisite high school courses for college admission.

The courts have only begun to test policies pertaining to (excessive or irrelevant) competency requirements for university entrance and graduation. For example, some organizations representing minority groups have protested admissions policies of law schools and medical schools (e.g., the *DeFunis* case). However, entrance and graduation requirements are largely internal matters for educational institutions to be negotiated by the administration, faculty, and students. There does not appear to be a widely felt problem requiring Federal concern in this area.

In addition to providing greater equality of economic opportunity, the increasing attention given by the courts to excessive or irrelevant credentials is benefiting society by forcing employers and educators to communicate more often with one another. Each group has skills which the other needs to develop appropriate competency-based assessment techniques.[101] Perhaps more important is the fact that court decisions on the fairness of a credential affect its marketability; and educators concerned about enrollments will have to communicate continually with employers to determine the market value of the educational credentials which they provide.

Obviously, a credential is likely to be less marketable when a court rules that it is excessive or irrelevant. The educational institutions which provide such a credential have a choice of : (1) Eliminating it, (2) keeping it the same, (3) upgrading it so that it will become more competitive in those occupations where it still counts,[102] or (4) making it more relevant to performance in the particular occupation. From the institutional point of view, none of these options is better or worse than the others. The process of selecting among them, however, is likely to require employers and educators to communicate their needs and preferences to one another. Given the present and growing surplus of college graduates in the labor market and the declines in college enrollment likely to result,[103] the survival of many educational institutions and programs may depend ultimately on the feedback that educators get from employers with respect to the marketability of educational credentials. Education is a business, too.

The self-interest of employers is no less served by attention to credentialing practices than the self-interest of educators. In collaboration with trade and professional associations and labor unions, employers are increasing efforts to apply competency-based assessment techniques to assure that the best people will be hired and promoted. Though educational credentials still serve to limit the pool of applicants for certain jobs, personnel officers use a variety of assessment instruments to select among the "qualified" applicants. In fact, many industries now have their own assessment centers to help identify or train promising job aspirants from both within and outside the firm, especially in the management and supervisory occupations.[104] Federal, State, and local government agencies are also using assessment centers to improve their internal selection and promotion decisions, as well as to enhance staff development.[105] Government agencies, however, infrequently use assessment centers for hiring from outside of government.

Although decisions about the validity, fairness, or constitutionality of credentialing practices will continue to be a matter of contention between employers and the courts, there are a number of reasons why the Federal Government should help employers and educators advance the state of the art in validating techniques for assessing occupational competence and educational achievement. First, Federal interest in competency-based assessment is likely to play a catalytic role in persuading educational institutions to become more explicit about the skills they are teaching ("truth in advertising") and thereby aid the student (or "consumer") in purchasing educational services. Second, improved competency-based assessment practices are likely to decrease educational costs while increasing instructional effectiveness. Third, competency-based assessment will break the hold of schools and professional associations on the gateways to economic opportunity by eliminating irrelevant criteria for certification. Fourth, improved assessment practices can upgrade the quality of promotion decisions and facilitate career change among workers who want it by helping employers evaluate the worker's present skills prior to determining whether they are transferable or useful to the new job. And fifth,

Federal interest, in this area is likely to bring the worlds of education and work closer together by requiring employers and educators to help one another improve their respective credentialing practices.

HEW activity to promote and improve competency-based assessment practices is a fairly recent phenomenon. For the most part, such support has been in the form of research and development under the auspices of the Fund for the Improvement of Postsecondary Education (FIPSE) and NIE. During 1972–76, FIPSE spent $6.5 million on 40 innovative demonstration projects in competency-based education. Generally, these projects require that the school or college prove through various assessment techniques that students actually learn the skills that it claims to be teaching (e.g., Alverno College in Milwaukee, Wis.). Since 1973, NIE has spent $1 million on competency-based projects having something to do with occupational or educational credentialing. The largest portion of this by far ($800,000) is for the evaluation of Oregon's new law which requires that school districts establish and test requisite competencies for high school graduation. Among the other competency-based projects sponsored by NIE is one which examines the fairness of college entrance tests.

Both NIE and FIPSE intend to continue projects either to study output-oriented projects in their natural settings or to develop them in new settings. Furthermore, both agencies intend to continue projects aimed at improving generic evaluation methodologies and competency-based assessment techniques which are applicable to any occupational field or kind of training. Finally, a better conceptual framework for the field will be developed by attempting to answer such questions as: (1) What are the problems associated with implementing and replicating output-oriented models of schooling? (2) What are the effects of these reforms on the structure and productivity of schools? and (3) What are the effects on student learning and attitudes?

Given the current temper of the courts and the absence of any pending conceptual breakthrough which is generic to the measurement and assessment of occupational competencies, the Federal role with respect to competency-based education ought to be catalytic and not programmatic. Federal R. & D. activity in this rapidly expanding area should continue, but there is no clear case for a large-scale or categorical Federal program to develop competency-based tests for occupational certification. None of the conditions normally advanced for advocating a national program are met.

The first condition for advocating a national program is its likelihood to serve some overriding national or collective interest. This condition is met only in part. On the positive side, it would be in the national interest to give employers the tools with which to make more rational employee selection and promotion decisions. But, from the negative viewpoint, to increase the number of people who hold occupational credentials at a time when an oversupply of credentialed workers already exists in many fields (especially college graduates) would likely cause employers to unnecessarily raise their hiring standards again and thereby exacerbate the problem of excessive credentials. In other words, a large-scale Federal program to resolve the problem of irrelevant credentials might contribute simultaneously to the problem of excessive credentials by vastly increasing the number of people with them, as might well be the case because competency-based programs allow people to acquire competencies in a variety of settings and circumstances. At best, an expansion of competency-based credentialing practices may prevent some marginal participants from being certified and help some outstanding persons with exceptional experience to earn degrees with less effort. [106]

Knowledge of solutions for a national problem might be a second condition for starting a Federal program. Unfortunately, the present state of the art with respect to the validity of competency-based tests and the ambivalence of the courts regarding their use suggests that Federal guidelines and standards for such tests would be highly premature at this time. Continued R. & D., on the other hand, might bring some solutions which could be replicated on a wider scale.

A third condition for a Federal categorical program is that efforts being made to resolve the problem (by the private sector or by State or local governments) are not adequate and have little likelihood of becoming so in the near future. Even though the adequacy-of-effort condition is not being met by any sector, it would be difficult to begin any new widely targeted program because there is no agreement on how to develop valid competency-based tests for most occupations.

A fourth condition might be that the Federal Government possesses expertise in the problem area that is largely unavailable elsewhere. In the case of competency-based assessment, both the Federal Government and the private sector possess expertise, but little of this has been coordinated or analyzed. Business and industry are already heavily involved in developing their own tests and assessment techniques; witness the widespread establishment of assessment centers. Of the Federal agencies, prehaps the Department of Defense is the most active in developing competency-based tests; these qualify individuals to enter and remain in various military occupations.

The fifth and final condition of this hierarchy of conditions for starting a Federal program is that the benefits of such a program are likely to justify the cost and are more worthwhile than other government services which could be purchased for the same cost. In the absence of knowing or being able to quantify either the benefits or the costs of a general program to expand competency-based tests for occupational certification, this condition is not even close to being satisfied. Federal R. & D., however, could increase the likelihood of this condition being fulfilled by addressing the question of the costs and benefits of competency-based assessment in different settings.

Inadequate Credentials. Though there are still many workers in need of skill training and career development, occupational competency in American society has generally improved along with the expansion of knowledge and technology. In order to assure occupational competence, public and private employers, labor unions, professional and trade associations, and special accrediting agencies have all developed their own licensing procedures. When a State or local community becomes dissatisfied with private licensing or accreditation practices because of the poor quality of work provided by the incumbents of a certain occupation, it may develop its own licensing standards. For the most part, however, communities and States rely on the licensing and accrediting practices of trade and professional associations. So does the Federal Government.

Like the problem of excessive or irrelevant credentials, the problem of inadequate credentials is best addressed by specifying and measuring to the extent possible the competencies which are required for occupational or academic success. This process is enhanced when having employers and educators systematically communicate their needs to one another and thereby influence the credentialing practices of each. The earlier recommendation to stimulate such employer-educator contract through the funding of innovative competency-based testing and education programs is applicable here as well.

Perhaps the most inadequate credential of all, and the one which the Education Division ought to be the most concerned about, is the high school diploma. In most States and communities, graduation from high school is based more on "seat time" than demonstrated competencies or academic achievement. Only one State, Oregon, requires that LEA's establish and test requisite competencies for high school graduation. California is moving in this direction by allowing high school students to graduate a year early if they can pass certain competency-based tests.[107] Both the Oregon and California experiences are being monitored and evaluated by NIE. New statewide experiments to introduce competency-based graduation requirements should be monitored and evaluated as well. A more activist Federal role in promoting the adoption of competency-based graduation requirements would be premature until more evidence of positive outcomes from the current programs becomes available.

Inaccessible Credentials. The confusion about desirable credentials necessarily spills over into the organization of experimental programs for acquiring these in nontraditional settings. Many of these programs have come about in response to the demands of adults who wanted to earn credentials but who did not have access to the traditional programs because of the lack of time or money or the imposition of home or family responsibilities. External degree or nonresidency programs, continuing education and extension programs of universities, and home correspondence programs are some examples of the kinds of nontraditional credential-granting programs available.

Concern about the quality and subsequent marketability of credentials obtained in nontraditional programs has led many of the providers of these programs to emphasize the competencies needed for certification, while giving less emphasis to the manner or setting in which they are acquired. By permitting individuals to acquire requisite competencies by different routes, these nontraditional programs contribute to equity of access to further education, greater efficiency, and greater self-determination on the part of the student in selecting his or her educational experiences. Equity of access is strengthened because of: (a) The use of more objective, i.e., competency-based, criteria (at least in theory) for admission or certification, and (b) a reduction in the opportunity cost in attending, (i.e., the opportunity to obtain the credential in less time and hence at lower cost). Efficiency is strengthened because students need not take courses covering study areas in which they can demonstrate competence or relevant previous experience. Finally, self-determination is enhanced because a student is given greater choice as to how he might plan his education in order to acquire the requisite competencies for graduation.

While nontraditional programs have proliferated at the postsecondary level, nontraditional means of obtaining the high school diploma are becoming more popular, also. The proportion of students who pursued such means increased from 3.2 percent in 1961–62 to 7.6 percent in 1972–73.[108] More than 250,000 people per year earn high school diplomas through nontraditional means. The examination they usually take is the general education development (GED) test. In most States, high school students are not permitted to take these examinations before the age at which most students normally would have been graduated (age 18 or 19).[109] The main exception is California, which administers its own test of high school equivalency to students who wish to graduate a year early.[110]

Though the number of people who earn their credentials through nontraditional programs is increasing at both the high school and postsecondary levels, the use of competency-based assessment techniques as a means for validating the credential is becoming much more evident in the postsecondary institutions. Possibly, one reason is that postsecondary credentials are more directly related to employment requirements. More important, perhaps, is the fact that a few of the important assumptions and concomitant structural aspects of public education would be threatened substantially by the widespread adoption of competency-based assessment techniques.

Public education in the United States generally has operated under the premise that being involved in the process of education (attending school) would guarantee the desired outcomes (learning something). Moreover, it has been assumed that the student must be taught what he or she already may have learned. Allowing students to earn their diplomas by substituting competency-based assessment for either "seat time" or "being taught" or both, challenges both of these assumptions, as well as two important structural aspects of public education which have grown out of these assumptions. One is teacher tenure. If students do not have to be taught what they already learned elsewhere, many teachers, were it not for tenure, would lose their jobs on the grounds of reduced productivity. Another structural feature which would be challenged by a shift to competency-based assessment is the widely used method for distributing State funds to LEA's on the basis of average daily attendance. If students are not coming to school because they are busy acquiring competencies in the workplace or community, the allocation of funds according to attendance becomes anachronistic.

The sum of efforts to allow people to earn high school and college diplomas through nontraditional programs and to assure the quality of many of these programs through competency-based assessment techniques has been to make credentials more accessible. From the standpoint of equity, greater accessibility of credentials may be in the national interest, from the standpoint of occupational opportunity, maybe not. Easier access to credentials will help the midcareer worker who wants to change careers, but it may prove a hindrance to the worker who is unemployed or underemployed because of an oversupply of workers in his/her field. As stated earlier, when greater numbers of people possess credentials because they are more accessible, the individual worker's problem of being either overqualified for the job or unable to find a job which utilizes his/her skills may well be exacerbated. Federal programs, then, which would make credentials more accessible; e.g., to expand external degree programs and the like, might not be desirable. Furthermore (as is noted in the adult section), nontraditional programs are developing fast without Federal assistance.

While Federal programs to make credentials more accessible through nontraditional means are not indicated, Federal efforts to determine the labor market utility of such credentials and to improve their quality might well be justified. Such descriptive and evaluative studies and projects (which could be conducted by NIE) would help potential consumers of nontraditional education select their programs of study, as well as help providers of nontraditional education improve their offerings.

The labor market utility of nontraditional degrees or credentials could be determined by longitudinal studies which compare the labor market experience of individuals who obtain credentials from traditional and nontraditional programs at the same time. One item which should be assessed is the differential labor market and postsecondary education experience of regular high school graduates and those who graduate a year early or who pursue their high school diploma through nontraditional means. The same could be done to compare the experience of holders of traditional and nontraditional degrees from postsecondary institutions.

As stated earlier, the Federal role in competency-based assessment is essentially to fund and/or evaluate innovative demonstration projects and to pull together and disseminate periodically what has been learned from these projects. Many of the experiments in nontraditional education which have employed competency-based assessment techniques have had Federal support at one time or another, either through OE, NIE, or FIPSE. These experiments attempt to specify more objectively the performance needed to obtain a diploma or credential and thereby make an institution more accountable for the quality of its graduates. Most of the OE-funded projects in this area have been for teacher education, whereas the NIE and FIPSE efforts have not been so exclusively focused.

At the present time, no one has attempted to pull together, evaluate, and disseminate the results of educational programs which use competency-based assessment techniques. NIE is conducting pilot studies to determine how such evaluations can best be done. In the meantime, continued Federal support for planned variation in competency-based education is recommended. Continuity of Federal funding, albeit at a modest level, will help assure that all the rich experience in this rapidly expanding area is captured.

Conclusion. The problem of school leavers who cannot find appropriate work or educational opportunities because their competencies are not certified in a useful way is not likely to disappear soon. The refinement of competency-based assessment techniques slowly will contribute some solutions, but ambiguity and uncertainty in this field are likely to remain for a long time.

In the absence of any pending conceptual breakthrough which is generic to the measurement and assessment of occupational competencies, a cautious and systematic approach is to be preferred over large-scale Federal action. Given the present state of the art and the current lack of unanimity in judicial opinion as reflected by recent court actions, the appropriate Federal role ought to be catalytic and not programmatic with respect to competency-based education. Federal R. & D. activity in this rapidly expanding area should continue, not only to capture and disseminate rich experience worthy of widespread utility, but to bring employers and educators together around a common problem (certification) and to persuade educational institutions to be more forthright and explicit about what they are teaching.

Perhaps one service of a programmatic nature which government could provide at this time would be to continue and expand efforts to inform students and jobseekers about current occupational and educational entrance requirements. No doubt changes in these requirements will accelerate as court cases pertaining to occupational certification proliferate (NIE estimates that since 1972 there have been 135 such cases). Information systems, like those described earlier, would attempt to keep abreast of new developments in credentialing practices and in other career-related topics.

Job Placement Assistance

Over the years, public concern has shifted from preventing the too early employment of children to insuring that they find work when they are ready for it. Nevertheless, the least help is provided to those who need it most. Thousands of public dollars are invested in providing one young person with years of preparatory higher education, but very little is put into seeing what can be done about another's moving directly from high school to work. In no sense has this developed retributively. It's just bad business to which attention is now, belatedly, being given.

Although Federal youth employment programs have appeared from time to time during the course of our history, it was not until 1950, some 17 years after the Wagner-Peyser Act created the U.S. Employment Service, that a formal Employment Service (ES) program for youths got underway as a cooperative program with public schools. At best, it was a one-shot service; ES personnel came to the school, registered seniors not going on to college for job placement, and perhaps offered a series of tests and a counseling interview. The number of high schools involved grew impressively, to the point that by 1963 some service was available in 50 percent of the schools with two-thirds of the total number of graduates. During that year the program was credited with the actual placement of a modest 113,000. A peak figure of over 1.8 million placements of all persons under 22 years of age was reported for 1966.[111] (The reporting system was corrected in 1970 to record individuals—a significantly lower number—instead of placements.)

With the assumption of higher priorities in the mid-1960's; i.e., the need to place disadvantaged workers and veterans, the Employment Service school cooperative program declined considerably. A 1974 field survey of 24 cities in 9 randomly selected States, for example, indicated that the outstationing of ES personnel in schools was taking place in only 5 cities.[112] However, an inhouse survey indicated that ES offices in some 100 cities supplied schools and other interested institutions with daily computer printouts of the local job bank data. But this included only that information that comes from job orders filed by local employers. Most employers don't use the Employment Service to recruit part-time student employees except for a few limited types of jobs.[113]

Though Department of Labor data show that ES serves a considerable and growing number of youths (1.2 million under age 22 were placed by ES in fiscal year 1975, compared to 800,000 in fiscal year 1972), these data cannot be disaggregated to show the extent to which ES serves the particularly critical teenage group. Surveys which collect placement data from the youths themselves suggest that ES is reasonably effective for those in the age 20-or-over bracket, while it provides very little service to teenagers, especially those in school. The available evidence indicates that only about one out of 6 teenagers (age 16 to 19) looking for work even goes to the Employment Service (ES) ; among those who are out of school, one out of four visits ES.[114] Among out-of-school teenagers who are employed, only about 4 percent surveyed in January 1973 credit ES with directing them to their present jobs. The overwhelming percentage of jobs obtained are found through friends and relatives (27 percent), or by going to the employer directly and independently (32 percent). Some 10 percent get their jobs through want-ads, only 6 percent through school placement offices or teachers, only 5 percent through private employment agencies; and 10 percent through other means.[115] These Bureau of Labor Statistics data on jobseeking methods employed by out-of-school youth are corroborated by two somewhat older analyses of the National Longitudinal Survey (NLS) cohort of 5,000 young men 14 to 24 years old. In one study, Kohen and Andrisani found that among June 1969 male high school graduates who had changed employers (in the civilian sector) between the 1968 and 1969 surveys (which were conducted in November), the most frequently used job-search methods were through friends and relatives (52 percent) and direct contact with the employer (24 percent). Formal job placement assistance through either school, public, or private employment services helped only 11 percent of these graduates find their new jobs.[116] In another study of the NLS cohort of young men, Saunders found almost identical percentages for types of job-search methods used among those who were out of school with less than 4-years of college completed.[117]

Students are even less likely than out-of-school teenagers to get help from formal placement services in finding jobs. Again using NLS data for the cohort of young men, Parnes and others found that among teenage students (age 14 to 19) who were employed in 1966, less than 1 percent found their jobs through ES or through some private employment agency while 9 percent were helped by the school placement service; 53 percent were aided by friends or relatives; 23 percent went to employers directly; and the remaining 15 percent used want-ads or some other method or combination of methods. [118] A more recent study indicated that only 29 percent of the Nation's high school seniors in 1972 felt that schools provided satisfactory job placement assistance, whereas 77 percent believed that schools should help students find jobs when they leave school.[119]

Since neither the school nor the Employment Service provides much job placement assistance to students, neither has much influence on a student's career plans. When a national random sample of high school seniors in 1972, for example, was asked to indicate which categories of persons influenced very much their post-high-school plans, parents and friends were the most frequently named (43 and 25 percent, respectively), while only 10 percent named a teacher, 9 percent named a guidance counselor, and 1 percent named a State employment service officer.[120] We would hypothesize that ready access to job placement services would augment these institutions' influence (hopefully positive) on students' future plans.

As the presence of the Employment Service in the schools declined in the face of rising youth unemployment rates during the late 1960's, the reaction in the public schools was to draw back from the job placement responsibility completely. They already had more to do than they could handle. The counselors continued their college placement mission but accepted beyond that only a nebulous area of responsibility for the development of self-awareness and at most a very general exposure to what work might look like in the pages of the *Occupational Outlook Handbook*. Job placement was marked, quite understandably, as somebody else's business.

A 1973 study conducted by the American Institutes for Research for OE concluded that no quantitative data are available on the scope of placement services in the public secondary schools.[121] Through some local school systems like Baltimore and Cleveland do operate effective job placement services, these benefits are not being provided routinely as an important part of counseling and guidance programs.

In response to renewed public interest in the problems of youth unemployment and the transition from school to work, the National Center for Education Statistics (NCES) recently surveyed a national sample of some 520 school districts to determine the extent to which public high school students are served by school-based placement services. The study found that the number of job placement programs for these students has been increasing rapidly. More than half of the programs were developed in the last 5 years, and 44 percent of school districts nationwide enrolling two-thirds of all public secondary school students now have some sort of placement service. In addition, the study found that school staffs alone were involved in job placement in 54 percent of the districts having programs, while local employment services staffs had roles along with school personnel in 38 percent of the districts. The remaining 8 percent of districts with placement services each report having a formal agreement with a local employment service which provides working staff.[122]

The rapid growth in the number of school-based placement services is probably due to several factors: (1) the increase in teenage unemployment and labor force participation rates, which at once show their need and desire for work; (2) the 1968 Vocational Education Act Amendments which permit school districts to use their block grant funds to support placement services; and (3) the demonstration effect of the better community colleges and proprietary trade and technical schools, which attract students by devoting serious attention to the placement of those who finish their courses.

At the present time, no OE programs exclusively support guidance and counseling and placement. However, OE (categorical) program funds authorized by titles I and III of the Elementary and Secondary Education Act (ESEA), part B of the 1968 VEA, and section 120 of the 1976 VEA (limited to those who have successfully completed vocational education programs) can be spent on guidance and placement activities at the discretion of the recipient State or local education authority.[123] The aggregate amount of Federal funds spent by State and local education agencies for such activities cannot be estimated precisely with present data, but best guesstimates are in the $20 million per year range.

Until very recently, little effort has been made to bring students who want to work in contact with people who provide it. Despite students' overwhelmingly belief that schools ought to provide placement assistance,[124] most schools are still reluctant to provide it. Instead they prefer to concentrate their scarce resources on traditional academic concerns.[125] The Public Employment Service, also, has viewed student placement as a low-priority item, especially when so many adults are out of work. In sum, no institution perceives youth job placement as its responsibility. Despite the unusually and excessively high youth unemployment rates, youth and student job placement has been accepted no better than as an unwanted child.

So the superior force of institutional habit has had its victories over good sense. Proposals for new ways to fuse workaday realities and academic processes must, therefore, include consideration not only of: (1) How to provide high school age students with going-to-work counseling at least as effective as the traditional going-to-college counseling, and (2) how to give youth job placement at least as much attention as adult job placement, but also of (3) how to combine these youth counseling and job placement functions regardless of the minor earthquakes incident to doing so will cause in stratified established bureaucracies.[126]

Expanding local interest in providing school-based placement services suggests that now may be a propitious time for the Federal Government to provide some guidance and support to help assure that the services are of high quality. Though the recent one-page National Center for Education Statistics survey did not intend to assess the quality of the school job placement services, it did provide some evidence to suggest that many of the programs leave something to be desired. For example, among the school districts providing placement assistance to high school students, only 62 percent listed "job order taking and listing" as a function of this service; only 59 percent listed "job solicitation." [127] These job placement functions, in addition to the usual "referral to job openings" are thought to be crucial to the success of a placement program, yet are absent in a sizable minority of them.

Federal leadership might well be required to prevent the youth placement function from continually being lost in the cracks, or from being carried out in an unprofessional or inept manner. What to do is not the question. There are already several successful school placement models from which to draw. The difficult questions are: Who should do it? Who should lead it? How much Federal financial incentive is required?

Compared to other Federal human resource programs, the amount of money needed to establish placement services in high schools on a widespread basis is not large. An expenditure of $50 million, for example, could provide enough professional placement specialists to serve one-third of the Nation's high school students (grades 10 to 12), assuming a ratio of 1 placement person for every 1,500 students. If States or local agencies were to match such a figure on a dollar-for-dollar basis, two-thirds of the Nation's high school students could be served.

As to whether federally subsidized school placement officers should be employees of the Employment Service, of the schools themselves, or of some other agency like a local CETA agency or an education and work council, an approach which permits participation of different delivery agencies in different localities seems preferable. Whatever agency is used, the school placement service should coordinate with the Employment Service or other manpower agency contracted by the CETA prime sponsor to do placement work and rely on it for central referral of job orders. Moreover, any new Federal program to support school placement services should take into account ES's concern that these services could well reduce its potential number of placements and hence its budget for the subsequent year, inasmuch as placement credits are the main determinant of an ES office's budget allotment. Possibly, an exception to present ES regulations ought to allow ES to be credited with at least a portion of placements made by a school's program.

Another concern in the establishment of school placement offices is the need to continually follow up graduates, whether they get their jobs through the school placement program or not. Followup data should include enough specific occupational assignment and wage data to permit future graduates to better assess their probabilities for obtaining employment in certain fields. The mere accounting of whether a graduate is employed or not and whether this employment is in a training-related field (viz., the federally required vocational education placement form) is not sufficiently detailed to help placement officers with their responsibilities. Possibly, Federal aid could be directly tied to conducting sufficiently detailed followup studies of graduates. The cost of such a multiyear followup does not become so prohibitive when samples of graduates are surveyed rather than the entire graduating classes (the present OE regulation calls for the followup of all graduates for 1 year).

Ultimately, the success of placement services for students is largely determined by external economic factors and the availability of jobs. Accountability of guidance-placement programs based solely on placement "batting averages," therefore, is probably ill advised. For now the greatest justification for having school-based placement services is that students expect such assistance and want the school to demonstrate some concern about what happens to them after they leave school. Placement services are evidence of such concern and should become more widely available to students, regardless of their subsequent impact on unemployment rates.

Marketable Skills
(Basic Skills and Vocational Education)

For some time a debate has been raging about how much specific job preparation ought to take place in secondary schools. Should schools equip all students with skills that are salable in the labor market? Or, should schools tend to their traditional business of teaching basic skills while performing certain socialization and custodial functions?

The dispute begins with a calm assertion by teachers of vocational education that without a specific occupational skill, young people have a hard time finding jobs. But skeptics retort that in a rapidly changing technological era highly specific skill training is in danger of obsolescence and may not foster movement up career ladders. Proponents of this view contend that schools should emphasize basic literacy and computational skills, the most marketable skills of all, and should help students learn how to learn and solve problems.[128] The compromise position, endorsed by many proponents as well as critics of vocational education, holds that while schools should stop short of equipping students with specific job skills, they should provide preoccupational or "cluster" instruction, which aims at teaching general familiarity with a field, easily transferable skills within an occupational cluster, good work habits, reading capability, and sound thinking—all of which begins to sound suspiciously like what any good education is supposed to do.[129]

Employers and the general public are as split on their views as are educators. Many employers prefer to hire young people who have had a good general education and then teach them specific job skills in their own training programs. Most often, these employers are large companies in high technology fields that must continually improve their products and provide training in order to remain competitive.[130] Other employers want school leavers to be as job ready as possible and do not want to invest in their training.

All employers seem to want young people who are both trainable and adaptable. But many continually complain that young people lack the work habits and basic skills needed to learn on their own. Employers have always felt this way. The question remains whether there are grounds for this feeling at present. How well do schools equip students with skills to enter work? Moreover, to what extent do Federal programs help schools contribute effectively to students' eventual employability?

Basic Skills. Few educational issues in recent years have gripped the imagination of the popular press like declines in college admissions and achievement test scores. In view of the sparse factual information that is available about the changing results or outcomes of our educational institutions, it is no wonder that reports of these findings have attracted so much attention and reinforced feelings by many that something is or may be wrong with our educational enterprise. As educational policymakers consider whether or not declining test scores indicate that today's high school graduates are less well prepared to enter the labor market or postsecondary education than graduates in previous years, they should explore the nature of the problem and develop interpretations that are consistent with the facts.

First of all, it can be stated with reasonable assurance that most achievement test scores have been declining since the mid-1960's in all grades from five upward. This conclusion holds across most different assessment instruments, alterations in these over time, and varying compositions of the types of students taking these tests.[131]

Among the tests applied to high school students, the results are summarized as follows:

- *Scholastic Aptitude Test (SAT)*: College-bound high school seniors show a decline in verbal and mathematical scores over the past decade.
- *American College Testing Program (ACT)*: Supports downward trend of SAT scores in English and mathematics. Only natural science scores have remained at the same average level over the past decade.
- *Preliminary Scholastic Aptitude Test (PSAT)*: The scores of high school juniors do not show systematic declines.
- *Minnesota Scholastic Aptitude Test (MSAT)*: High School juniors in Minnesota show a decline in verbal and mathematics scores since the mid-1960's.
- *Iowa Tests of Educational Development (ITED)*: Iowa high school students manifest same test score patterns over time as SAT, ACT, and MSAT.
- *National Assessment of Educational Progress (NAEP)*: Declines in science achievement and writing skills over a 4-year period were observed for a national sample of 17-year-olds. However, the results for the reading-literacy assessment show an opposite trend.
- *Project TALENT:* No significant difference was found in reading comprehension among high school juniors between 1960 and 1970; the same test was administered to students in each of these years in 134 of the original Project TALENT schools.

Second, score declines are more pronounced in higher grades and in recent years. Third, declines are more severe for tests probing verbal than mathematics achievements. These findings are in contrast to the 20-year period prior to the mid-1960's when achievement test scores steadily increased. [132]

The causes of declining achievement tests scores are not well known, but there are plenty of theories and countertheories. Among the more plausible hypotheses about factors which might contribute to test score decreases are: (1) Substantial decreases in general or academic course enrollments, especially in the proportions of pupils taking the traditional basic courses of the college preparatory curriculums; (2) fewer high scoring students taking the tests in their senior year (i.e., taking them instead in their junior year); (3) fewer less affluent gifted students applying to selective private institutions; (4) a decline in the caliber of teachers, particularly with respect to their verbal and mathematical skills; and (5) a perception by students that test scores are not predictive of future academic nor occupational success, hence the diminished effort to do well on them.

Several scholars are attempting to test these and other rival hypotheses which explain the decline in test scores. [133] In some cases the data are sufficient; in others, they are not. Improvements in programs of performance data collection and continuing school surveys will no doubt help to clarify what is now a very confused situation. One of the most promising lines of analysis of the declining test scores situation is to disaggregate the verbal and mathematical scores into their respective constituent abilities. Such disaggregation of scores already is beginning to show why trends across different assessment instruments do not coincide more than they do. For example, while almost all tests of general verbal ability show declining scores, those which measure reading ability only; e.g., the reading tests of Project TALENT and the National Assessment of Educational Progress (NAEP), do not show such declines. [134] Aspects of verbal ability which concern writing skill (sentence and paragraph construction and spelling) and vocabularly, however, have declined significantly, as seen in a comparison of 1960 and 1975 results for students in 17 secondary schools using the same Project TALENT tests, as well as in a comparison of 1969 and 1974 results for 17-year-olds using the NAEP writing mechanics test. [135]

A similar state of affairs obtains when the decline in general mathematical ability is analyzed. Flanagan,[136] for example, showed that when mathematical ability is disaggregated into its constituent parts, a 1960 to 1975 comparison of Project TALENT test results revealed significant decline in computation and quantitative reasoning while abstract reasoning and the ability to apply elementary concepts in mathematics improved slightly. Perhaps these latter abilities are more important to succeed in mathematics than the more mechanical skill of computation, which the pocket calculator is rendering somewhat less important. Generally speaking, then, it is likely that an analysis of test scores without disaggregating them into constituent abilities will lead to misleading interpretations and inappropriate policy recommendations. Specific skills which appear to be deteriorating are those which are more rote or mechanical (computation and writing) or time-bound (vocabulary) in nature, while less deterioration (science achievement), or outright improvement is observed for skills relevant to problem solving (abstract reasoning and creativity).[137] Both positive and negative conclusions can be deduced from such findings. Without further data one can only speculate that perhaps some of the attention being given by teachers and students to problem solving and project activities of a more practical nature is beginning to show results.

Reluctance at this point to characterize declining test scores as a national problem should not lead us to dismiss the possibility that national programs impact upon the scores themselves. Indeed, a considerable amount of Federal money under ESEA title I is spent by local school districts to improve the basic skills of their students, particularly students from disadvantaged backgrounds. Most of these funds are targeted to elementary school students. The fact that achievement test scores did not decline, and in some instances improved, for the first four grades raises the question whether Federal funding to assist low achieving primary school students helped to prevent the kind of aggregate decline seen at the secondary school level. Similarly, in those few places where ESEA-title I funds were targeted at secondary school students, did changes in average test scores improve upon or merely reproduce the national results? Until these and related questions about the causes of test score trends are resolved it will be difficult to contemplate a revised Federal role.

While some time may pass before the declining test score controversy is resolved, the possibility still remains that the sharp decline in the last 2 years of high school especially (e.g., Iowa testing programs data) is symptomatic of the progressive deterioration of secondary education. By themselves, declining test scores are a merely symptomatic of a larger problem. When combined with other indications like increasing school vandalism and delinquency, drug abuse, alcoholism, and higher rates of suicide and running away among teenagers, a picture of an institution unable to cope with the needs of the modern adolescent emerges.

Vocational Education. The issue of how much specific job training ought to take place in the schools as opposed to workplaces has been debated vigorously both in the United States and abroad.[138] Proponents of school-based vocational training claim that such training will prevent many students from dropping out and lead to greater early labor market success as expressed by higher earnings, more time employed compared to time unemployed, more highly skilled jobs, and greater job satisfaction. Detractors from this position say that not only will vocational training at the secondary school level fail to achieve the aforementioned goals, but also that such training may be harmful in the long run by consigning vocational students to low-paying jobs for the rest of their lives. Furthermore, the detractors contend, job training can be accomplished more effectively and at less cost by business and industry due to their greater likelihood of having modern equipment and qualified, up-to-date instructors to teach people how to use, maintain, repair, and modify this machinery.

Orgies of studies at the local, State, and national levels have attempted to investigate the certitude of these claims and counterclaims.[139] Microstudies; e.g., those at the local and State levels, normally yield widely different conclusions about the worth of vocational education. These studies are usually flawed by their inability to control for local economic conditions and to keep track of graduates for long enough periods of time to accurately assess their early labor market experience. The mobility of graduates from one part of the country to another is a particularly perplexing problem for those who conduct these local or State studies. Other methodological errors commonly seen in them include: (*a*) Collecting earnings data from all graduates during the summer following high school graduation, and then comparing the wages of vocational education graduates with college-bound graduates who fully expect to give up their low-paying temporary jobs upon entering college in the fall; (*b*) including industrial (practical) arts and business courses in the definition of vocational education, or not using uniform terminology for each study; (*c*) aggregating female and male data despite the generally more unstable work experience of young women and the fact that their response rate to questionnaires is higher than men's; and (*d*) comparing the unemployment rates of vocational education graduates, which are derived from the annual vocational education followup survey taken within 8 months after graduation, with the national unemployment rates of the 16- to 19-year age group. The latter are derived from the more rigorous Current Population Survey conducted monthly by the Bureau of the Census. There are two serious analytic errors associated with this technique of comparing unemployment rates: (1) There is a selection bias in the vocational education followup survey in that the response rate is typically much lower than for the Current Population Survey and the vocational graduates who choose to answer tend to be the most satisfied alumni who have jobs; (2) Comparable groups are not being studied when the employment status of vocational graduates age 18 to 19 years is related to that of the 16- to 19-years-old population as a whole, especially when one considers that unemployment rates among 16- to 17-year-olds are much higher than among 18- to 19-year-olds.

National longitudinal studies which compare over several years the labor market experience of vocational and nonvocational high school graduates who do not attend college, and which include statistical controls for background and aptitude variables, are the most likely to assess accurately the unique outcomes of vocational education. Three longitudinal data bases have been used for this effort: Project TALENT, which sampled 400,000 secondary school students in 1,353 public and private high schools around the country, including 5- and 10-year followups since 1962; the National Longitudinal surveys of labor force behavior conducted by Prof. Herbert Parnes and associates at Ohio State University, which tracks the labor force experience of a national sample of 5,000 young men and 5,000 young women 14 to 24 years of age; and the National Longitudinal study of the high school class of 1972, conducted by the Educational Testing Service for the National Center of Education Statistics, which tracks the labor force and educational experience of 18,000 young men and women who were high school seniors in 1972.

Collectively, the studies which have compared the experience of vocational and nonvocational students by using these three national longitudinal data sets have shown that vocational education does not do any harm. Specifically, the studies, with occasional exceptions, conclude variously that vocational students or graduates are:

1. no more knowledgeable about the world of work than nonvocational students; [140]
2. as likely as other graduates to seek or obtain postschool training (i.e., vocational training in high school does not preclude the need for subsequent training and learning) ; [141]
3. as likely to drop out as other students; [142]
4. somewhat more likely than nonvocational graduates to obtain jobs within 16 months after graduation doing work in which they expect to use their training—especially true among women; [143]
5. getting jobs not too unlike the kinds which nonvocational graduates get within 3 years after graduating; [144]
6. no more likely than other students to obtain well-paying jobs or jobs requiring high levels of skill; [145]
7. only somewhat less likely than nonvocational students who also received training to believe that they could have gotten their job without the training; [146]
8. among blacks, no more likely than other students to obtain well-paying jobs, even with increased work experience and additional vocational training; [147]
9. among whites, more likely than nonvocational graduates to get well-paying jobs if they receive additional postschool training; [148]
10. no more satisfied with their jobs than graduates of the general track, and somewhat less satisfied than commercial and college preparatory graduates.[149]

Despite the evidence that longitudinal studies show that vocational education overall creates no labor market advantages for its graduates, vocational education programs are popular among students and the general public and constitute the fastest growing segment of the educational sector.

The last decade (1965–75) has witnessed a tenfold rise in outlays for vocational education. As Federal financial support for vocational education grew slowly in recent years, local and State contributions rose much faster. In fiscal year 1975, Federal assistance for vocational education amounted to $0.5 billion compared to $0.3 billion in fiscal year 1970 and $0.2 billion in fiscal year 1966 while the local and State contribution added to $3.2 billion in fiscal year 1975 compared to $1.5 billion in fiscal year 1970 and $0.6 billion in fiscal year 1966.[150]

Suggestions to reduce the amount of vocational training in secondary schools usually originate in the premise that it is more costly per student than other curriculums. Unless the benefits of this experience justify the costs, so goes the argument, vocational programs are a luxury that the schools can ill afford, especially during times of declining school revenues.

This type of argument, no doubt, will persist for many years.[151] From the standpoint of Federal policy, it is largely irrelevant— school districts have the right to determine for themselves which programs are worth what costs. As far as the Federal Government is concerned, what students learn when they are standing, moving about, and manipulating things is just as valuable as what they learn sitting from books, blackboards, and lectures. That vocational education contains more of the former than the latter is of no particular Federal concern, so long as no harm comes of it, and there is little evidence of any damage.

A picture of studied Federal neutrality with respect to the comparative worth of school-based vocational training is far from the actual case, however. Since the early 1960's, the Federal Government has given vocational education a priority accorded to no other kind of high school education.[152] The Federal policy to increase enrollments in vocational education has been eminently successful. At the same time, a large infrastructure of federally aided vocational education boards, planning bodies, and advisory councils was put in place to improve the quality of vocational education.

When the VEA legislation was passed (1963) and later amended (1968), widespread and persistent manpower skill shortages were assumed along with the rationale that out-of-school youth could not get jobs was because they lacked skills. Federal legislators and officials thought that more manpower and vocational training would decrease unemployment and eliminate manpower shortages. Hence, federally supported job training would be in the national interest .

Subsequent investigations failed to turn up massive skill shortages (job vacancies did not go begging in the skilled areas) and federally subsidized vocational training did little to change the unemployment rate nor improve significantly the labor market experience for all but the most disadvantaged participants (e.g., Job Corps). In short, there was a shortage of jobs, not skills, a condition which was partially alleviated by the war in Vietnam.

Today, a postwar United States continues to face a shortage of jobs. Our economy is becoming more and more marked by skill surpluses than by skill shortages; people with skills, as well as those without specific occupational skills, frequently cannot find appropriate (or any) employment. In view of the negligible public and private benefits of federally supported occupational training for youths, the fact of more or fewer of them engaged in such training does not now appear to concern the national interest.[153]

A case can be made, then, for turning Federal attention away from the amount or quantity of vocational training which occurs in public high schools. Past experience with Federal manpower and vocational training programs suggests that if a State or LEA wishes to reduce its vocational education enrollment, there is no national interest which would be subverted by so doing. Our vocational education legislation, nonetheless, clearly prohibits such cutback and provides aid to expand the number of vocational training opportunities.

While the number of school vocational training opportunities is becoming an irrelevant Federal issue, a continued Federal responsibility to help upgrade the quality of vocational education is evident. Many students are learning obsolescent skills which offer neither payoff in the labor market nor any general education utility. Once begun, a vocational program is rarely terminated; manpower demand and supply information seldom influences vocational education planning decisions and is hardly ever disseminated to students in such a way as to influence their decision to enroll. [154]

A new Federal strategy for vocational education might diminish concern for the quantity of vocational education and focus on the quality. Such a strategy might include the following actions:

1. improve the use and understanding of labor market information for vocational education planning and vocational course selection by students;
2. improve and expand the followup of vocational graduates so that prospective students will have a better idea of their probabilities for obtaining employment in a field related to their training;
3. focus support for occupational training on relatively few centers of excellence, expanding on the idea of regional skill centers;
4. develop flexible vocational curriculums which help students learn skills that are transferable to several occupations and evaluate such curriculums by determining the occupations where preemployment training provides the greatest economic return to graduates;
5. integrate instruction in basic skills (literacy and computation) with vocational training on a larger scale than at present; and
6. develop alternative ways to help students in the latter years of high school get occupational training either not offered by the school, or of higher quality than that offered by the school, including experimental use of entitlements or stipends which would enable secondary school youths to purchase occupational training from nonschool sources, including employers, labor unions, proprietary schools, and community colleges.

A new Federal role, then, would focus on technical assistance, dissemination, and research and demonstration. A catalytic function would replace the operational task of expanding vocational education opportunities. Fewer students might be served, but those served would be served better.

FEDERAL ROLE

Federal assistance to help localities improve the school-to-work transition can be justified on several grounds

1. The problems are of sufficient magnitude and are sufficiently widespread.
2. Efforts to resolve the problems by the private sector or by State or local governments are not adequate and show little likelihood of becoming so in the near future.
3. For most of the problems there are solutions already tried and tested.
4. The Federal Government has a sufficient degree of expertise in the problem areas to be able to help most localities and States.
5. The benefits of the proposed Federal activities or program are probably worth the cost.

Despite the justification for Federal involvement, this question can still be raised: Why can't the States and communities do it? Answer: They can, and some are; but the process of bringing the worlds of education and work closer together will move along faster if the Federal Government plays a catalytic role.

A more fundamental question, perhaps, is: Why has the Nation permitted education and work to become so isolated from one another? There are several reasons. First and foremost, education has been viewed uncritically for so long as a way to get ahead that few people considered the importance of relating its systematically to the world of work. In the sellers market which prevailed during the quarter century following World War II, employers could do little else than accept the products of the schools, for no other supply sector was doing any better and industry needed educated, or, at least, literate people. In the buyers market of the 1970's, however, when skill surpluses rather than shortages prevail, employers have become more selective and schools have begun to get pressure from parents to teach their children the competencies needed to become employable.

Other reasons for the progressive isolation of the worlds of education and work, especially for high school students, have been: the post-Sputnik emphasis on recruiting more high school graduates for professional careers requiring college preparation, with correspondingly less emphasis on placing the non-college-bound graduates into jobs (although Federal vocational education legislation did attempt to redress this imbalance); the "equality of educational opportunity" movement which similarly stressed movement (of the disadvantaged and minorities) into further education, while assuming that this would improve access to jobs (economic opportunity); the rise of a number of school trends such as pass-fail grading, grade inflation, automatic promotion, and open enrollment—all intended to motivate students to learn but yet they made it more difficult for students to become sufficiently aware of their abilities and aptitudes to be able to match them with the requirements of different occupations; the rapid growth of community colleges and proprietary vocational schools which enabled many more students to obtain specific occupational skills and placement assistance, thereby making it less necessary for high schools to concern themselves with the transition to work; and the progressive reluctance of school officials to hire professional personnel who lack teacher certification or who offer extensive experience in noneducational work. This situation evolves chiefly from the increasing power of teacher organizations to influence school employment practices and, in part, from the declining growth rates of school budgets.

To a considerable extent, then, the progressive isolation of the worlds of work and education grew out of well-intended national policy to increase the Nation's supply of highly trained manpower while achieving a greater degree of social justice by making postsecondary education more accessible and attractive to more people. This policy has largely succeeded, though somewhat at the expense of youths' preparation to enter the world of work, whether or not they go on to college. Perhaps it is time to evaluate and reemphasize this preparation-for-working-life function of education, not to give it more priority than other legitimate educational functions, but merely to allow it to finally attain a place among the most important.

FEDERAL POLICY OPTIONS

To increase the supply and quality of jobs available to youths is perhaps the most effective way to assure their successful transition from school to work. If young people are reasonably confident that hard work in school will be rewarded by suitable job opportunities, they are more likely to strive to acquire in school the skills and knowledges which will enhance their employability. Improving youth job opportunities is easier said than done, however, there is little consensus on which macroeconomic or manpower policies ought to be followed. Alternative strategies which are currently being discussed and debated include: (1) Policies to promote general economic expansion, (2) financial incentives to employers for hiring youths, such as tax credits, or a lower minimum wage for youths, (3) public works and public service employment, including required public service for the young, and (4) job sharing or redistribution of work. The major unresolved problem is how to create useful and productive employment for youths without taking jobs away from adult workers.

Although some time may elapse before consensus is rallied around a plan to improve the youth employment situation, there are a few actions which the schools could take to help young people make their job search more efficient and their subsequent work more personally satisfying. In general, the options put forth here are intended to help young people approach career decisionmaking with a greater sense of realism about themselves and about the labor market. In addition, they call for more direct assistance from the school in helping young people make contact with both employers and workers. These school-based activities will not have any major effect on the youth employment situation. To the extent, however, that these activities decrease job search time (because of knowing what one wants and getting assistance to obtain it) and quit rates (because of wanting to keep satisfying work), youth unemployment rates would be reduced, also.

On the assumption of relatively constant Federal expenditures for education and work, a strategy to effect a more successful transition from school to work would gradually shift the Federal funds used to support school-based vocational training to other activities which appear at this time to be more strongly associated with a successful transition.[155] Possible Federal actions classified by problem areas are identified under the options which follows.

Options To Improve Students' Knowledge of the Labor Market

Of the various ways to improve secondary school students' knowledge of the world of work, affording them career-type work experience (i.e., work offering advancement potential and training for skill development) and providing them direct access to occupational data (especially realistic job outlook forecasts) through information systems or guidance-placement programs are the most effective. While some classroom based career education programs have expanded the career awareness of students, evaluation evidence accumulated thus far suggests that incorporation of occupational information into secondary school curriculums is generally not effective, unless students are actively involved in using the information in learning by doing contexts. Public policy should emphasize the expansion and qualitative improvement of paid and unpaid work experience programs for secondary school students, as well as the development and dissemination of comprehensive, high quality occupational and educational information.

1.—Provide Secondary School Students With More and Better Work Experience Opportunities (see chart 1). Supervised and planned experience in the workplace can help some students acquire academic knowledge as well as help them learn about work. Many successful work experience models exist. Minimally, a Federal effort should be made to classify and evaluate these models by type of school setting and then to disseminate the results. This effort could be aided considerably by OE's National Diffusion Network System and the Joint (NIE–OE) Dissemination Review Panel, which seek to identify and disseminate successful educational practices. In addition to this technical assistance effort, HEW might wish to invest more of its discretionary funds in a wider demonstration of the more successful work experience programs, like the experience-based career education (EBCE) and the executive high school internships programs (which use the workplace as a setting for learning) and the Canadian youth opportunities programs (which pays students to create their own public service jobs). Those models which encourage youth entrepreneurship in the private sector might be demonstrated as well. If more Federal funds were to become available to increase substantially the number of work slots for students, priority ought to be given to youths in high unemployment areas; and care should be taken to assure that their work experience has some educational value. Work experience programs which segregate younger workers should be avoided, because they tend to end in transfers of income and not the accomplishment of real work with defensible performance standards (e.g., Neighborhood Youth Corps). Young workers need to interact with older workers for the employment experience to have either productive or educational value.

2.—Provide Students With More and Better Career Information (see chart 2). Students are not getting the information they need for intelligent job choices. Yet knowledge of occupations is associated with early labor market success. Lack of Federal initiative in this area will perpetuate a situation where much misinformation about the labor market is disseminated to students. Regardless of labor market conditions and the possibility that better occupational information may not improve access to jobs for many, people still have the right to get the most accurate information available.

A range of Federal activities to provide students with accurate, up-to-date, and locally relevant career information ought to be considered. Modest amounts of Federal dollars would support a variety of technical assistance and training activities, including the development of short courses and materials in the *Interpretation and Utilization of Labor Market Information*, and the dissemination of effective models of occupational and educational information systems, career education, vocational guidance, and career exploration. More money would enable HEW to demonstrate on a larger scale some of the more

Chart 1.—Options to Provide Work Experience to Students

		Range of options (from little to considerable Federal involvement and support)				
		Little support			Considerable support	
		I	II	III	IV	V
Problem	Program objectives	Demonstration of local education and work councils	Federal technical assistance and training	Expansion of demonstration programs	Federal student volunteers program	Federal student work experience program
nadequate knowledge of the labor market.	To encourage communities to provide more and better work experience opportunities which will allow students to learn about work by participating in it.	Bring trade associations, service organizations, unions, public and private employers together to generate more work experience slots for students.	Identify and package effective models of paid and unpaid work experience, classify and rate these by type of school setting. In collaboration with interest groups and associations, disseminate information about these models and develop a public information program to persuade local authorities and employers to increase the number and quality of work experience slots for students. Sponsor conferences, workshops, etc. for work-study coordinators ($1,000,000 to $2,000,000 per year).	Fund more demonstrations of EBCE program through VEA exemplary projects and NIE laboratories ($4,000,000). Fund demonstration program to encourage youth entrepreneurship along lines of Canadian youth opportunities program. National Commission on Resources for Youth might be willing to develop and administer some models ($4,000,000 to $6,000,000). Fund NIE to demonstrate feasibility of exploratory work experience programs for junior high school students ($400,000). Expand DOL/USOE WECEP. Extend best of NIE-developed career exploration models for postsecondary students to more institutions ($800,000).	New legislation to provide students in high-youth unemployment areas with paid community service opportunities ($330,000,000).	Legislation to give schools financial incentives to increase the number of work experience slots. (On the assumption that the cost of creating one new slot is $500 per year, and that it is desirable to give work experience to 10 pct (2.4 million) more high schooll students, the annual cost would be $1.2 billion).

KEY TO ABBREVIATIONS

EBCE = Experience-based career education.
VEA = Vocational Education Act.
NIE = National Institute of Education.

DOL = U.S. Department of Labor.
USOE = U.S. Office of Education.
WECEP = Work experience and career exploration program.

successful models for providing career information. For example, HEW could help DOL extend its eight-State demonstration to three or four more States and could provide funds and guidance to improve the educational information contained in the systems. In addition, HEW could extend to more areas the best projects which help students understand and use career information materials.

Moving beyond technical assistance and demonstration programs, HEW and DOL should jointly consider establishing career information systems in all parts of the country. Their involvement might be in the form of "seed money" to persuade States to develop their own systems which would become self-supporting within a few years, or a full-fledged federally supervised and funded system might be instituted. At present, the country is moving in the direction of State-operated rather than federally run career information systems, witness the DOL eight-State demonstration program which utilizes the "seed money" approach just mentioned. Regardless of which strategy is employed, DOL would be concerned mostly with the quality of the occupational information in the system, while HEW would be responsible for the quality of the educational information.

Options To Improve Self-knowledge of Abilities and Aptitudes

Several recent school phenomena in combination have made it more difficult for students to know where they stand in relation to their ability to enter work or pursue further education. These include pass-fail grading, grade inflation, automatic promotion, open enrollment in courses of study and educational institutions, and the lowering of academic standards and entrance requirements to assure full enrollments in many postsecondary institutions. On the other hand, the Family Education Rights and Privacy Act of 1974 (Buckley amendment), which guarantees students and parents access to the school's information about them, is likely to help students learn about their abilities and aptitudes. Given the fact that few schools have enough personnel who can help students understand and intelligently use such information, this act needs to be supplemented by activities which will help students become more knowledgeable about themselves. Examples of possible Federal initiatives include (see chart 3):

1. Development and testing of a new course or module in *Consuming Postsecondary Education* which would help high school students learn how to ascertain the veracity and usefulness of information obtained from schools and colleges.
2. Development of easily understood materials that would help students interpret their performance on standardized achievement, aptitude, and interest tests.

Chart 2.—Options To Provide Career Information to Students

Problem	Program objective	Range of options (from little to considerable Federal involvement and support)				
		Little support			Considerable support	
		I	II	III	IV	V
		Local education and work councils	Federal technical assistance and training	Expansion of demonstration programs	States grants program to establish career information systems	Federal career information system
Inadequate knowledge of the labor market Students don't know much about working and lack information about the nature and requirements of different occupations, about employment prospects, and about the educational and experience requirements for career entry and progression.	To provide students with more and better career information (i.e., occupational and educational information).	Small grants to 15 to 30 communities to establish councils, which would disseminate local occupational data and information to schools and encourage visits, field trips, etc. to bring students into greater contact with employers and workers. $1,000,000 to $2,000,000.	Through HEW–DOL–occupational Information Coordinating Committee: Sponsor short courses in **Interpretation and Utilization of Labor Market Information** for State and local manpower and education planning staff, vocational counselors, work experience coordinators, etc. Develop LMI dictionary and users manual ($300,000 per year). Identify and package effective models of occupational and educational information systems, career education, vocational counseling and exploration, etc. Collaborate with associations and interest groups to identify such models and disseminate information about them ($2,000,000 per year).	Extend DOL 8-State demonstration of **Occupational Information Systems** to 3 to 4 more States with HEW participation ($1,000,000 per year). Extend best of FIPSE educational information projects to more areas ($1,000,000 per year). Extend to more areas best of projects which help students understand and use career	New legislation to expand DOL, OIS program to all States with HEW participation. DOL responsible for quality of occupational information. HEW responsible for quality of educational information. Local user agency assumes delivery or equipment costs. State systems to become self-supporting within 4 years (DOL and HEW each contribute $5,000,000 per year for 5 yr.).	Legislation to establish federally supervised and funded system to provide career information to students and adults. DOL and HEW share cost and responsibility for demonstration and delivery of occupational and educational information, respectively (each agency contributes $15,000,000 to $20,000,000 per year).

In 8 States having DOL OIS program, fund a State vocational education board staff member to work with OIS staff and serve as program's "extension agent" to manpower and vocational education planning bodies ($200,000 per year).

Require all public, proprietary, and home study schools receiving Federal aid to report program completions by appropriate OE education course codes and DOL **Dictionary of Occupational Titles** codes.

information materials ($1,000,000 per year).

KEY TO ABBREVIATIONS

HEW = U.S. Department of Health, Education, and Welfare.
DOL = U.S. Department of Labor.
DOC = U.S. Department of Commerce.

OIS = Occupational information system.
FIPSE = Fund for the improvement of postsecondary education.
LMI = Labor market information.

3. Development of a series of State-specific booklets or course modules in conjunction with the States themselves which inform dropouts about the alternatives available to them if they do not return to the regular high school.
4. Expansion of research on how test scores predict successful job performance in different occupations.
5. Development of experimental educational brokering services which would remove some aspects of counseling from the high school and put them directly at the service of the student and his/her family. (Different methods of financing such brokering services ought to be tried, including counseling vouchers given directly to the student.)
6. Help to reform counseling in schools to reflect a consumer advocacy approach by providing counselors with inservice and preservice training in : (a) How to consume postsecondary education, (b) how to interpret student scores on standardized tests, (c) how to interpret and use occupational information in career decision-making, and (d) juvenile law and children's rights.

These options are not mutually exclusive. All are low cost and could be implemented singly or in various combinations.

Options To Reduce Extent of Restricted Occupational Socialization

Despite some progress in reducing occupational stereotyping in schools, the great majority of them still use materials which perpetuate the problem by showing women in subordinate roles and primarily as teachers and nurses. State legislation, such as the California statute prohibiting the use of public funds to purchase school texts that reinforce such stereotypes, can be supplemented by Federal efforts to develop films, TV and radio programs, counselor and teacher guides, etc., which characterize occupations in a sex- and race-fair manner.

HEW's Education Division has rapidly expanded its activities in this area during the past 2 to 3 years, and the Education Amendments of 1976 authorize even more vigorous activity (e.g., $2.6 million is authorized now under vocational education legislation to provide each State with staff responsible for eliminating sex stereotyping). During fiscal year 1976, the Education Division spent some $6 to $8 million on projects to reduce sex-role stereotyping compared to about half that sum during the previous year. In the absence of performance standards or criteria which indicate success, however, it is difficult to determine how much Federal initiative is enough. As HEW continues and expands its research and development (R. & D.) and dissemination activities to reduce occupational stereotyping, the department should develop appropriate goals and performance criteria to permit more coherent planning. Moreover, the various agencies

Chart 3.—Options To Help Students Get Accurate Feedback About Their Academic Performance and Aptitudes

Problem	Program objective	Options (not mutually exclusive)		
		I Develop materials to help students learn about themselves in relation to future educational and occupational choices	II Research, development, and demonstration	III Federal technical assistance and training
Students have inadequate knowledge about their own abilities and aptitudes which might be useful in selecting an appropriate career or further education.	Reform counseling in schools to reflect a consumer advocacy approach, which focuses on helping students get accurate feedback and information about their academic achievement and aptitudes.	Develop and test materials for new course or module in **Consuming Postsecondary Education** which would help high school students learn how to ascertain the veracity and usefulness of information obtained from schools and colleges ($250,000). Have each State develop a booklet and/or a short debriefing module or course which informs dropouts about alternatives if they do not return to the regular high school ($20,000 per State=$1,000,000). Develop easily understood materials that would help students interpret their scores on standardized achievement, aptitude, and interest tests ($300,000).	Supplement industry-based research on how test scores predict successful job performance in different occupations ($1.5 million). Develop experimental educational brokering services which remove some aspects of counseling from the high school and put them directly at the service of the student and his/her family. Include counseling vouchers for students as one way of paying for such a service ($1.5 million). Develop experimental student advocacy service in high school where students would participate along with school authorities in selecting counselors and structuring their tasks ($1.5 million).	In collaboration with interest groups and associations, provide inservice and preservice training to counselors in: (a) How to consume postsecondary education and training. (b) How to interpret student scores on standardized achievement, aptitude, and occupational interest tests. (c) How to interpret and use occupational information in career decisionmaking. (d) Juvenile law and children's rights ($3,000,000 per year). Furnish local education agencies with footlocker of best materials on how to help students with self-appraisal. Continually update this package ($2,000,000).

within HEW which are concerned about this area should coordinate their activities in order to avoid needless duplication of effort while assuring dissemination of the most promising projects or practices.

Options To Provide More Functional Ways of Certifying Competencies

Given the current trend of the court decisions and the absence of any pending conceptual breakthrough which is generic to the measurement and assessment of occupational competencies, the Federal role with respect to competency-based education ought to be catalytic and not programmatic. Federal R. & D. activity in this rapidly expanding area should continue, not only to capture and disseminate rich experience having widespread utility, but also to bring employers and educators together around a common problem (certification) and to persuade educational institutions to be more forthright and explicit about what they are teaching or certifying.

In addition to developing and evaluating innovative competency-based education and assessment techniques which help people earn occupational licenses and educational credentials, the Federal Government should closely monitor and evaluate State and local efforts to award competency-based high school diplomas (e.g., Oregon and California).

Options To Help Students Find Work and Develop Jobseeking Skills

Thousands of public dollars are invested in providing one young person with years of preparatory higher education, but very little is put into seeing what can be done about another's moving directly from high school to work. School guidance personnel, for example, help many graduates proceed to college yet they seldom help workbound students find jobs. Though there are several successful school placement models, most schools still do not routinely provide such services; and the U.S. Employment Service serves only a minute percentage of students (ES does serve many out-of-school youths, however). On the optimistic side, a recent national survey of school districts, indicates that this situation is improving rapidly—over half of the school-based placement programs now in existence were begun during the last 5 years. Expanding local interest in school-based placement services suggests that the late 1970's may be a propitious time for the Federal Government to lend some guidance and infuse some support for this movement in order to help assure that high quality services are provided.

On a spectrum of little to considerable involvement and support, four Federal strategies which would stimulate schools and other local agencies to provide students, recent graduates, and dropouts with job placement assistance ought to be considered: (1) Establish local education and work councils; (2) provide technical assistance and training; (3) conduct a large demonstration and comparative evaluation of alternative placement models; and (4) provide grants to local areas to establish high schol placement programs. These can be considered either as mutually reinforcing or competing (mutually exclusive) strategies (see chart 4).

The least costly option would be to demonstrate the feasibility of local education and work councils, which would bring several community agencies and interest groups together to provide services, including job placement, that would help students make a more successful transition from school to work. Although the Federal Government could earmark some council funds for placement, most resources for this purpose would come from the local institutions themselves.

Another low-cost way to divert local resources for job placement assistance would be to provide Federal technical assistance and training. Under this strategy, the Federal Government could: (*a*) disseminate information about successful school placement models through conferences, workshops, public information programs, and the like; (*b*) designate Employment Service personnel to lend technical assistance to school-designated placement coordinators, and (*c*) comparatively evaluate the various courses or modules in *Job Search Techniques and Achievement Motivation for Youths* which have been developed under the auspices of career education, and disseminate information about best practices to schools, perhaps with the help of business and trade associations.

A somewhat more ambitious and expensive Federal strategy, though still within the framework of existing legislation and appropriation levels, would be to conduct and evaluate large demonstrations of two or three successful school placement models in each State (see chart 4). This would require considerable planning and coordination between HEW and DOL. A related demonstration activity would be to fund several LEA's with high youth unemployment to stagger summer vacations or use the quarter system so that large numbers of students would not be entering the labor market simultaneously.

A fourth strategy to provide students and recent school leavers with job placement assistance would establish high school placement services on a widespread basis with the help of Federal grants. The Federal cost of $50 to $150 million per year could be reduced by requiring the school districts to match funds or gradually take over the entire financing of the program.

Chart 4.—Options To Provide Placement Assistance to Students and School Leavers

Problem	Program objective	Range of options (from little to considerable Federal involvement and support)			
		Little support		**Considerable support**	
		I	II	III	IV
		Demonstration of local education and work councils	Federal technical assistance and training	Large demonstration and comparative evaluation of successful models	Grants to LEA's to establish high school placement programs
Students and school leavers conduct job search in a haphazard and ineffective manner. The great majority of students expect their school to help them find jobs, but few schools do.	Provide more job placement services that help students, graduates, and dropouts find part-time, full-time, and summer jobs.	In addition to other activities to improve the school-to-work transition, bring together schools, local employment service, trade and service organizations, unions, etc. to develop appropriate type of job placement service for students ($1,000,000 to establish 15 to 20 councils). Earmark special funds for placement services in cities having an education-work council ($100,000 per city or $1.5 million total).	Identify and package effective school placement models. In collaboration with interest groups and associations, disseminate information about these models through regional conferences, workshops, etc. and develop public information program to persuade local authorities to adopt a suitable placement model, if not already in place ($2,000,000). Employment Service would designate 1 placement specialist to lend technical assistance to school-designated placement coordinators in each of 200 major school districts ($4,000,000). Comparatively evaluates courses or modules in **Job Search Techniques and Achievement Motivation for Youths,** which have been developed under auspices of career education. Identify best	Fund each State to establish and comparatively evaluate 2 to 3 delivery systems for school placement services: (1) Outstationing of Employment Service personnel in schools. (2) Hiring of placement staff by LEA. (3) Hiring and supervision of placement staff by education-work council, industry-education council, local CETA planning council, and the like ($15,000,000 per year for 3 yr). Fund 20 LEA's in areas with high youth unemployment to experiment with the quarter	Program would provide 1 placement specialist for every 1,500 students in grades 10 to 12. Such personnel would take and list job orders, refer students or school leavers to job openings, solicit jobs from employers, provide job counseling and instruction in job search techniques, conduct followup studies, and seek assistance from community volunteers. School may choose a variety of delivery systems (see strategy III). **Cost:** Assuming unit cost of $20,000 per specialist: Coverage of ⅓ of high school students—$50,000,000.

practices and disseminate materials and hold regional conferences, workshops, etc. ($4,000,000).

system or staggered vacations so that large numbers of students are not entering labor market simultaneously ($5,-000,000 per year for 2 yr).

Coverage of ⅔ of high school students—$100,000,000.

Coverage of all high schools $150,000,000.

Note.—Federal costs could be reduced by requiring school district to match funds or gradually take over financing of program. School districts already having a placement service would get funds anyway.

KEY TO ABBREVIATIONS

CETA = Comprehensive Employment and Training Act.

LEA = Local education agency.

Integrative Options

In addition to Federal categorical assistance where new programs are developed to address specific problems, forms of Federal assistance which address problems through building local capacity should be considered. Demonstration of the feasibility of local education and work councils consisting of representatives from the schools, manpower agencies, and business and industry has been mentioned as an example of such an approach. Through better coordination and utilization of resources these councils attempt to improve the effectiveness of local institutions in helping people integrate their education with their work. In so doing, they may opt to address one or several of the problems described previously.

Better coordination among local institutions need not be the only means for helping young people make more successful transition from school to work. The councils might wish to institutionalize reform, also. An example of such a reform would be to establish local/regional 1- or 2-year institutions equivalent to the 12th and possibly a 13th grade year of secondary school. These institutions would be governed by some type of multisector consortium, like an education and work council with a strong employer and industry flavor. The institution would be judged by the success with which it assists young people in making successful transition to work. Programs would presumably: (*a*) Provide students with information about the nature, requirements, and employment prospects of different occupations; (*b*) help students develop a better understanding of their own abilities and aptitudes; (*c*) certify student competencies in a way useful to entry and progression in various occupations; (*d*) improve student jobseeking skills; and (*e*) establish paid and unpaid work experience, information, and placement liaisons with local and regional employers. For students selecting this track, the institution would arrange for the completion of any residual requirements for high school graduation as it seeks to place the student in a post-high-school, career-type job.

Federal research and development funds might be used to demonstrate the feasibility of this and other ways of institutionalizing a closer integration between education and work. Alternative ways of financing such institutional reform should be tried on an experimental basis, also. For example, students selecting the "education and work track" might bring all or some percentage of their 12th grade year entitlement (the annual per pupil cost) with them. Such an approach gives the high school student more options at a time when these are most needed and appreciated.

Inasmuch as the 12th grade is largely empty academically, with increasing numbers of students finding ways to avoid it (e.g., the California program which allows students to graduate after the 11th grade if they can pass certain tests), new institutional alternatives might be necessary to motivate students to take advantage of this last year of high school for serious planning of their own lives. The experimental introduction of such alternatives makes the most sense in the final year of public school, when critical career decisionmaking takes place for many students and where experimentation is likely to do the least harm if it should fail.

Implementation of Federal Initiatives to Improve the School-to-Work Transition

With the exception of programs to increase the number of work slots for students, it is unlikely that the total cost of vigorous Federal activity in all five of the problem areas would exceed $200 million per year over a period of 4 to 5 years. Funding of this magnitude would support the following kinds of activities (those requiring the largest outlays are listed first) : (1) Direct placement services to help secondary school students and graduates find part-time, full-time, and summer jobs; (2) directly provided useful occupational and educational information to students through information systems or guidance-placement programs; (3) providing secondary school students with more diverse and higher quality work experience opportunities, both paid and unpaid, through technical assistance and vigorous dissemination of research and evaluation results; (4) development and dissemination of sex- and race-fair curricular materials used at primary school level; (5) development and dissemination of materials and provision of technical assistance to reform career counseling in schools from a directed guidance approach to a consumer advocacy approach, which focuses on helping students get accurate feedback and information about their school performance and personal aptitudes and abilities; and (6) development and evaluation of innovative competency-based education (CBE) and assessment projects which help people credential themselves through different routes.

The Vocational Education Act or the Comprehensive Employment and Training Act (CETA) would have to be amended to effect the two most important and costly changes, namely, the provision of school-based placement services and the establishment of State career information systems. Federal activities in three of the five problem areas—certification of competencies, occupational socialization, and self-knowledge of abilities and aptitudes—fall entirely within the categories of R. & D. or technical assistance and training and could be funded under current discretionary authority and budget levels.

Adults: Career and Life Redirection and Renewal

AN EMERGING PROBLEM: INEQUITABLE DISTRIBUTION OF WORK IN AMERICAN SOCIETY

The basic human resource problem among adults in the United States is not a shortage of skilled individuals, but a shortage of jobs—unskilled or skilled. The problem is larger than just the current economic situation. For the last half century, society has not been able to provide jobs during peacetime for everyone able and willing to work.

This undercapacity to provide jobs has given rise, in part, to a variety of social ills—a large, expensive, inefficient, and degrading welfare system, crime, mental illness, etc. These ills have been borne disproportionately by minority groups, women, youths, and older persons. Though employment discrimination against these people remains a problem, some progress has been made in eliminating it for minority group members and women; but, not so for youths and older people whose positions in the job market have deteriorated steadily during the last several decades.

Although the compression of work into the middle period of the lifecycle merely confirms a long historical trend which has had basically healthy features (e.g., child labor laws and the possibility of retirement with a pension), there is evidence that the course has run too far. As work, especially career-type work, has become monopolized more and more by the middle-aged cohort of the population, the entry of many young people into career-type work has been deferred for an unnecessarily long period, meanwhile the age of compulsory retirement has been lowered to the point where retirement for many has become a predicament rather than a welcome rest from a life of work. [1]

The progressively inequitable distribution of career-type work among the three large age cohorts has led to a rigid sequence—from school during youth to work during midlife to leisure during old age. The lockstep is especially frustrating for youths and retirees, who both want more work, independence, and responsibility.

There is also evidence, which will be presented later, that a significantly large minority of middle-aged workers want more leisure without having to sacrifice too much in the way of economic security and job status to get it.

INEQUITIES IN THE DISTRIBUTION OF LEISURE AND EDUCATION

Disregarding for a moment the problems of younger and older workers in getting a "fair" share of the preferred career-type jobs, we should note that within the cohort of middle-aged workers (age 25 to 60), there are also great inequities. Obviously, not all or even most middle-aged workers can be expected to get high-status, well-paying jobs. But those who hold the low-status, unskilled, and low-paying jobs are the ones who have the least leisure time and educational benefits. Highly skilled, unionized or professional persons who work for large companies that adapt continually to rapid technological development have the best of all worlds: their work is challenging and secure (at least they feel that way); and their vacation and education benefits exceed those granted to other workers.

On the other hand, employees of smaller firms are heavily over-represented among those who do not get any paid vacation (30 percent of all workers in 1972) or less than 2 weeks (47 percent of workers in 1972); yet vacation time for all but the newest employee in collective bargaining units of 1,000 or more personnel is a minimum of 2 weeks; and vacations as long as 5 or 6 weeks are common for seniority employees.[2] Indeed, in 1973, 41 percent of workers in collective bargaining units over 1,000 were under contracts which provided maximum vacation benefits of 5 or more weeks.[3]

Opportunities to participate in education and training are also inequitably distributed among middle-aged workers. These benefits overwhelmingly go to employees who are well educated already and who are in occupations requiring a high level of preparation; e.g., professional-technical occupations (see tables 8 and 9). Moreover, the opportunities to participate in education and training are allotted disproportionately among workers in industries that undergo rapid technological development and accordingly require programs to upgrade and keep skills current and/or supplant skills made obsolete by technological displacement (see table 10).[4] The great majority of America's workers however, are not employed in these industries and therefore have relatively few opportunities to upgrade or renew their occupational skills.

Table 8.—Participation Rates in Adult (Part Time) Education by Educational Attainment, 1969, 1972, and 1975

Education	1969		1972		1975		Percentage Change in rate	
	Eligible population [1] (in thousands)	Rate (percent)	Eligible population (in thousands)	Rate (percent)	Eligible population (in thousands)	Rate (percent)	1969–72	1969–75
Total_____	119,597	10.9	127,263	12.4	131,019	13.0	1.5	2.1
None to 8th grade___	30,540	2.1	28,559	2.1	25,764	2.1	0	0
9th to 11th grade____	21,770	9.4	21,859	6.6	21,303	5.7	−2.8	−3.7
High school_____	42,861	11.8	47,753	12.4	50,188	12.7	.6	.9
Some college_____	12,380	20.8	14,727	22.9	16,673	22.0	2.1	1.2
College graduate____	7,510	26.3	9,207	28.0	10,692	28.9	1.7	2.6
College plus_____	4,607	31.7	5,157	34.8	6,334	33.5	3.1	1.8

[1] Noninstitutionalized persons age 17 or over who are not regular full-time students.

Note.—All changes in rate significant at 0.5 level of confidence.

Source: National Center for Education Statistics; published and unpublished data from "Triennial of Adult Education Survey" 1969, 1972, 1975.

DESIRE TO REDISTRIBUTE WORK, LEISURE, AND EDUCATION

There are several strong indications that Americans would like to alter the current distributions of work, leisure, and education. Those who traditionally have not been workers—women and students—now want more work.[5] Prime-age, full-time workers, about two-thirds of whom are men and who have been provided generously with employment, are working about as many hours per week as they did 30 years ago[6] but they indicate, nevertheless, that they would like more free time.[7] A sizable proportion of retired workers would prefer to continue working, though perhaps for fewer hours per week, rather than retire. Finally, adults of all ages appear to want additional and more varied education opportunities.[8]

Despite the desire by many for a more equal allocation of work, leisure, and education among the various cohorts in the adults population, it is likely that a combination of social and demographic forces will soon exacerbate the inequities in their distribution. Secure, stable, protected, full-time career-type work with the usual leisure and occasional education benefits will become harder, not easier, to get. Younger and older people will experience even greater difficulties than before in getting or keeping this type of work. Youths will compete directly with middle-aged women who are reentering the labor force for the entry-level, career-type jobs and will be forced, increasingly, to prolong the period of credentialization or schooling while they work part time in noncareer jobs to support themselves. Prime aged (25 to 45 years old) workers will find it more difficult to get career-type work if they don't have it; and if they do, they will find it harder to get promoted or to change into some other occupation providing similar job

Table 9.—Participation Rates of Workers in Adult (Part Time) Education by Occupational Group, 1969 1972, and 1975

Occupation	1969		1972		1975		Percentage change in rate	
	Eligible [1] population (in thousands)	Rate (per-cent)	Eligible population (in thousands)	Rate (per-cent)	Eligible population (in thousands)	Rate (per-cent)	1969–72	1969–75
Total labor force_____	74, 487	14. 0	78, 989	15. 8	82, 052	16. 6	[2] 1.8	[2] 2.6
Professional/technical_____	10, 413	32. 0	10, 977	35. 0	11, 875	35. 8	[2] 3.0	[2] 3.8
Engineers_____	1, 132	33. 2	1, 127	30. 7	NA	NA	[2] −2.5	_____
Medical/health_____	1, 631	23. 9	1, 809	32. 2	NA	NA	[2] 8.3	_____
Teachers excluding college_	2, 416	42. 9	2, 977	47. 6	NA	NA	[2] 4.7	_____
Other professional/techni-nal _____	5, 234	29. 3	5, 175	28. 9	NA	NA	−.7	_____
Farmers, farm managers, fore-man, and laborers_____	3, 263	4. 8	2, 850	6. 1	2, 800	6. 1	1. 3	1. 3
Managers and administrative___	8, 001	14. 2	7, 917	16. 9	8, 568	16. 8	[2] 2.7	[2] 2.6
Sales_____	4, 172	14. 3	4, 675	16. 5	4, 659	17. 8	[2] 2.2	[2] 3.5
Clerical_____	12, 203	14. 3	12, 991	15. 9	13, 095	17. 6	[2] 1.6	[2] 3.3
Craftsman and kindred_____	9, 806	12. 9	10, 354	13. 8	10, 282	14. 0	.9	1. 1
Operatives_____	13, 289	7. 3	12, 686	7. 7	11, 533	7. 4	.4	.1
Service workers domestics, and nonfarm laborers_____	11, 337	8. 9	12, 904	11. 0	12, 739	11. 8	[2] 2.1	[2] 2.9
Unemployed_____	2, 002	12. 2	3, 658	14. 6	6, 502	12. 5	[2] 2.4	.3

[1] Noninstitutionalized persons age 17 or over who are not regular full-time students.
[2] Change in rate significant at 0.05 level of confidence.

Source: Unpublished data, National Center for Education Statistics, "Triennial Survey of Adult Education," 1969, 1972 1975.

status and pay. This job stagnation or reduced occupational mobility will occur precisely at a time when other social forces will act to increase the desire for both vertical and horizontal occupational mobility. The resulting dissatisfaction with career progression could well result in diminished worker productivity.

What, then, are the social and demographic forces which are likely to inhibit occupational mobility while other forces increase the desire for it? First is the imminence of a "promotion squeeze" or a lesser amount of vertical career mobility within the middle-aged cohort, as members of the large, well-educated baby-boom generation (born between 1947 and 1961) attempt to move above the lower rungs of the occupational ladder, as the younger better educated members of minority groups seek the job opportunities denied their parents, and as more women become full-time career workers.[9] More people simply will compete for the relatively stable number of preferred jobs, and because of the higher occupational expectations resulting from higher levels of educational attainment, a higher proportion of middle-aged workers than in the past, particularly white males, will become unhappy with their progress.

The "promotion squeeze" will hit the postwar baby-boom generation first, if not hardest. This generation, which crowded our school

Table 10.—Participation Rates of Workers in Adult (Part Time) Education by Industrial Group, 1969, 1972, and 1975

Industry in Which Employed	1969 Eligible[1] population (in thousands)	1969 Rate (percent)	1972 Eligible population (in thousands)	1972 Rate (percent)	1975 Eligible population (in thousands)	1975 Rate (percent)	Percentage change in rate 1969–72	Percentage change in rate 1969–75
Total labor force	74,487	14.0	78,989	15.8	82,052	16.6	[2] 1.8	[2] 2.6
Agriculture	3,520	5.1	3,231	6.8	3,189	6.4	[2] 1.7	[2] 1.3
Mining	532	11.5	621	10.2	754	16.7	−1.3	[2] 5.2
Construction	4,712	9.6	4,964	10.1	4,693	11.0	.5	1.4
Manufacturing	20,541	12.5	19,233	12.4	17,777	12.8	−.1	.3
Transportation and public utilities	4,918	12.8	5,216	14.5	5,121	15.5	[2] 1.7	[2] 2.7
Wholesale, retail	12,376	10.3	13,778	11.8	14,422	12.1	1.5	[2] 1.8
Finance, insurance, and real estate	3,530	20.6	4,036	22.6	4,260	23.8	2.0	[2] 3.2
Private household servants	1,571	4.2	1,432	6.6	1,101	5.4	−1.4	1.2
Public administration	4,167	22.6	4,369	23.4	4,327	25.7	.8	[2] 3.1
Miscellaneous services	16,615	19.9	18,443	23.8	19,908	24.8	[2] 3.9	[2] 4.9
Business and repair	2,207	12.5	2,339	14.2	NA	NA	[2] 1.7	____
Forestry and fisheries	91	12.1	78	7.7	NA	NA	−4.4	____
Personal, except private household	2,383	8.2	2,217	9.4	NA	NA	1.2	____
Entertainment and recreation	578	5.9	555	13.5	NA	NA	7.6	____
Medical except hospitals	1,451	19.1	1,842	21.8	NA	NA	2.7	____
Hospitals	2,457	19.6	2,666	23.9	NA	NA	[2] 4.3	____
Welfare and religion	754	19.5	959	23.7	NA	NA	4.2	____
Education	5,371	31.0	6,193	34.8	6,575	32.2	[2] 3.8	1.2
Other professional services	1,315	16.9	1,602	22.1	NA	NA	[2] 5.2	____
Unemployed	2,002	12.2	3,658	14.6	6,502	12.5	[2] 2.4	.3

[1] Noninstitutionalized persons age 17 or over who are not regular full-time students.
[2] Change in rate significant at 0.05 level of confidence.

Source: Unpublished data, National Center for Education Statistics, "Triennial Survey of Adult Education," 1969, 1972, 1975.

systems in the 1950's and 1960's and swelled the ranks of teenage workers, is now meeting difficulty in breaking out from the lower occupational levels. Large portions of this age group have deferred their entry into career-type work while prolonging their education, in part because of the fierce competition for jobs. As members of this age group move into middle age, they will experience more competition than previous generations in progressing up the ladder; and they will find it harder to change into some other occupation providing similar status and pay. Further, this state of affairs will work to the disadvantage of young workers from the subsequent post-baby-boom generation, who will not be able to dislodge experienced workers who are stuck above them. For the next 30 years, the increased competition for work, especially preferred work will bring pressure at once for earlier compulsory retirement, more jobs, and greater sharing of existing jobs.

In contrast to sharp projected increases in availability of workers for higher status (predominantly white-collar) jobs between 1970 and 1985, we can expect substantial reductions in the proportion of workers who will be available for the lower level occupations. This will result mostly from the projected slowdown in the growth in the number of younger workers, who had accounted for a large and growing segment of the "low level" labor force during the 1960's.[10]

Recent experience suggests some of the ways in which the labor market is likely to accommodate to these altered conditions. At the upper end of the job spectrum, as the supply of better educated workers becomes more plentiful, employers are likely to respond by reducing relative wages and by raising selection standards. Conversely, as some lower level jobs become harder to fill, a number of options will be open, depending in part upon the elasticity of demand for such workers. In some occupations, such as domestics, a further employment decline can be expected: an increasing proportion of families will be obliged to seek substitutes for the services of paid domestics, either through product substitution, such as increased use of commercial services, or simply by doing more of their own household chores. Conversely, in the case of occupations such as construction laborers and hospital attendants, the more probable longer range outcome is for an increase in relative wages, accompanied by other efforts to make these jobs somewhat more attractive. In the case of low-wage industries, such as apparel manufacturing, adjustment might also take the form of continued geographical shifts to States or regions where there are residual reserves of low-wage labor or increased reliance upon finished goods imported from low-wage countries.[11]

Some of the problems associated with these trends are visible already; others can be expected to become evident as we move into the 1980's:

- The better educated young workers who have recently entered the labor market, or who will be entering it in the coming decade, can expect increased competition in seeking preferred jobs depending upon their area of specialized training and they may be forced to stay in or accept jobs not utilizing their education. Recent surveys have indicated that between one-fourth and one-third of American workers already consider themselves overqualified educationally for their jobs and that these workers have significantly lower levels of job satisfaction than others.[12] An acceleration of these trends, in turn, can be expected to intensify problems associated with poor worker morale.

- Minority workers and women, seeking a fair share of the preferred jobs, face increased competition from majority worker categories, with a consequent danger of increased confrontations on issues relating to equal employment opportunity. These issues become even more critical in periods of substantial unemployment (such as the mid-1970's), since such workers—because of lower seniority—are often the first to be laid off.

- Although employers will have a greater choice of applicants in many professional, managerial, and other higher status occupational fields, they may be faced with high job vacancy and turnover rates—and with related problems of poor worker morale—in low-skilled, low-status jobs.

- Institutions of higher education, already beset by serious financial difficulties, will be forced to reevaluate their educational programs and their enrollment prospects in the light of the altered labor market outlook for college-trained personnel.

- Youth employment prospects for all but the lowest skilled jobs will be diminished by the increasing employment trends among adult women (who are significant job competitors with youths) and the sizable pool of adult unemployed workers—many of whom have substantive job skills and experience. It will become more difficult than ever for youths to get career-related work especially those whose educational levels are below the norm; contrariwise, youths will be expected to hold onto lesser skilled work longer than ever, frequently until their mid-20's, as the attrition rates among those entrenched in the better jobs drops lower and opportunities for newer aspirants dwindle. A slight compensation is that these unskilled jobs will fetch better wages than in the past.

- Worker dissatisfaction resulting from reduced likelihood of promotion, especially among members of the baby-boom generation, together with higher occupational expectations resulting from higher levels of educational attainment, might well increase the desire to change careers; or such discontent might persuade more workers to seek a greater share of their life satisfaction outside of work.[13] Workers who cannot step up, in others words, will look more favorably on the option of stepping out.

As demographic trends make promotions more problematic, the ever-present job shortage situation will weaken chances to change jobs and careers. Public employment programs might increase the number of jobs, but they are unlikely to satisfy the demand for career-type jobs, if our experience with these programs is any indication. Holders of preferred jobs are less likely to give them up in a slack labor market—witness the greatly decreased turnover in the teaching profession during the last few years.[14]

The reduced possibilities for changing careers and getting promoted are likely to increase the number of workers who feel locked in or powerless to alter their career direction once having embarked along a career path. Studies undertaken at the University of Michigan show that many workers feel trapped, that because of circumstances they will never achieve more—even though they deserve more. These feelings are primary sources of dissatisfaction with life and work and correlate highly with problems of physical and mental health.[15] Nevertheless, in order to upgrade one's job through additional training, or seek a new employment which will provide more personal satisfaction, workers frequently must quit their present job and thereby sacrifice whatever income and seniority benefits they might have accrued. The individual who is willing to take these continued risks and personal upheavals is truly exceptional.[16]

FACTORS WHICH WILL INCREASE DESIRE
FOR CAREER CHANGE

While our present economic situation discourages occupational mobility, the desire to change careers is heightened by: (1) The increased awareness of different kinds of work, due to a more highly educated work force and increased coverage by the mass media; and (2) increased willingness to risk leaving one's job or occupation as larger proportions of adults are free of dependents for greater portions of their lives. These decreasing dependency ratios are due to increasing propensities of Americans toward later marriage, smaller families, nuclear families (no more than two generations in residence), double income households (both spouses working), more frequent divorce, and financial self-reliance during old age.[17]

Though, as suggested, there are forces at work in the United States which should increase the desire for career change among workers as their prospects diminish for vertical career mobility, there are neither attitudinal nor behavioral data which confirm that such a trend is underway. Some studies indicate that substantial numbers of workers do think about changing their jobs,[18] but these studies do not differentiate between careers (or occupations) and jobs nor determine whether such attitudes are changing over time. Actual career change data show that the percent of workers who change occupations from one year to the next has remained fairly constant since 1961. Three Bureau of Labor Statistics (BLS) studies of current population survey data conducted in 1962, 1967, and 1973 show that the yearly rate of occupational change from one to another of 440 detailed 3-digit occupational groups has stayed at about 9 percent.[19]

According to Bureau of the Census data, 1 out of 5 workers moved from 1 of 12 major occupational groups to another between 1965 and 1970. Unlike the three BLS studies of current population survey (CPS) data which used more detail in classifying occupations, the census report grossly understates the amount of occupational mobility, because it does not include any changes made within large groupings. For example, a change within the category of professionals, from social worker to teacher goes unrecorded. So too does a change from tool-and-die maker to carpenter, since both occupations are classified under craftsmen.

Using both census and CPS data, the Department of Labor estimated in 1964 that a 20-year-old man would make between six and seven job changes over the course of his working lifetime.[20] Most of these moves would not involve a change in occupation. According to a more recent study, this same man will, on the average, make one or two shifts (the figure comes out at 1.7) in major occupational grouping.[21]

Despite our expectations of increased desire among U.S. workers for career change and improvement, economic and demographic factors during the rest of this century are probably too strong to permit a satisfying degree of occupational mobility. Unless there are major and sustained periods of accelerated economic expansion, we can expect—under the current system for allocating work—continued high unemployment along with increasing amounts of job stagnation, boredom, and the underemployment of skills and knowledge provided by formal education. This state of affairs could lead to diminished worker productivity and other signs of discontent such as increased absenteeism and industrial sabotage. Society might well begin to consider alternative ways to restructure or redistribute work in order to prevent such problems. A negative aspect of redistributing work, however, is that higher aggregate wage costs for an industry might be associated with constant output, thereby reducing productivity.

PUBLIC POLICY CONSIDERATIONS IN THE DISTRIBUTION OF WORK, LEISURE, AND EDUCATION

To alter the distribution of work, leisure, and education in the United States is far from being a resolved matter of public policy. While Americans appear to want to diminish the inequities in the distribution of these facets of life, there is considerable confusion and controversy over how this should be done. Some would redistribute more equitably the amount of time people work, by introducing a shortened (4-day, 32-hour) workweek, by limiting the work year, or by prohibiting forced overtime; others would effect such a redistribution by expanding the total amount of employment through Government-subsidized public works and/or public service employment. Still others would redistribute more equitably the quality of work; i.e., the preferred career-type jobs, through such schemes as job sharing and the creation of more part-time jobs in highly skilled occupations. Schemes to redistribute leisure include guaranteed minimum amount of paid or unpaid annual vacation, extended vacations (like the steelworkers have) as rewards for length of service, greater opportunities to take leave of absence without pay, and laying off workers (when that is required) in reverse order of seniority, which is the case for some workers who qualify for supplemental unemployment benefits. Finally, schemes to redistribute education more equitably among adults include a variety of education entitlement or voucher plans, paid or unpaid educational leave, work sabbaticals, and the countercyclical use of unemployment insurance to support job-related education and training (see chart 5).

Obviously, there is considerable overlap among proposals to redistribute work, leisure, and education. Redistribution in one area is almost certain to effect a redistribution in the other two. If a person works less, he is almost certain to have more leisure hours and hence more time, if not money, to engage in further education. If an individual continues his education, he will become somewhat more likely to obtain employment, especially higher skilled work. If someone gets higher skilled work, he is likely to be offered more opportunities to participate in further education, et cetera.

Despite general agreement that the present system of progression from school during youth to work during adulthood to retirement during old age is too rigid, there is little agreement about how to move to a more cyclical or rhythmical life pattern.[22] People concerned with full employment tend to focus on proposals to expand the number of jobs and to redistribute work. People concerned with the arts and

Chart 5.—Proposals for Distribution of Work, Education, and Leisure

WORK

Public service employment
Public works projects
Youth domestic service corps (e.g., Civilian Conservation Corps)
Work/job sharing
Creation of more skilled part-time jobs
Creation of own public service jobs
No forced overtime

        LEISURE

        Shortened workweek
        Longer annual vacations
        Extended vacations or sabbaticals
        Gradual retirement plans
        Earlier retirement
        Fuller vesting of pensions
        Supplemental unemployment benefits for workers with seniority
        Leave of absence without pay
        "Cafeteria" benefit plans featuring leisure

                EDUCATION

                Entitlements or vouchers
                Paid and unpaid educational leave
                Educational sabbaticals
                Tuition assistance for low-income adults (part-time study)
                Tuition aid or refund
                Countercyclical use of unemployment insurance for education
                Public adult and continuing education
                Vestibule training
                Job Corps.
                Opportunity Industrial Centers

other cultural activities tend to be more attracted to proposals which increase the amount of discretionary leisure time. And educators, naturally, will look favorably on proposals to promote education among adults who have had lesser amounts of it. The present state of knowledge, unfortunately restricts rational choice among the many alternatives.

What About "Recurrent Education"?

Of the many proposals to redistribute work, leisure, and education, one of the most visible and heavily publicized has been called lifelong learning or recurrent education. Advocates of this approach assume that greater equality of economic opportunity will result from greater equality of educational opportunity; i.e., if adults with low incomes and lesser amounts of education are provided with more education, their economic and occupational status will improve. There is very little evidence, however, which corroborates the view that removal of inequities in education will lead to less inequity in the distribution of preferred, stable, protected, career-type employment. In reality, the extent to which further education and training contributes to the employability and job and life satisfaction of U.S. workers is not easily determined. Available data reveal a very complex and ambiguous situation with respect to the relative importance of educational opportunity for adults:

- While recent studies indicate that several million Americans would participate in additional education if certain obstacles were removed; [23] these same studies as well as others [24] indicate that: (1) A large and increasing proportion of workers already participate in education, (2) millions of others don't take advantage of such opportunities even when they are made available, [25] and (3) among the additional fringe benefits desired by American workers, education and training benefits are given very low priority. [26]

- While many people achieve low levels of education or are functionally incompetent, [27] large and growing proportions of workers are becoming overqualified for their work, as their educational attainment and concomitant acquisition of skills increases faster than the skill levels needed to perform jobs. [28]

- While many workers face job obsolescence and experience periods of unemployment or underemployment, most workers in this category eventually do obtain the job training or retraining they need to maintain marketable skills.

- While many women have difficulty getting the education and training they need to reenter the labor force, many other women do get it. [29]

While many workers appear frustrated at not being able to change their present job and occupation, workers as a whole continue to change jobs and careers at about the same rates as 10 years ago.[30]

The overwhelming impression left by these studies, then, is that America already is a Nation of students—a large and growing proportion of the adult population acquires knowledge through some type of formal or informal arrangements. Estimates of the total annual dollar effort directed to the education of adults in the United States (excluding on-the-job training offered by business and industry and Government) ranges between $50 and $60 billion. According to the 1973 *Annual Report of the National Advisory Council on Extension and Continuing Education*, the Federal share of this total is about $8.3 billion. The remaining activities are sponsored by business and industry, labor, public schools, community service organizations (foremost among which are the church organizations), and private nonprofit institutions and associations.

The degree of participation in educational activities by adults is not uniform across all categories. Compared to the average adult in the United States, the participant is younger, better educated, more affluent, more likely to be living in an urban area, and more likely to be in the labor force (i.e., either working or looking for work).[31] A majority participate in adult studies to improve or acquire marketable skills.

Given the large and increasing amount of resources directed toward adult learning, the question is raised whether the present volume is sufficient and whether there is any national interest served by accelerating the rate of growth. Advocacy of the "more is better" doctrine is based frequently on the notions that: (1) The present amount of education and training is inadequate to enable society to meet the demands made by a rapidly changing technology, and (2) higher levels of education and training maximize the probabilities of becoming and staying employed, and (3) adults simply want more educational opportunities and are frustrated at not being able to overcome barriers to their participation. Each of these assertions can be disputed, however.

Adapting to technological change.—First, there is little evidence that the work force is or will be too slow in adapting to technological change. At present, job vacancies in the highly skilled technical occupations are not going unfilled for long periods of time. If anything, the rate at which workers are acquiring education is outstripping the rate of increase in the skill content of jobs within homogeneous skill clusters.[32] Furthermore, the level of educational attainment [33] is not related to job performance as rated by employers in the great majority of occupational groups.[34] In short, work today calls for a good deal less educational preparation than people are able to bring to it. And there is some indication that this disparity is increasing rapidly.

The contention that workers of the future will need vastly increased amounts of job training and retraining, because accelerating technological change will require them to change their occupations more often, also lacks empirical foundation. The radical change in the sectoral (industrial) distribution of employment which has occurred over the recent past, especially since 1945, is now virtually at an end. Since 1930 the change in the sectoral distribution of employment has been primarily the consequence of the extreme decline in the relative importance of agricultural employment, with the agricultural share of the labor force falling from 19 percent in 1929 to less than 4 percent in 1969, and to a lesser extent, the consequence of the relative growth of government, which increased its share of employment over the same period from 7 percent to 18 percent.[35] While particular sectors may expand or contract greatly, no individual sector is of sufficient relative magnitude to produce a similar shift in the overall composition of employment within the foreseeable future; and current indications are that no significant change in the sectoral composition of employment will be observed between 1970 and 1980.[36] Massive efforts, then, to retool the labor force to adapt to great and imminent increases in the rate of technological change do not appear to be warranted.

Maximizing employability.—The second argument put forth by proponents of accelerating the growth of adult education is that higher levels of education and training maximize the probabilities of becoming and staying employed while increasing earnings. The argument is extended further by claims that improved earnings and lower unemployment due to additional education and training will be in the public interest by increasing the tax base while decreasing income maintenance or welfare payments. The evidence on this is mixed. An analytic discussion of the subject requires that the public and private benefits be considered separately.

Taking the private benefits first, we observe that some publicly subsidized education and manpower training programs do yield earnings benefits to low-income adult participants while others do not. On the positive side, a recent study which compared the earnings experience of a matched sample of GI bill users and nonusers who separated from the military service in fiscal year 1969 revealed that those who used their education entitlement for vocational training by March 1974 increased their earnings to a level about 10 percent above what they would have earned in the absence of training (i.e., 10 percent above the earnings of nonusers who had similar demographic characteristics and earnings capacity as measured by prior labor market experience).[37] The same study demonstrated that vocational training is particularly valuable for blacks who take greater advantage of the GI bill than do nonblacks within each ability test score (Armed Forces Qualification Test) and prior education group. The former tend to gain $500 to $600 per year more in annual earnings than do otherwise similar nonblack trainees. (The earnings history was not sufficiently long to compare the labor market success of groups of GI bill users who attended college with nonusers who did not.) Finally, it was shown that while veterans with less prior education use benefits at a lower rate than those with more prior education, even when race and test score are held constant, this gap in usage is narrowing.

In contrast to the private benefits obtained by disadvantaged and minority group users of the GI bill during the early 1970's, the Federal manpower training programs of the 1960's, on the whole, did less to improve the employment and economic status of the disadvantaged, though some benefits were gained.[38] O'Neill and Ross [39] speculate that the reason voucher funding (via the GI bill) produces a greater increase in earnings than did institutional training under the Manpower Development and Training Act is either: (a) The voucher trainee has been able to select courses more to his taste and he therefore performs better, or (b) training provided in response to demand expressed through the market is more closely alined with job opportunities for trainees. The researchers did not attempt to ascertain the veracity of this explanation and left it as a subject for future investigation.

While evidence on the private benefits of publicly supported education and training for adults is mixed, there is precious little evidence that the public benefits are worth the public costs. The mere expansion of education and training opportunities is unlikely to resolve the job shortage problem. If more training were the answer, aggregate unemployment rates ought to decrease as the general education level of the population goes up. This has not happened. Instead, further education and training merely improves the participant's position in the employment queue while displacing the nonparticipant to the rear. Such substitution has little to do with the number or kind of jobs available.

Evidence is accumulating that the amount of education and training received by a worker is just as likely to result from the kind of job that he/she has as to lead to such a job. An analysis of the triennial adult education survey conducted by the Bureau of the Census for OE shows that the increase in the participation rates of workers in part-time education from 1969 to 1972 and 1975 occurred among those in the industries and occupations which must adapt to continual technological development and accordingly provide programs to upgrade or renew skills (see tables 9 and 10). Hence, the participation rates grew most during this 6-year period for the better educated who tend to work in professional or technical occupations. Leading the advance were those in the medical and health fields. When classified by industrial group, the greatest increase in participation rates between 1969 and 1972 occurred in the professional service industries, including entertainment and recreation, hospitals, and education. The lowest participation rates, and the lowest 6-year growth in these rates, occurred among workers who had jobs which require little additional education and training; namely, operatives, service workers, domestics, and nonfarm laborers. Individuals in the sales and clerical occupations manifest participation rates and growth in these rates which are typical for the work force as a whole (14 to 16 percent).[40]

Further indication that training results from job holding as well as vice-versa is suggested by an analysis of collective bargaining agreements which contain education and training provisions. In 1966–67, the last time complete company training data were collected by the Bureau of Labor Statistics, only one-third of workers in large companies (i.e., under collective bargaining agreements involving 1,000 or more workers) were covered by contracts which contained training or retraining provisions.[41] Almost all of these workers were in knowledge- and technologically-intensive industries; e.g., transportation equipment, primary metals, electrical machinery and equipment, communications, etc., where continual training is essential to maintain marketable skills. More recent but less complete information from BLS suggests a significant increase in the number of workers who are covered by contracts which contain training provisions. In 1972, about two-thirds of the workers in large companies were covered by contracts with such provisions. Most of these workers, however, are still in the technologically progressive industries.[42]

It should be noted that most company-provided training is not under collective bargaining agreement. Companies provide such training when they perceive it to be in their economic interest to do so. Whether they give enough training (from the workers' point of view) or whether this training is of sufficiently high quality is another issue. The point here is that the companies which have been the most active in providing their own training have been those which need to secure a certain amount of technological superiority among their employees in order to maintain a competitive edge over other companies producing similar products. That Xerox, International Business Machines Corp, Eastman Kodak, Kimberly-Clark, American Telephone & Telegraph Co., etc., have huge education programs and benefits is not accidental—clearly these benefits serve the respective corporate interests. Workers who receive such training not only become more technically qualified, but also they more likely prefer to stay with the company when their skills are continually being upgraded. Job satisfaction improves when workers believe that they are continually learning.[43]

3 *Elimination of barriers to participation.*—The third argument put forth by proponents of increased public subsidies for adult education

is that people want it. This view is buttressed by studies by the Carnegie Commission, the Commission on Non-Traditional Education, the National Opinion Research Corp., the U.S. Office of Education, and the National Advisory Councils on Adult Education and Continuing Education, and by the Faure report to UNESCO. All state that millions of adults want to continue their education—many for occupational purposes—but that they are prevented from doing so by a variety of barriers and practical problems. Of these, lack of money and time were seen as the greatest obstacles by most people. Lack of transportation, child care, and information about available programs were also frequently cited.[44]

For policy purposes these studies are difficult to interpret. All are attitude- and opinion-type inquiries and suffer from the lack of comparative data on how people would spend their time and money if options besides continuing one's education were included. When an individual is asked whether he would like to participate in a good thing, and in America education is perceived as such, the most common response is, "Of course!" Social science methodology would criticize this kind of question on three grounds. First, there is the problem of the "acquiescence response set," where people tend to answer "yes" more often than "no." Questions oriented to a negative response are needed to balance those with a positive bias. Studies which have been designed to ascertain adult education's "felt needs" do not meet this requirement. Second, comes the problem of the "socially acceptable response set" where people tend to give the interviewer the answer they think he wants. As already suggested, in America getting more education is usually the socially acceptable response. Third, and finally, is the problem of "compared to what," or presenting other options to the individual about what else he or she would do with the extra money or time. Unless alternatives are offered, the strength of preference for any one activity like adult education cannot be ascertained. Adults were not asked to make such tradeoffs in the aforementioned studies.

There are a number of behavioral and attitudinal studies which indicate that the majority of adults do not assign very high priority to obtaining educational opportunities for themselves. Most convincing are two studies which show that workers do not take great advantage of education or training opportunities provided by employers. According to the 1972–73 *Quality of Employment Survey* covering a national sample of all workers, employees took only moderate advantage of training programs available through their employers; among workers who report the availability of training which is considered part of the jobs [45] (about 43 percent of all workers), only 60 percent participated in one or more of these programs.[46] A conference board study of *Employee Tuition Aid Plans* (under which firms normally reimburse employees for courses taken after working hours) shows even less interest in further education among workers— only 5 percent of approximately 3.6 million eligible employees participated.[47]

In addition to the aforementioned behavioral data, surveys of workers' desires for additional fringe benefits indicate that they assign very low priority to educational benefits. Unlike the single option-type questions which appear in most studies of adult education, a few surveys do enable the respondent to react to different options and assign priorities accordingly. Two national surveys conducted by the University of Michigan's Survey Research Center in 1969–70 and 1972–73; for example, asked workers to assign priorities to the kinds of benefits desired. Fewer than 1 percent of the workers cited educational benefits as the single additional benefit most wanted.[48] In another survey on the present and desired benefits of workers, educational benefits are mentioned so infrequently that the item does not even appear in the relevant tables.[49] More paid vacation and additional health (e.g., dental care) and retirement benefits are of much higher priority.

Though a case cannot be made for either: (1) A widespread overwhelming desire on the part of adults for further education, or (2) the national interest being served by increasing the number of adults who participate in formal education or training, it is true that substantial minorities who would like to pursue further education are prevented from doing so by a variety of barriers. Despite the fact that there is evidence that many of the obstructions in many parts of the country are being eliminated (witness the growing rates and amounts of participation by adults in education), the obstacles still remain for a significant number of people. The question remains whether society benefits more from eliminating barriers to education or from ridding itself of other kinds of blockage to economic opportunity, such as employment and housing discrimination and inadequate health care.

Even though evidence does not corroborate fully the hypothesis that removing barriers to education for adults would substantially improve their economic status, advocates of increased public subsidies for adult education claim that these obstacles ought to be eliminated anyway because the education that people would receive would be good for them and therefore good for the country. Yet there is little evidence that participating in adult courses, generally, is any better (for the individual or for society) than other wholesome ways and spending one's discretionary time and income; e.g., conducting an extensive search for a new job or career, participating in community service activities, learning or practicing recreational skills, traveling or taking a vacation, improving one's personal property, spending time with one's family, or going shopping. In the absence of any greater national interest being served by participating in one of these activities and not the others, there is no reason for singling out adult education for increased Federal subsidy.

Possibly another reason for not having a program targeted to eliminate financial barriers to education among adults is that it would likely result in regressive taxation. If a program were to become universally available to all adults, the poor would probably end up subsidizing the education of the nonpoor, because the better educated and more affluent adults are much more likely to participate in additional education.[50] A program targeted to disadvantaged adults only might also be regressive. The occupational status and income of the participants might not improve much as a result of their participation, especially if the unemployment rate is high, while the individuals who would benefit would likely be the middle-class providers of the educational services.[51]

The assumption that financial difficulties prevent huge numbers of low income adults from participating in part-time education can also be challenged. The 1972 Survey of Adult Education conducted by the Bureau of the Census indicated that 48 percent of the 3.7 million courses taken by some 2.3 million part-time participants having family incomes of less than $6,000 per year were paid for by the participants themselves or their families. For the adult education population as a whole, the corresponding figure was 56 percent. Though it is true that people with higher incomes are more likely to pay out of pocket for their courses than people with lower incomes, a substantial portion of low-income people are able to pay for the courses they take. The average price of each adult education course was $75.

A final point to be made on whether or not there should be additional subsidies for adult education is that it has been growing and flourishing without significant increments in Federal assistance or guidance. According to the triennial survey of adult education conducted by the Bureau of the Census for OE, the participation rate in part-time education increased from 11 percent in 1969 to almost 13 percent in 1975, or an increase of more than 4 million adults. During this same period the participation rate among workers increased from 14 to 16 percent with almost all of the increase occurring among better educated workers in professional occupations.[52] The growth in these programs is not so much a result of broadly conceived public policy as it is a response to a consumer demand for these opportunities. The demand is not for a further extension of the years of conventional schooling but a demand for more kinds of postsecondary education with more points of access and exit; and a demand for educational programs tailored to the time requirements and energy limits of the many individuals interested in further education who cannot spend full time at it or who cannot participate within the time frame of the regular academic calendar.[53]

A New Problem: Overqualification for Jobs and the Underutilization of Skills

The great and growing desire of Americans for more education is beginning to result in a problem which is quite different than the one envisioned by advocates of expanded learning opportunities for adults. The trouble is that we are developing more highly educated people faster than we are creating jobs that traditionally required so much education (see table 11).[54] Inherent in this disparity are degrees of overqualification, underutilization of skills, and a resulting social discontent among those who feel they are overqualified and underutilized.[55] O'Toole [56] suggests by way of analogy that the situation is nearly Malthusian in its proportions: levels of education attainment have tended to climb in almost geometric progression, while the number of jobs that require higher levels of education has tended to grow at a much slower pace.

The problems of overqualification and the underutilization of skills are exacerbated because the United States is still creating many more lesser than higher skilled jobs. This is most convincingly demonstrated by Freedman's analysis of structural arrangements that segment the labor market into jobs at various earnings levels in 1960 and 1970. Using occupational and age data from the 1960 and 1970 censuses, she found that expansion of employment in the 1960's was predominantly in lesser skilled, low-paying occupations. Moreover, this expansion was greater in the less stable segments of the labor market; i.e., the expansion tended to be in part-time and/or part-year nonunionized jobs with few fringe benefits and employment security protections.[57] The

Table 11.—Actual and Projected Shares of Professional-Technical Employment for College Graduates, 1960–85

Year	College graduates as portion of total civilian labor force (percent)	Professional-technical workers as portion of total civilian employment (percent)
1960	10.0	11.0
1965	11.7	13.0
1970	13.2	14.2
1975	16.9	15.0
1985 [1]	20–21	[2] 14.9–15.4

[1] Projected estimates.
[2] Proportion of managers in labor force will decline by about 1 to 2 pct between 1975 and 1985.

Source: 1985 projections by Bureau of Labor Statistics and by Joseph Froomkin, "Supply and Demand for Persons With Postsecondary Education," Policy Research Center paper prepared for the Assistant Secretary for Education, U.S. Department of Health, Education, and Welfare, Washington, D.C., 1976.

increased low-paying, low-skilled jobs in the less stable segments of the labor market between 1960 and 1970 were filled disproportionately by women and youths (see table 2), whose labor force participation rates increased substantially during that period.[58]

The increase in the number of low-level jobs is occurring in both the public and private sectors. In the private sector, for example, much of the increase in part-time work during the 1960's was the result of more people contributing fewer hours of work in lesser skilled occupations in retail trade.[59] In the public sector—especially in State and local governments where one out of three new jobs is being created—most of the rapidly expanding demand is for services (in hospitals, police, maintenance) or for jobs with service characteristics (typing, clerical work). When teachers are subtracted from the total of government employes, the two largest remaining categories are clerical and service workers who, together, account for 78 percent of the remaining jobs.[60] According to Ivar Berg, 60 to 70 percent of the new public jobs being created are "in the categories of aide, attendant, and assistant, clerical workers, custodian and semiskilled blue collar." [61] And now with revenue sharing and public service employment dollars gushing into State and local coffers, many more public jobs offering low pay and little in the way of career opportunities are likely to be created.

Despite the fact that more lesser skilled than higher skilled jobs are still being created, the number of jobs in the professional and technical categories is increasing. Nevertheless, these jobs are increasing at a lesser rate than the number of people who are qualified to fill them. BLS estimates that between 1974 and 1985 there will be a surplus of 950,000 college graduates, or an average surplus of 86,000 per year; i.e., there will be job openings (demand) for 12.2 million out of 13.1 million college graduates (supply) during this 11–year period.[62]

In terms of the total labor force in 1985, BLS projects that 20.4 million college graduates, or about 22 percent of the total labor force, will be available to fill some 18.8 million jobs requiring at least a college degree, leaving an overall surplus of 1.6 million graduates (another 4.5 million graduates will not be in the labor force in 1985).[63] This estimate might be too conservative, however. Other analysts posit an even greater oversupply of college graduates. Joseph Froomkin,[64] for example, estimated that if the ratio of college graduates in each industry remains at the 1970 level, the year he feels a good balance was struck between college graduates and jobs,[65] some 14.2 million jobs will be available in 1985 for between 21 and 23 million persons with college degrees; if the 1975 relationships and projected employment are used to calculate the number of suitable jobs, the number increases to about 16.2 million. Hence, depending on whether 1970 or 1975 employment patterns are used, the projected surplus of college graduates would be between 6 and 8 million, or roughly 4 or 5 times the BLS figure.

The underutilization of skills will not be confined to college graduates. Individuals with some college will also experience difficulties in obtaining jobs requiring their level of education. Froomkin estimates that like the college graduate situation, there will be a shortage of 6 to 7 million suitable jobs for persons with some college (1 to 3 years) preparation.

Froomkin's estimates of the supply of college-educated persons is somewhat higher than BLS's because he assumes a higher labor force participation rate and level of educational attainment among women. BLS apparently is less likely to posit such accelerated cultural change. Froomkin's estimate of the demand for persons with college degrees is lower than BLS's because he assumes a greater degree of technological advancement and automation in supporting both professional and managerial occupations; i.e., machines will increasingly replace manpower in these two occupations. In fact, the rate of growth in the professional occupations has already started to decline. Whereas the proportion of professionals in total employment increased from 11 percent in 1960 to 13 percent in 1965 and to 15 percent in 1970, this proportion failed to increase a full percentage point in the subsequent 5 years.[66] Froomkin argues, also, that current BLS projections are too high in the employment of both professionals and managers in education. BLS apparently believes that student/teacher ratios will decline and the number of school and college administrators will increase in the face of unchanging enrollment levels; Froomkin is not so optimistic.

Perhaps the most serious problem for future college graduates will be the slower-than-hitherto-projected growth of the nonprofit and government sectors, where a large and increasing proportion of new jobs for college graduates has been created. Whereas 71 percent of the new jobs created for college graduates between 1970 and 1975 came from this sector of the economy (13 percent more than in the previous decade), this proportion will decrease considerably as the growth of employment in this not-for-profit sector slows due to the current disenchantment with big government and declining or stable enrollments in schools and colleges.[67] Froomkin estimates that during the decade following 1975 roughly 40 percent of the new jobs filled by college graduates will be in the nonprofit sector, as contrasted to 71 percent in the past 5 years.[68] For persons with less than a college degree, only one-fifth of the jobs are projected to materialize in the nonprofit sector, as contrasted to more than half of the total in the past 5 years.

The main result of the slowing rate of growth in the nonprofit and government sectors of the economy is that college-trained persons, in order to find work at all, will have to accept jobs in other than professional or administrative fields. This trend has already started to manifest itself. For instance, in both 1960 and 1970, some 84 percent of all college graduates reported working as either professional or as managerial and administrative employees. By 1975, this proportion declined to 76 percent, mostly due to the lower proportion of college-educated persons able to find jobs in the professions.[69]

There is also some evidence that the quality of jobs filled by younger college graduates is deteriorating, as their earnings have been growing more slowly than those of persons with a high school education. Between 1969 and 1974, the mean earnings of male college graduates aged 25 to 34 increased by 19 percent, while those of high school graduates increased by 32 percent.[70] In real terms, the earnings of college graduates, after deflation by the Consumer Price Index, were reduced by some 13 percent during the 5-year period, in contrast to those of high school graduates which declined by less than 2 percent.[71]

The difficulties which college graduates have experienced in landing jobs are also reflected in their higher unemployment rate. College graduates under age 25 had a 6.4-percent average unemployment rate in 1975, as contrasted to 2.4 percent in 1970. While the overall unemployment rate less than doubled over these 5 years, the rate among young college graduates nearly tripled.[72]

Though investigators disagree on the extent to which there will be oversupply of college graduates, most agree that there will be an excess—even among those who posit a sharp decline in enrollments. If enrollments decline by a third, as postulated by Dresch [73] who noted the recent decline in the proportion of high school graduates enrolling in higher education, the number of graduates would be reduced only by 3 million, and the balance between supply and demand is not likely to be restored by 1970 or 1975 standards.[74] Furthermore, the enrollments are not likely to decline as drastically, since education, in all probability, is viewed as both a consumption and an investment good and a worthwhile alternative to young people who experience difficulty in finding jobs.

The increasing degree of overqualification for work in the United States is already having negative effects. First, employers have set educational entrance requirements which are far too high for the jobs to be performed, a condition which tends to discriminate against poor people, women, minorities, and youths. Berg,[75] for example, estimates that about 80 percent of American college graduates are taking jobs that were filled previously by workers with lower educational credentials. Freeman [76] found that this is occurring primarily in the white-collar managerial and sales fields.

A second negative consequence of the rising degree of overqualification in the U.S. work force is its likely contribution to poor morale and feelings of job dissatisfaction among overqualified workers. The huge Department of Labor-sponsored *Survey of Working Conditions*, for example, showed that feeling overqualified for one's work was one of the strongest correlates of overall job dissatisfaction.[77] The total number of workers who feel overqualified for their jobs is already substantial—35 percent in 1969 and 27 percent in 1973.[78] Although aggregate levels of job satisfaction have not changed much over the last 10 years,[79] the fact that the probabilities for vertical career mobility will diminish in the future because of demographic trends should cause some concern. What is clear from almost every study of job dissatisfaction is that the placing of intelligent and/or highly qualified workers in dull and unchallenging jobs is a prescription for pathology—for the worker, the employer, and the society.[80] For example, O'Toole [81] reports a study undertaken by Sandia Laboratories which indicates that intelligent (not dull) blue-collar workers are the ones most responsible for damage, low productivity, errors, and accidents in the workplace.

On the positive side, the increasing overqualification of workers, who, ironically, have the educational backgrounds to articulate their dissatisfactions, could result in an overall improvement of working conditions, the creation of more interesting jobs (as employers consider how to adjust the demand to fit the supply), and greater amounts of industrial democracy with more workers sharing in corporate decisionmaking. Though the increasing educational attainment of the labor force has not had such an impact thus far, we must remember that the oversupply problem is still somewhat new, having begun only in the past 5 years.

From the economic perspective, there is some evidence that this inflation of educational credentials may lead to an actual lowering of productivity. It was argued in the 1960's by Theodore Schultz and the "human capitalists" that investments in education were investments in the gross national product. These economists felt that upgrading the work force educationally would lead to high productivity as underqualified workers were replaced by those with greater skills.

Ivar Berg has argued that the reality of the process is quite different from the economists' model. What actually happens is a process of unproductive job dislocation—more highly qualified workers who may be forced to stay in or accept jobs not utilizing their education, "bump" slightly less qualified workers from their jobs. No increase in productivity occurs because the nature of the jobs is usually such that they do not require higher skills. Productivity may actually drop because the more highly qualified worker is likely to be dissatisfied with the job. In sum, increasing the educational level of the work force above a certain level, without concomitant changes in the structure of work to capitalize on the increased capabilities of workers, will probably exert a slightly negative impact on productivity.[82]

In the last two decades, universities, corporations, and the government have all adopted the human capitalist mode of calculating the return of investment per year of education. Ironically, as the economic ceiling on the need for more highly qualified workers is being reached, the increasing supply may actually be driving down the market value job. In sum, increasing the educational level of the work force above of educational credentials. As it becomes clear that education will not pay off as promised, there is a very real possibility of a massive buildup of disillusionment and a sense of betrayal among those stuck with a bad investment.

On the other hand, there is no reason to assume that college students will view education solely or even primarily, as a passport to a good job. They might instead view education as an important ingredient of the good life whether or not their education is relevant to their jobs. Time series data are needed to determine whether students' perception of the value of education is accommodating itself to the changing values of educational credentials in the job market.

Despite ample evidence which indicates diminishing probabilities of being able to turn educational credentials into well-paying and high-status jobs, other evidence suggests that young people still in school have high educational and occupational aspirations. For example, a recent American college testing service study showed that 65 percent of 11th graders plan to attend college for 2 or more years and 46 percent plan to attend for 3 years or more.[83] In a study of college freshmen, Alexander Astin found that 57 percent plan to go to graduate school.[84] An Office of Education survey reported that over 54 percent of a national sample of 18,000 high school seniors desired professional or managerial-level jobs.[85] A more recent study conducted by the National Assessment of Educational Progress confirmed these earlier results by showing that 44 percent of American 17-year-olds wanted professional careers, approximately double the portion of professional and managerial jobs currently in the economy.[86]

Though there is nothing wrong with having high educational or occupational aspirations, the fact that there is a strong positive correlation between the two raises the question whether an increase in educational attainment of the work force will lead to even higher occupational expectations and subsequent frustration at not being able to fulfill them. Future research ought to keep abreast of this issue. If increasing levels of educational attainment appear causally related to increased levels of job dissatisfaction (because of perceived under-utilization of skills on the job) and there are no compensating features such as increased productivity, then society ought to contemplate a reduction in public subsidies for postsecondary education. If, on the other hand, there are no such ill effects of higher educational attainment, then society must ponder whether the non-employment-related or social benefits derived from postsecondary education outweigh the advantages of other socially oriented programs deserving of public subsidy.

Student Aid for Part-Time Students?

Federal and State financial aid programs for postsecondary students tend to ignore part-time students, or those who attend less than half-time. Among the eight Federal programs which assist postsecondary students, part-time students who attend less than halftime are excluded from all but the State student incentive grant (SSIG) and GI bill programs administered by OE and Veterans Administration, respectively. Full-time attendance is also a requirement under the Social Security Survivors Benefits Plan of the Social Security Administration. At least halftime attendance is required by OE's basic educational opportunity grant (BEOG), supplemental educational opportunity grant (SEOG), and the college work-study (CWS) programs. Eligibility for OE's subsidized insured loan (SIL) and direct student loan (DSL) programs varies by State; some specify full-time enrollment.

State aid is usually granted on the basis of need and most often requires full-time enrollment. Almost 740,000 students in 28 States benefited in 1973–74 from State-funded programs. Only 15 percent of the States make financial assistance available to part-time students.[87] The Federal BEOG program makes it possible for States to support part-time students but not at the expense of full-time students. Occasionally part-time attendance is discouraged by the tuition policies of the institutions. The American Council on Education reported that 66 percent of the institutions in its survey charged higher tuition per credit-hour to part-time than to full-time students (1975).

Though part-time students do not benefit much from Federal and State student aid programs,[88] there are other programs in both the public and private sectors which can assist them. In the public sector, the community college, which normally charges very low tuition, is the logical choice of the part-time adult student lacking funds. In the private sector, employers frequently make available financial assistance for job-related education and training. Employer plans usually require the employee to obtain company approval for the course(s) he/she intends to take. Upon evidence of successful completion of the work at an approved institution, tuition is refunded. While estimates of private sector expenditures are difficult to obtain, their value for employees seeking educational and occupational advancement may go as high as $500 million yearly, if fully utilized.

Little evidence is available on the extent to which the educational opportunities offered by community colleges and private industry are sufficient to meet the demand for them by low-income working adults.

The poor methods used to estimate the strength of the desire for educational benefits among adults have been discussed. Evidence which compares the desire for further education among adult workers with desires for other social benefits indicates clearly that education is given very low priority, especially by low-income workers. Nevertheless, the extent to which insufficient funds among working adults constitutes a barrier to participation is still an open question in the absence of programs which provide workers with such funds.[89] Federally funded but locally administered manpower training programs under CETA do provide training to low-income workers, but the worker's choice is limited to the kinds of occupational training which the local authorities decide to offer.

Given the lack of compelling evidence that there is a barriers-to-education problem among low-income workers, the Federal Government would be wise to proceed cautiously in this area. One possible Federal activity would be to monitor and evaluate programs conducted by States and local areas which provide low-income workers with funds to continue their education on a part-time basis. Occasionally, such programs are federally funded. Portland, Oreg., and Baltimore for example, are providing work incentive programs (WIN) to welfare clients by issuing vouchers which will enable them to purchase occupational training. The Bureau of Social Science Research is evaluating this experiment for the Department of Labor.[90]

Of all the States, perhaps Massachusetts is the closest to passing a law which would provide low-income adults with part-time educational opportunities. In 1975 and 1976 a bill was introduced to create an *adult recurrent education entitlement voucher program*. The proposed legislation followed a comprehensive study of educational opportunities for adults in Massachusetts,[91] which found the existing system of continuing and part-time postsecondary education to be more sensitive to adult needs and more reflective of current educational reform than the more traditional full-time day system of higher education. The new bill would encourage and enable adults of low income and meager previous education to take advantage of part-time study opportunities by offering vouchers to cover the cost of courses taken in the public and private institutions which constitute this nontraditional system.

To be eligible the participant must have earned less than $15,000 in the previous year, have fewer than 4 years of college credit, and be at least 25 years of age. The amount of the entitlement is graduated depending on the applicant's income and previous level of education. The maximum entitlement is $50 per credit, and the maximum utilization rate is two three-credit courses per semester. The voucher would be given to the provider institution, which in turn, would submit the voucher to the State treasury for reimbursement. Participating institutions would have to meet the eligibility requirements of OE's Federal student assistance programs.

As conceived now, the proposed program in Massachusetts would be budget limited to an annual appropriation of $2 to $4 million; i.e., vouchers would be distributed on a first-come first-served basis until the appropriation runs out. Though not yet enacted, this program would strengthen the nontraditional postsecondary education sector, but not at the expense of the traditional sector nor of the interests of younger students who desire to study fulltime. Economic circumstances might force such tradeoffs, however.

If, indeed, the Massachusetts recurrent education bill becomes law, the Federal Government should monitor and evaluate it closely. Unfortunately, the budget-limited or first-come first-served feature of the bill might make it impossible to ascertain the unsatisfied demand for additional part-time study opportunities for low-income individuals. No doubt the first people to use their vouchers will be from the more affluent and highly educated group within the eligible population. A GI-bill-type model which guarantees all members of the eligible group full benefits is the only model which will provide the necessary experience to determine the extent to which the barriers problem is perceived by low-income adults who wish to undertake part-time education.

Regardless of whether or not the proposed Massachusetts model is enacted, there is little reason for the Federal Government to consider replicating it at this time. Aside from the fact that such a program would not address any particular national need or problem, a national replication could be extremely expensive. Based on national participation rates in part-time education from a 1972 survey conducted for OE by the Bureau of the Census, an annual Federal expenditure of $180 million could be expected from a plan which would provide tuition assistance to adults earning $6,000 or less per year (the Massachusetts plan specifies a maximum income of $15,000). This $6,000 figure is derived from data which show that in 1972 some 2.3 million adults with an annual family income of under $6,000 took 3.7 million courses, 1.8 million of which they paid for themselves.[92] If the Government were to subsidize these 1.8 million courses (previously paid for out of pocket) at a rate of $100 per course, the cost would be $180 million. Increased participation rates or larger stipends per course or enlarging the pool of eligibles would result in a program costing hundreds of millions of dollars. One way to reduce the contemplated expenditure would be to focus on an even smaller target group; e.g., individuals who continue to earn less than $6,000 per year for 3 or more consecutive years. Such a modification would address more specifically the locking in problem which causes people to feel year after year that they are unable to return to school in order to improve their occupational status because of economic circumstances. If the Federal Government were to contemplate any kind of tuition assistance for low-income adults, it would be wise to focus on or begin the program with the group that is chronically low income; i.e., the most locked in, and not just low income once in a while.

Two other options to consider which would give low-income adults greater flexibility for combining work and education would be either to raise the ceiling on income which an independent or self-supporting student may earn and still remain eligible for the basic educational opportunity grant (BEOG) program or to permit part-time (less than halftime) students to take advantage of this program. Either strategy would enable many more working students to participate. If this were done and BEOG funding levels were to remain the same despite the expanded supply of eligibles, the average grant, logically, would be reduced. This, in turn, would limit further the kinds of institutions that eligible students could afford to attend.[93] As a likely consequence, a greater portion of BEOG recipients would be forced to reduce their course work and/or work more hours. Possibly, taking longer to complete college course work would encourage these low-income recipients to integrate their course work more closely with their career plans.

Recent evidence indicates, however, that there is no economic advantage in combining part-time work and part-time study. Specifically, O'Neill and Ross [94] found that veterans who use their GI bill benefits to support part-time vocational-technical study have better jobs to begin with; therefore, in the posttraining period, they have higher earnings than full-time vocational-technical participants. Hence the researchers conclude that the effect of training per se on earnings is greater for the full-time users than for the part-time users.[95]

Raising the amount of income an independent student may earn and maintain eligibility for a basic opportunity grant has more cost disadvantages than permitting part-time (less than halftime) study while holding eligibles' income constant. Making part-time students eligible does not expand the number who would qualify for grants under the current income test, while raising the amount an independent or self-supporting student may earn does increase the supply of income determined eligibles. Moreover, there is no evidence to suggest that opening the program to part-time students would increase participation to the point that it would either increase the total cost of the program (if fully funded) or reduce significantly the size of the grants available to full-time and halftime users (if limited funded). In terms of cost, the main disadvantage in extending eligibility to part-time students is the likelihood of an increased number of grants with a lower average stipend, thereby increasing the paperwork and hence administrative costs per grant.

In terms of the national interest, there is no reason why the BEOG program should not include part-time students, even if the program did not receive full funding and the size of grants for full-time students had to be reduced. No evidence suggests that the ratio of full- to part-time students in the Nation should be of concern. If there were, objections would have been heard by now concerning our largest entitlement program, the GI bill, which has existed for several years without discriminating against part-time users.

Arguments in favor of extending BEOG eligibility to part-time students are: (1) That low-income individuals (the client group of BEOG) who do not have the energy, capacity, or circumstances to take on at least halftime study (e.g., handicapped, elderly, house-wives, etc.) ought to have the same opportunity to enrich their lives with education as low-income individuals who do not have such problems (the equity argument); and (2) that chronically unemployed youth or young people (from poor families) with low-paying, dead-end jobs who are trying to get better jobs can't afford time away from their job search to permit halftime study, but they could combine work/job search with further education if the opportunity to obtain part-time grants were available (the flexibility for combining work and education argument).

Arguments against extending BEOG eligibility to part-time participants are: (1) That students who study less than halftime miss out on much of the informal learning which occurs in an institution when people are on campus long enough to partake in it; (2) that part-time students will be less likely than full-time students to take courses having job-related value and more likely to take courses for consumptive or recreational reasons; (3) that a greater portion of BEOG funds would flow to proprietary schools, which tend to have higher rates of Federal student aid program abuse than nonprofit institutions; and (4) administrative costs of the program would increase due to handling a larger number of grants.

None of the arguments, pro or con, are empirically supported. From the standpoint of equity, however, part-time students should become eligible. Perhaps this notion should be experimented with for a couple of years in order to determine the costs and benefits. One low-risk way of starting would be to permit part-time study for no more than one or two consecutive quarters or semesters. Such variations could be tried in a few institutions or States before attempting national implementation.

Summary

Evidence has been marshaled to show that from the job-related point of view, no cogent case can be made for significantly increasing Federal expenditures for adult and continuing education. From what is known at this time, the number of people who participate in these activities or the types of courses they take has no particular bearing on the national interest:

- Chronic long-term skill shortages in the labor market do not appear to exist. If anything, our economy is characterized more by a shortage of jobs, not skills. The American system has done a better job in helping workers maintain marketable skills than to market them.
- Overqualification for work and the underutilization of skills of persons with college training is becoming a national problem. Between one-fourth and one-third of American workers feel overqualified for their jobs. National programs which promote further education among adults might exacerbate such feelings by raising occupational expectations which are not likely to be fulfilled.
- Participation in career related educational activities among adults is as likely to result from the kind of work that one does as to lead to such work.
- Adult education is flourishing and growing without significant increments in Federal support or guidance. This growth is not occurring for all segments of the adult population, however. Most of the growth has occurred among better educated workers in professional occupations.
- Significant future increments in the amounts of education and training pursued by adults are more likely to result from a more equitable distribution of work and leisure among demographic groups in the United States than from increased availability of educational programs per se.

Although there is no empirically supported rationale for increasing the Federal financial contribution to adult and continuing education, there is no reason for excluding low-income adults who wish to study part time from current Federal student aid programs. Almost all of these postsecondary programs require at least halftime enrollment. If eligibility were to be extended to part-time (less than halftime) students as well, low-income youths and adults would gain additional flexibility in combining work and education. In the absence of data which indicate whether full-time enrollment has any greater public or private benefits than part-time enrollment, Federal student aid programs, especially the basic opportunity grant (BEOG) program, might well begin to make part-time students eligible at least on an experimental basis. It is unlikely that an extension of eligibility to part-time students would significantly increase the participation rate and hence the total cost of the program (if fully funded) or the size of the average stipend going to recipients who are enrolled on a halftime to full-time basis.

RECOMMENDATIONS FOR FEDERAL POLICY

The (aggregate) job shortage problem is not likely to be resolved by a mere expansion of education or training opportunities. Past Federal investments in education or training programs have not expanded the national supply of jobs. Even if we were to assume that increased enrollments of adults in education or training programs serve the national interest, such increments are as likely to result from a more equitable distribution of work and leisure as from augmented availability of educational programs per se. Evidence suggests that once a person advances in age beyond his/her mid-twenties, participation in educational activities for the purpose of improving or maintaining career status is as likely to result from the kind of work that one does as to lead to such work.

The job shortage problem is most likely to be resolved by a strategy which promotes macroeconomic expansion as well as greater flexibility in working life through a more equitable distribution of work, leisure, and education among the younger, middle-aged, and older cohorts of the population. Although a policy to provide more career-related work to younger and older people while affording more leisure and educational opportunities to midcareer people is appealing, there is little likelihood that the Nation will make a major effort in the near future to restructure or redistribute work. It is recommended, nonetheless, that a variety of Federal activities be pursued which would contribute in a modest way toward making worklife more flexible while supplying valuable information which would be needed before contemplating more dramatic steps. In order of progressing degrees of involvement, the Federal Government could: (1) Expand research to assess the kinds of life scheduling patterns which appeal to people as well as serve the collective public interest; (2) help States establish occupational and educational information systems as well as consumer-oriented "brokering" services which would help individuals of all ages make more intelligent choices about careers and educational and leisure activities; (3) through public information programs, conferences and the like encourage labor and management to negotiate plans to allow individual employees to choose among varying amounts of and ways of scheduling work and time off; and (4) consider legislation which would enable more workers to take a temporary leave of absence from their jobs in order to participate in activities which might facilitate career or life improvement, renewal, or redirection. Details of these four types of activities follow.

RESEARCH ON CAREER
AND LIFE REDIRECTION AND RENEWAL

In contrast to the school-to-work transition problem among youths, where evidence has lead us to propose some concrete public policy and programs, the vast area of career and life redirection and renewal among adults is much less well-defined and, at this time, much less amenable to public solutions. Most studies of the need for more adult and continuing education can be characterized as reflecting a cause in search of a problem. True public interest research which attempts to compare the need or desire of adults for more educational opportunities with other kinds of needs and desires is almost nonexistent. Such research is essential before major new Federal undertakings in this area are attempted.

A research strategy to assess the need to provide more opportunities to change careers and participate in renewal activities would consist of four parts: (1) A wants/needs assessment through the use of— (a) Survey research which would force respondents to make tradeoffs between different mixes of work, leisure, and educational opportunities, and (b) incentives research which would provide workers with real human resource development alternatives from which to choose; (2) public interest research which would attempt to determine whether investment in career/life redirection or renewal opportunities yields a greater public benefit than some other type of public investment; (3) public policy modeling which would attempt to determine how proposals to significantly change work-leisure-education scheduling patterns would impact on the U.S. economy and polity, as well as on educational institutions and Federal education programs; and (4) research on support systems such as information and brokering projects to acquaint adults with human resource development opportunities. Research results would be forwarded to a clearinghouse, which, in turn, would disseminate this information to interested parties through a variety of methods.

Wants/Needs Assessment: Survey Research

Surveys to determine adult education needs or barriers to pursue further education and training traditionally have been biased in favor of providing more subsidy for these activities inasmuch as the respondent rarely is permitted to compare his preference for education with other ways of spending extra money or time. New surveys, therefore, to find out why adults don't participate in further education and training are largely a waste, at least for the Federal Government. Local providers of educational services might want to conduct such market research for their own purposes, but inasmuch as the number of adult education participants is of no particular Federal concern, no federally sponsored market research is necessary.

The national interest, however, would be served by surveys which attempt to find out what people want by having them make tradeoffs between several desirable commodities: Money, the amount and allocation of worktime and leisure time, educational opportunities, and other health and welfare benefits. Surveys, ought to ask people what they would give up in order to get certain human resource benefits. Nealey and Goodale;[96] for example, asked 200 auto workers to decide (hypothetically) in what form they would like a 2-percent increase in benefits over the course of a year; interestingly, a straight 2-percent increase in wages came in fourth place after: (1) An additional week of paid vacation, (2) five additional Fridays off, and (3) greater retirement benefits. Studies like this—but more comprehensive and on a larger scale—would have to be undertaken in order to provide some solid hypotheses on which to base experimental studies on how people would behave if real and not hypothetical alternatives were available.

Wants/Needs Assessment: Incentives Research

Behavioral research can be relied upon much more than attitudinal or opinion research to discover what people want. Making selections among hypothetical alternatives is no substitute for real alternatives. While a full-fledged experimental manipulation of incentive structures would be tremendously useful to determine which work-leisure-education scheduling patterns appeal to different categories of people, it is unlikely that sufficient Federal funds will become available in the near future to conduct such broad, large-scale experiments. However, there are smaller scale and geographically limited experiments which are federally funded and which should yield valuable information about the kinds of human resource development opportunities that adults want. For example, HEW and DOL have introduced the use of occupational training vouchers for welfare recipients in work incentive programs (WIN in Portland, Ore. and Baltimore and for participants in income maintenance or negative income tax experiments in Seattle and Denver.

In addition to following closely the results of ongoing experiments, Federal research projects should attempt to assess the consequences of the manipulation of incentive structures which occur naturally in our society all of the time. For example, labor and management are constantly negotiating about the conditions under which employees can take advantage of educational benefits. Such conditions usually include whether or not the employee can: (a) Participate in the program during work hours, (b) continue to receive salary while participating in programs offered during normal work hours, and (c) take courses in vocationally relevant areas only. The consequences of manipulating any one or a combination of these conditions as well the amount of the training stipend itself, would be good nominations for research: that is, how do different permutations of eligibility and use requirements affect the participation rate in the program? If a little more money were available for this kind of research, the Federal Government could fund such experimental permutations of these educational benefits programs in order to find out how workers would respond. NIE is considering this kind of research.

Other variations of incentive structures which could be investigated include: (1) Introduction of changed eligibility criteria to participate in company-sponsored sabbaticals, extended vacations, paid education leave, leave of absence without pay, etc.; (2) introduction of job redesign and job enrichment programs (e.g., investigate their influence on voluntary participation in further education and training); (3) introduction of the "cafeteria plan" in collective bargaining agreements where the employee himself is permitted to structure his own package of fringe benefits, including medical, dental, life insurance, paid vacation, retirement, and educational entitlements; [97] and (4) introduction of changed eligibility criteria in Federal aid programs which would permit greater flexibility in the scheduling of work and education, like making part-time (less than halftime) students eligible for the basic opportunity grants program.

If Federal research efforts are to capture successfully the significance of these natural variations in incentive structures, it is essential that any investigations begin before the variations are introduced. Otherwise, local and State programs will be started, and researchers will never reap the benefit of a pretest which is essential to discover what difference was made by the particular program. Improved lines of communication, therefore, are needed between the research agencies and local and State governments.

Public Interest Research

In the area of adult and continuing education, federally sponsored research should attempt to determine whether or not public investments in this kind of activity yield greater public benefits than some other type of public investment. A particularly ripe subject for such "tradeoff research" would be a comparison of the relative benefits of investments in education with investments in health and welfare. For example, the health of older citizens might improve more from a public policy to encourage them to participate in physical fitness activities than a policy which would build more hospitals and provide more Medicare. Or stated another way, perhaps paying older citizens to take classes in yoga or aerobic dancing is more cost effective than investing a similar amount in increased Medicare, or subsidies to purchase drugs. A longitudinal study, obviously, would be required to test such a hypothesis.

Another kind of tradeoff experiment would compare the labor market benefits of providing education and training to welfare recipients with the benefits derived from providing an equivalent value of short-term wage subsidies to employers who would agree to hire these people and keep them on the job for at least a minimum period.

113

Possibly, direct employment experience will make an unemployed person more employable than additional training.

A final type of public interest research might seek to determine how plant and worker productivity is affected by taking advantage of educational opportunities. For example, if an employer decided or could be persuaded to allow his full-time employees to spend up to half a workday a week (4 hours or 10 percent of the workweek) in educational activities of their choice, a carefully designed research project could attempt to determine the effects of such time away from work on overall plant and worker productivity, as well as on the productivity of individual workers who took advantage of such opportunities. It might well be that taking time off for educational purposes will have negligible effect on or even improve productivity, to say nothing of job satisfaction and worker health and feelings of well-being. Again, such hypotheses are worth testing if we are to learn how the extent to which individual wants can be made compatible with collective benefits.

Public Policy Modeling of Viable Alternatives To Create Greater Flexibility in Worklife

Several schemes have been proposed in the last few years to provide people with greater opportunities to renew or redirect their lives and/or careers. These have included educational entitlements, voucher, and tuition assistance plans; paid and unpaid educational leave; work sabbaticals or extended vacations; countercyclical use of unemployment insurance funds to support training and education; more flexible seniority systems; fuller vesting of pensions; gradual retirement plans; work sharing; and more flexible occupational licensing and educational credentialing practices. Though these schemes vary widely with respect to the problems and target groups addressed, all are directed toward minimizing somehow the problems created by our overly rigid system of (lock step) progression from school to work to retirement.[98]

Given the attractiveness and intuitive appeal of many of these schemes and the fact that they are being widely talked about, it would make sense to systematize the study of them and bring order and substance to further public discussion and debate of them. A major study of the most viable public policy alternatives to achieve greater flexibility in working life is therefore recommended. Unlike most studies which have been commissioned on the subject, this one would pit each scheme against the others in terms of their expected costs and benefits and would estimate the relative impact of the different plans upon existing institutions and (human resource development) programs. Furthermore, very specific legislative proposals to implement the respective schemes would be submitted to a hierarchy of juries (e.g., groups of workers, professionals, politicians, students, retirees, home-makers, etc.), whose reactions would be duly recorded and summarized and included in the study's final report.

A comprehensive project of this type would involve several scholars and eventually hundreds of people who would react to their proposals. The major consequence would be an informed national dialog about alternative ways for scheduling or arranging work, leisure, and education among adults. No doubt such a study would be expensive and require a special authorization and appropriation from the Congress—for example, under the new Lifelong Learning Act of 1976.

Research on Support Systems

Earlier, federally sponsored programs to provide adults as well as youths with reliable, up-to-date, and locally relevant occupational and educational information were proposed. Better and more comprehensive information in combination with more consumer-oriented broker-ing or counseling services than are available now would facilitate more personally satisfying choices among these adults who wish to obtain additional education or training to upgrade their occupational status or change careers.

Though enough is known about career information systems and brokering services to begin operational programs, continued research would help to make these that much more effective and efficient. The utility of career information systems for adults, for example, would be enhanced by more detailed knowledge of occupational mobility and transferable vocational skills within occupational clusters. As knowl-edge of skill transferability becomes available, it can be included in occupational information files. Such information is likely to be very useful to an adult who wishes to know where his present vocational skills are marketable, especially if he or she desires to change careers but does not wish to spend excessive amounts of time training for such a shift. Adult entrants and reentrants into the labor force are also likely to consider the topic of skill transferability as they contemplate a particular kind of occupational training or further academic preparation.

HEW activity to identify skills and knowledges which are trans-ferable to several occupations began with the development of OE's 15 occupational curriculum clusters during the 1960's. These efforts resulted in the identification of a core of skills and knowledges which were common to most of the occupations within each cluster.[99] Voca-tional students would learn the core skills early on and obtain the more occupationally specific skills as their vocational training progressed.

NIE is attempting to update these earlier efforts through its current project on transferable skills being conducted by the Center for Vocational Education at the Ohio State University.[100] This project, which cost $300,000 in 1976, continues the search for transferable skills while attempting to describe occupational mobility in terms of workers' demographic and personality characteristics. The project also attempts to evaluate the utility of various data sources and occupational classification schemes for identifying transferable skills. The findings of this research will result, hopefully, in recommendations for improving educational programs as well as hiring and promotion decisions.[101]

Another research activity which would support the use of career information systems is continued experimentation with educational brokering projects. NIE and FIPSE have already funded the development of several such projects, which use various information retrieval and counseling techniques. New research in this area ought to focus on how to help these projects sustain themselves after their Federal grants run out. Indeed, planning for self-sustenance ought to become one of the criteria upon which new Federal awards are given for these projects.

Establishment of a Clearinghouse and Dissemination of Research Results

Establishment of a small unit in the Education Division is recommended to help individuals, companies, and government agencies learn about the various research and demonstration activities being conducted throughout the country on the flexibility of working life and lifelong learning. The clearinghouse would disseminate information on flexible work scheduling, extended vacation programs, sabbaticals, paid and unpaid educational leave, tuition aid programs, leave of absence policies, cafeteria-type benefit plans where individual employees can choose from a variety of fringe benefits (including education and paid vacation), labor-management productivity committees, and company- and union-sponsored education and negotiated career planning programs. In addition to providing descriptive information about such programs, the clearinghouse would keep records of relevant research and evaluation efforts and disseminate annotated bibliographies relative to them.[102]

On occasion, clearinghouse staff would prepare (inhouse) or contract for state of the art or policy analysis papers which utilize the research and evaluation studies stored in the clearinghouse. Of particular interest would be studies on how flexible arrangements for combining work, leisure, and education affect productivity, rate of job changing and turnover, total company employment, worker health and job satisfaction, family life, and worker educational attainment and participation in available education or training. Finally, technical assistance staff would constantly arrange conferences, meetings, workshops, and courses on the flexibility of working life, involving (when appropriate) other Federal agencies having relevant concerns (Labor, Commerce, Commission on Productivity and the Quality of Working Life, etc.).

CAREER INFORMATION AND GUIDANCE SYSTEMS

Earlier, a case was made to provide better career information and guidance to young people who are about to make the transition from school to work and who are in the process of career exploration and decisionmaking. The need to make informed career choices exists for adults also—whether the choice is to change jobs or careers or to leave the labor force and reenter it later. Though the type of information and guidance services for adults may be different than for youths, the need for accurate, up-to-date, locally relevant, and publicly accountable career information is the same.[103] Any extra or special information which might be incorporated within the system for adults; e.g., information on the transferability of advanced job skills, could be included at minimal extra charge once such information becomes available.

Several forces are at work in the society which might well make the provision of information and guidance services for adults much more important in the years to come. Most significant are the factors which are likely to result in greater desires for career change or horizontal career mobility. Among these are: (1) Greater competition for the preferred, higher skilled and better paying jobs as a result of a much larger number of workers who want and are qualified for these jobs; (2) decreasing dependency ratios, which give adults, on the average, greater portions of their lives free of dependents and hence more opportunity to take job-changing risks; and (3) the entrance and reentrance of a higher percentage of women into the labor force. In addition to fostering greater desires for career change, the reduced probabilities for promotion or career advancement might well increase the proportion of workers who will look outside of work for their primary sources of life satisfaction. Such workers are also likely to benefit from information and guidance services which help them learn about adult education or recreational activities in the community.

Dissemination of high quality, locally relevant, and up-to-date occupational and education-training information is not taking place to any large degree in the United States. Emerging, however, are several "educational brokering" projects around the country which attempt to do this as well as provide counseling, jobseeking techniques, and personal assessment to adults contemplating further education. NIE and FIPSE together spent about $2 million on such projects in fiscal year 1975. Much as these broker services for adult learners show promise, they have the same weakness as most of the career guidance and information systems which serve youths: they lack high quality occupational and educational information. Counseling for either group is more likely to be effective if there is accurate information to counsel with.

The development of reliable, up-to-date, and locally relevant career information in useful, easily understood forms and formats merits the highest Federal priority. What to do about this is discussed in more detail in the school-to-work transition section.

Whereas fairly specific Federal standards and guidelines ought to accompany the distribution of Federal funds to States for the purpose of developing occupational and educational information, the standards should be more flexible with respect to the manner in which the information is delivered or disseminated. At this time, a Federal effort to replicate a particular delivery system does not appear to be warranted, because no particular method of delivering occupational and educational information to adults has been proven to be superior over other methods. Federal research and demonstration grants should continue to encourage innovation in this area. Comparative research which emphasizes the relative costs and benefits of the various delivery systems for different adult target groups should be emphasized. In addition, the Federal funding of new demonstrations or the continued funding of older projects should be made contingent upon evidence that these projects develop and test marketing procedures which will help them become self-supporting or self-sustaining after the Federal grants run out.

TIME-INCOME TRADEOFF AND WORK SCHEDULING OPTIONS

Through a public information program, including the convening of representatives from labor and management in both the public and private sectors, the Federal Government should encourage the negotiation of plans and collective bargaining agreements that allow individual employees to choose among varying amounts of and ways of scheduling work and time off. The range of possibilities is enormous; many may be beneficial to both individual employees and their respective organizations. The Federal Government might apply this idea internally as a "demonstration case" as well as investigate the use of tax and other incentives to encourage management and labor to meet and consider the issue of additional flexibility in working life, and the various kinds of plans that might be instituted to bring about greater flexibility.

LEAVE OF ABSENCE WITHOUT PAY

Legislation should be considered that would enable more wage and salary employees, whether full time or part time, to obtain a certain number of weeks of release time after having worked for the same employer for a specific length of time. The duration of the leave of absence without pay would depend on the number of consecutive years worked—up to some maximum. If, for example, the legislation were to specify that the employee would earn 6 weeks of unpaid leave per year, after 3 years he would have earned 18 weeks, or the time equivalent of one semester of academic study. The precise period when the employee would be permitted to take leave—all or part of it—would require negotiation with the employer, including the provision of sufficient advance notice. Sweden has such provisions in its recent law on unpaid educational leave. Unlike the Swedish law, however, the leave of absence without pay envisaged here would be granted for any reason, not just education. Above all, the employee would be guaranteed reemployment at his old job or some equivalent job at no loss in pay or seniority when he or she returns from the leave of absence.[104]

A range of options along a spectrum of minimal to considerable amounts of Federal involvement or regulation should be evaluated. One type of option would provide financial or tax incentives for employers who agree to allow employees to take leave of absence. A more activist option would entitle employees by law to take temporary leave after meeting certain stipulated conditions. In both cases, the amount of leave would likely depend on the length of service with the employer. If, indeed, national consensus could be rallied around some plan, a plausible next step would be to find ways to maintain income during the leave of absence. Short of a Federal program to do this (e.g., loans, income tax deferments, etc.), labor and management might work out payroll savings or flexible pension plans and the like which could supply some income during this period.

A leave of absence law would help neutralize economic and demographic forces which inhibit risk-taking with respect to changing jobs or preparing oneself in school to qualify for another or a better job. It would also provide people the time to "do the things they've always wanted to do" before their retirement years. Finally, it would provide preretirees the opportunity to prepare for retirement or to experience it somewhat before it is actually upon them.

No evidence is available that could help determine the impact of such a law on employers and plant productivity. Workers who use their leave to look for another job are likely to be unhappy in their present job and seek a change. Employers most likely would not object to this kind of turnover; it might be a way to help unproductive workers find more suitable jobs. Workers who use their leave for some type of renewal or rejuvenation are likely to return to work more rested and motivated; hence they might become more productive.

Certainly, many workers would not be able to take advantage of such an opportunity because no income is paid by the employer during the leave of absence. Efforts to provide income during such leave time, even at a portion of the normal salary, would result in an expensive, full-fledged sabbatical-type program. In view of little likelihood of agreement on whether and how to do this in the near future, there is no point in proposing it here. Nevertheless, the possibility of extended time off with reemployment rights would at least give workers an additional option for combining work, leisure, and education. If workers know they will get the time off, they can plan how to support themselves during that time.

IMPLEMENTATION

An expanded research effort to assess the issues of redistributing work and facilitating career and life redirection and renewal would require additional research and demonstration funds, especially if some actual experimentation with incentive structures is contemplated. NIE should remain as the focus for this type of research within the Education Division. Because of the many sectors of society which would be influenced by such research, other Federal agencies ought to be involved as well, including the Departments of Commerce and Labor, and other agencies within HEW.

The establishment of a nationwide network of career information systems in all 50 States and other eligible areas would cost about $10 million per year over a 5-year period, assuming a gradual phasing in of about 15 States a year. All of the State systems would be expected to become self-supporting after an initial 3- to 4-year Federal grant. DOL and HEW ought to share in the funding and administration of the State grants. The Higher Education Amendments of 1976, in fact, authorize the establishment of education information centers, which is half of the career information system concept (the other half is the provision of occupational information). HEW should seek appropriations to implement this authority while encouraging DOL to expand its occupational information system grants program to more than the present eight States. An agreement between the two Departments would require a merging or common administration of educational information centers and occupational information systems when both are located in the same State. DOL would be responsible for the quality of the occupational information in any combined system, while HEW would be responsible for the quality of the educational information.

A Federal public information program to encourage a nationwide discussion of time-income tradeoff and work scheduling options would be carried out ideally by a multi-agency task force or consortium (principally the Departments of Commerce, Labor, and HEW) ; or the project would be housed in a private non-profit organization and draw its resources from the relevant Federal agencies. Wherever located, the project would convene representatives from business, labor, State and local governments to explore the advantages and disadvantages of providing employees with more options to choose among varying amounts of and ways of scheduling work and time off. A concerted and coordinated attempt would be made to disseminate the results and proceedings of these conferences, convocations, and seminars. Possibly, programs on the subject could be aired by or even developed by public or commercial television. The cost of a public information program, obviously, depends on the magnitude of the effort and the extent of participation by various groups.

Legislation to enable more employees to take a temporary leave of absence following a minimum length of service with an employer would be administered by the Department of Labor. The cost of such a program would depend on whether and to what extent financial incentives (in the case of voluntary collaboration by employers) or compensation (in the case of mandatory cooperation) were used to implement the law. One way to determine costs as well as program effects would be to try out different plans in different parts of the country on an experimental basis.

Footnotes

Youth: The School-to-Work Transition

1. In 1961 the labor force participation rate of teenagers 16 to 19 years old was 49.1 percent; in 1967, 50.5 percent; and in 1975, 55.2 percent. See *Employment and Training Report of the President 1976*, tables A–2 and A–3.
2. *Ibid.*, table A–6. For a recent analysis of the youth unemployment problem see George Iden et al., *Policy Options for the Teenage Unemployment Problem*, Congressional Budget Office Paper No. 13, Congress of the United States, Washington, D.C., September 1976.
3. "Jobs per capita" is calculated by dividing the average annual employment by the total noninstitutional population.
4. Approximately two-thirds of a national sample of 22,000 high school seniors in 1972 thought their schools should have placed more emphasis on vocational and technical programs, should have offered more practical work experience, and should help students find jobs when they leave school. See *National Longitudinal Study of the High School Class of 1972: Student Questionnaire and Test Results by Sex, High School Program, Ethnic Category, and Father's Education*, National Center for Education Statistics, No. 75–208, U.S. Department of Health, Education, and Welfare, U.S. Government Printing Office, Washington, D.C., 1975.
5. *Ibid;* David Gottlieb, *Youth and the Meaning of Work*, a report prepared for the Manpower Administration, U.S. Department of Labor, contract No. 81–11–72–04, 1973; Daniel Yankelovitch, *The New Morality: A Profile of American Youth in the 70's*. McGraw-Hill Book Co., New York, 1974.
6. In October 1974, the youth labor force (under age 25) numbered about 21 million. Of some 6 million enrolled in school, 13 percent were unemployed; of those at work, 82 percent had part-time jobs. Both the proportion of part-time workers and the unemployment rate were lower for the age 20–29 cohort than for the teenagers. There is also some indication that the unemployment rate of students is higher than that derived from data collected by the Bureau of the Census through their current population survey (CPS). Specifically, data collected through the National Longitudinal Survey of the Labor Force conducted by Herbert Parnes and associates at Ohio State University indicated that the unemployment rates for students were higher and for nonstudents were lower than the rates derived from CPS data. The discrepancy is probably due to the fact that the longitudinal survey obtains employment information directly from the workers, whereas the CPS data are obtained from an adult in the household. Hence, the desire for work among students is likely to be even stronger than the CPS unemployment data would suggest.

7. Sue Berryman Bobrow ("Reasonable Expectations: Limits on the Promise of Community Councils," a paper prepared for the National Institute of Education, contract No. 400–76–0120, 1976) summarizes a number of studies which suggest that unemployment is not a serious problem for youth in general. Though youth unemployment rates are high relative to adult rates, the difference in rates is largely attributable to high proportions of youth entries and reentries into the labor force. Much teenage unemployment, then, results from high rates of finding and quitting jobs as teenagers, especially students, experiment with a variety of jobs and use them to fulfill short-term goals. Bobrow notes, also, that the increase in the ratio of teenage to adult unemployment rates (a ratio which she corrects for changes in proportions of different age groups in the total population) is not so serious when one considers: (1) That teenagers are participating more in the labor force and are obtaining a larger share of the available jobs, (2) that most of the increase in teenage workers and teenage unemployment during the last 15 years has occurred among students who voluntarily enter, quit, and reenter the labor force at much higher rates than nonstudents, and (3) that teenage unemployment is seldom long term when compared to the experience of older unemployed workers. Many of these same points are made by other analysts, including: Iden, *op. cit.;* Herbert Parnes and Andrew Kohen, "Labor Market Experience of Noncollege Youth: A Longitudinal Analysis," in National Commission for Manpower Policy, *From School To Work: Improving the Transition*, U.S. Government Printing Office, Washington, D.C., 1976; Paul Barton, "Youth Transition to Work: The Problem and Federal Policy Setting," in *From School to Work: Improving the Transition*, 1976; Edward Kalachek, *The Youth Labor Market*, National Manpower Policy Commission Task Force, Washington, D.C., 1969.

8. During the recession year of 1975 the average unemployment rate was 36.9 percent for minority group teenagers (black youths or those of Mexican American, Puerto Rican, or American Indian descent), compared to 17.9 percent for white teenagers.

9. Iden, *op. cit.*

10. *Manpower Report of the President 1973*, table E–4.

11. Bernard Anderson, "Youth Employment Problems in the Inner City," in *The Teenage Unemployment Prob'em: What Are the Options*, report of a congressional Budget Office Conference on Teenage Unemployment, Congress of the United States, October 1976.

12. Unpublished data provided by Marcia Freedman, who developed the occupation-industry classification scheme in her book, *Labor Markets: Segments and Shelters*, Allanheld, Osmum, & Co., Montclair, N.J., 1976, pp. 71–82.

13. *Ibid.*, table 4.2, p. 75.

14. See, also, Iden, *op. cit.*, pp. 17–19.

15. Unpublished data from the first and second followups of the National Longitudinal Study of the High School Class of 1972, which were administered by the National Center for Education Statistics in October 1973 and October 1974, respectively.

16. Freedman, *op. cit.*

17. Paul Andrisani, "An Empirical Analysis of the Dual Labor Market Theory," unpublished Ph. D. dissertation, Human Resource Center, The Ohio State University, Columbus, Ohio, 1973; "The Dual Labor Market Theory and the Disadvantaged Labor Force: Issues, Evidence and an Appraisal," paper presented at Conference on Occupational Careers Analysis, Social Science Research Council, Greensboro. N.C., March 1976; "Discrimination, Segmentation and Upward Mobility: A Longitudinal Approach to the Dual

Labor Market Theory," paper presented at American Economic Association Meetings, Atlantic City, N.J., 1976.

18. Andrisani, "Discrimination, Segmentation and Upward Mobility: A Longitudinal Approach to the Dual Labor Market Theory," paper presented at American Economic Association Meetings, Atlantic City, N.J., 1976.

19. *Ibid.*

20. *Ibid.*

21. *Ibid.*

22. Anthony Pascal, "Youth, Schools, and the Labor Market," in Michael Timpane et al., *Youth Policy in Transition*, The Rand Corp., Santa Monica, Calif., prepared for U.S. Department of Health, Education, and Welfare, 1976.

23. James Coleman et al., *Youth: Transition to Adulthood*, Report of the Panel of the President's Science Advisory Committee, University of Chicago Press, Ill., 1974; John H. Martin et al., *National Panel on High Schools and Adolescent Education*, U.S. Office of Education, Washington, D.C., 1974; B. F. Brown et al. *The Reform of Secondary Education*, National Commission on the Reform of Secondary Education, McGraw-Hill, New York, 1973.

24. Timpane, *op. cit.*

25. A 1975 FBI report cited that 10 percent of 16,000 persons charged with homicide were under 18. Teenagers accounted for about half of those arrested for burglary, larceny, and bicycle theft. Nearly one-third of those arrested for robbery, 17 percent of those charged with assault, and 20 percent of those charged with rape were under 18. Teenagers were charged with 30 percent of the offenses that resulted in arrests, although they account for 16 percent of the population. The number of teenagers charged with one of these crimes was 9 percent higher in 1974 than in the previous year, while the number of adults arrested rose by 1 percent. Though these statistics are doubtlessly influenced by improved reporting practices, especially in schools, and though several hypotheses can be generated to explain their significance (e.g., adults are getting more sophisticated in avoiding arrest and/or conviction), these figures by any standard are too high. (See Margaret Gentry, *The Washington Post*, Nov. 18, 1975, p. A2.)

26. Office of Human Development, U.S. Department of Health, Education, and Welfare, *An Approach to Youth Participation*, Government Printing Office, Washington, D.C., 1975.

27. Roberta Rovner-Pieczenik, *The First Decade of Experience: A Synthesis of Manpower R. & D. Projects in Criminal Justice and Corrections*, 1963–73, Manpower Research Monograph No. 28, U.S. Department of Labor, Government Printing Office, Washington, D.C., 1973.

28. For example, participation in the out-of-school Neighborhood Youth Corps programs reduced the rate at which enrollees with police records (a substantial number) accumulated additional charges, but the program did not usually equip them for jobs that would pay enough to make criminal activity a less attractive source of income (Manpower Research Monograph, No. 13, 1970). A carefully constructed work experience program in Oakland, Calif., resulted in less delinquency (self-reported) in the experimental group than in the control group, but this resulted from no change in the experimental group while the control group increased in delinquency (*The Oakland Work Experience Program*. Behavioral Research Institute, Boulder, Colo., 1976). Other evaluations of work experience programs, however, show no improvement in juvenile delinquency; e.g., two programs conducted by the University of Colorado Youth Development Program and funded by HEW Office of Youth Development (*Youth and Work*, Goldberg, Talmadge, Bird, and Hunter, University of Colorado, 1975).

29. Paul Barton et al., *Juvenile Delinquency, Work and Education*, study prepared under auspices of National Manpower Institute for the Assistant Secretary for Education, U.S. Department of Health, Education, and Welfare, Washington, D.C., 1976 (mimeographed).

30. *Ibid.*

31. This issue is raised in the following articles: Milton Shore and Joseph Massino, "Employment as a Therapeutic Tool With Adolescent Delinquent Boys," *Rehabilitation Counseling Bulletin* 9:1–5, 1965; Milton Shore, "Youth and Jobs: Educational, Vocational, and Mental Health Aspects," *Journal of Youth and Adolescence:* 1(4) : 315–323, 1972; Regis Walther, "Strategies for Helping Disadvantaged Groups," paper for International Conference on Trends in Industrial and Labor Relations, Tel Aviv, Israel, 1972.

32. Adapted from a list found in *Education and Work Program Plan Fiscal Year 1977*, National Institute of Education, U.S. Department of Health, Education, and Welfare, Washington, D.C., May 9, 1975, pp. 5–6.

33. *Ibid*, pp. 2–3.

34. Purdue University, *Sources of Information for Career Decisions*, Opinion Poll No. 98, p. 5a; Purdue University, Vocational Plans and *Preferences of Adolescents*. Opinion Poll No. 94, May 1972, p. 3a; Gottlieb et al., *op cit.*, pp. 145–146; Richard Freeman, *The Market for College-Trained Manpower*, Harvard University Press, Cambridge, Mass., 1971, p. 194.

35. "Youth Attitudes: America's Teenagers Discuss Their Plans for Further Education and Their Career Choices," *Public Opinion Index* 28(20), Opinion Research Corp., Princeton, N.J., October 1970, p. 5.

36. Grace Massey, Mona Scott, and Sanford Dornbusch, "Racism Without Racists: Institutional Racism in Urban Schools," *The B'ack Scholar* 7(3) : 3–11, 1975.

37. *NIE Education and Work Program Plan Fiscal Year 1977, op. cit.*, p. 2.

38. William Fetters, *A Capsule Description of First Followup Survey Data*, National Center for Education Statistics, Government Printing Office, Washington, D.C., 1976.

39. Herbert Parnes et al., *Career Threshholds, Vol. 1*, Manpower Administration Research Monograph No. 16, U.S. Department of Labor, 1970, p. 101; *Job-seeking Methods Used by American Workers*, Bureau of Labor Statistics, Bulletin 1886, 1975, table C–1.

40. William Fetters, *A Capsule Description of High School Seniors: Base-Year Survey*, National Center for Education Statistics, Government Printing Office, Washington, D.C., 1974, p. 7.

41. A multivariate analysis of longitudinal data collected from a national sample of 5,000 young men indicated that for both blacks and whites the extent of a youth's knowledge of the world of work (as measured by an occupational knowledge test administered in 1966) has an independent effect upon his wage and occupational assignment (in 1968). See Herbert Parnes and Andrew Kohen, "Occupational Information and Labor Market Status: The Case of Young Men," *Journal of Human Resources* 10(1), winter 1975.

42. Thomas Hilton, "Counselor Questionnaire Results," in unpublished *Final Report of Base-Year Study, National Longitudinal Study of Class of 1972*, Educational Testing Service, Princeton, N.J., 1973.

43. Margaret Thal-Larsen, *Placement and Counseling in a Changing Labor Market: Public and Private Employment Agencies and Schools*, Institute of Industrial Relations, University of California, Berkeley, 1970.

44. Taking an even harder position, Sprinthal asserted in 1972 that "counselors try to perform jobs that are patently impossible; they are too few;

there is a bewildering plethora of activities they perform; the misperceptions of the work they do are staggering; and they themselves are unsure of what they are about." Echoing this sentiment, the National Commission on the Reform of Secondary Education declared that "in many schools, counselors are a hindrance, not a help, to adolescents who would benefit from career programs." (Cited in Beatrice Reubens, *Bridges to Work: International Comparisons of Transition Services*, Allanheld, Osmun & Co., Montclair, N.J., 1977 (in press), ch. 6).

45. *National Longitudinal Study of the High School Class of 1972, op. cit.;* "An Evaluation of the Role and Functions of the Guidance Counselor," report of the New York State Office of Education, Albany, September 1974 (mimeographed).

46. John Grasso, *The Contributions of Vocational Education, Training and Work Experience to the Early Career Achievements of Young Men*, Center for Human Resource Research, The Ohio State University, Columbus, 1975.

47. Fetters, *A Capsule Description of High School Seniors, op. cit.*, p. 9.

48. See, for example, *Applied Research Projects Supported in Fiscal Year 1975 131(a) of Part C of the Vocational Education Amendments of 1968*, Bureau of Occupational and Adult Education, U.S. Office of Education, Washington, D.C., 1976: *Profiles of Career Education Projects: First Year Program, Fiscal Year 1975 Funding*, Office of Career Education, U.S. Office of Education, Washington, D.C., December 1975.

49. A typology by which many of these career information systems are compared and contrasted is found in Barry Stern, "Application of Information Systems to Career and Job Choice," in Seymour Wolfbein (ed.), *Labor Market Information for Youth*, Temple University School of Business Administration, Philadelphia, 1975, pp. 208–219.

50. *Ibid.;* Barry Stern, "Labor Market Information for Counselors and Students," unpublished staff paper prepared for the Assistant Secretary for Policy, Evaluation, and Research, U.S. Department of Labor, Washington, D.C., 1972.

51. J. Weinstein, *Computer-based Vocational Guidance Systems*. U.S. Department of Health, Education, and Welfare, Government Printing Office, Washington, D.C., 1969.

52. *Occupational Information Systems Grants Program: Standards and Guidelines*, U.S. Department of Labor, Government Printing Office, Washington, D.C., 1974; Barry Stern, "The Occupational Information Systems Grants Program of the U.S. Department of Labor," *Vocational Guidance Quarterly* 23(2) : 202–209, March 1975.

53. *Occupational Information Systems Grants Program: State Project Summaries 1975, 1976*, National Occupational Information Service, Employment and Training Administration, Washington, D.C.

54. Many of these are listed by John Harris, "Occupational Information Projects: An Exploratory Study," prepared for Office of the Assistant Secretary for Policy, Evaluation, and Research, U.S. Department of Labor, contract No. L–74–11, 1973 (mimeographed). Also, see annual research and demonstration project summaries prepared by the Bureau of Occupational and Adult Education and the Office of Career Education, U.S. Office of Education.

55. David Evans and A. Russell Marshall, *Matching Occupational Classifications to Vocational Education Program Codes*, Tomorrow's Manpower Needs, Supplement 3 (revised), Bureau of Labor Statistics, Washington, D.C., 1975. Another example of collaboration is the use by DOL of the

NIE-funded Career Decisionmaking program (developed at the Appalachia Educational Laboratory) in revising the *Dictionary of Occupational Titles*.

56. NIE funding for school-based career education models was discontinued in fiscal year 1975. Almost all of the Federal classroom-based projects in career education are now funded by OE's Office of Career Education.

57. Donald McLaughlin, *Career Education in the Public Schools, 1974–75: A National Survey*, American Institutes for Research, Palo Alto, Calif., 1976. For a recent statement on the philosophy of career education, see Kenneth Hoyt, *Career Education Contributions to an Evolving Concept*, Olympus Publishing Co., Salt Lake City, 1975.

58. Council of Chief State School Officers, *The Status and Progress of Career Education*, Washington, D.C., 1975.

59. Comptroller General of the United States, *Career Education: Status and Needed Improvements*, Government Printing Office, Washington, D.C., January 1976.

60. McLaughlin, *op. cit.*

61. Courses which focus on the direct teaching of occupational information do not fare well either. A detailed review of courses in vocational orientation in New York State, for example, revealed considerable dissatisfaction with such courses by school personnel, and students, generally reported that the classes were dull and that they did not profit from the exposure (see Eli Ginzberg, *Career Guidance*, McGraw-Hill, New York, 1971, p. 196).

62. "Evaluation of the Group Guidance Program," prepared for Texas Education Agency by Education Systems Associates, Austin, Tex., June 1975 (mimeographed) ; Carol Ramirez, "Final Report: Group Vocational Guidance Program," prepared for Education Service Centers Consortium (regions 4, 5, and 6), Houston, Tex., 1975; Patricia Marshall, "Career Guidance Through Group Dynamics," *Manpower*, February 1974, pp. 12–18.

63. An example of permitting school personnel to engage in work outside of formal education is the employment service-school counselor summer program in California. This program enables school counselors to experience various aspects of work in the public employment service, including employment counseling, placement and job development, test administration and interpretation, and development of occupational information from data collected by the employment service.

64. In the long run NIE's efforts to infuse sex- and race-fair occupational information into basic primary text revisions and now texts might be the most consequential element of elementary school career education. The removal of stereotypical pictures and words from textbooks and audiovisual materials is likely to result in very different occupational expectations than people have now, particularly among girls and women.

65. Coleman, *op. cit.;* Martin, *op. cit.;* Brown, *op. cit.*

66. William Pierce, "Remarks on Cooperative Education," *Congressional Record*, Senate, June 24, 1976.

67. *National Longitudinal Study of the High School Class of 1972, op. cit.*

68. Grasso, *op. cit.*

69. Most of these enrollment and cost figures come from *Annual Evaluation Report on Programs Administered by the U.S. Office of Education, Fiscal Years 1974, 1975*, Office of Planning, Budgeting, and Evaluation, U.S. Office of Education, 1975, 1976.

70. See *Continuous Longitudinal Manpower Survey, Report No. E: Characteristics of Enrollees Who Entered CEIA Programs During Calendar Year 1975*, prepared for Employment and Training Administration, U.S. Department of Labor, Washington, D.C., November 1976.

71. *Ibid.*

72. Robert Smith and Hugh Pitcher, "The Neighborhood Youth Corps: An Impact Evaluation," Technical Analysis Paper No. 10 prepared for the Office of the Assistant Secretary for Policy, Evaluation, and Research, U.S. Department of Labor, 1973 (mimeographed).

73. Ernest Stromsdorffer and James Fackler, *An Economic and Institutional Analysis of the Cooperative Vocational Education Program in Dayton, Ohio*, prepared for Manpower Administration, U.S. Department of Labor, contract No. 82–18–71–24, 1973.

74. Steven Frankel, *An Assessment of School-Supervised Work Education Programs*, prepared by System Development Corp. for U.S. Office of Education, contract No. OEC–0–72–5024, Washington, D.C., 1973.

75. Stromsdorffer compares cooperative education students with other students enrolled in academic, vocational, and general tracks, whereas Frankel's comparison group includes only those noncoop students who have jobs while they are enrolled in school.

76. The two studies present an image of a coop student who perceives his high school education as instrumental toward achieving short-range career goals. He selects his coop work experience in a purposeful way and organizes his curricular experiences toward a carefully considered post-high-school work goal. He believes that his work and vocational training experiences are more important to him than other school experiences such as sports and social activities. He knows that he is less likely to pursue higher education than his more academically oriented colleagues and consequently realizes that his high school experiences should contribute directly to his earnings capability over the short run. In short, the coop student is busy, purposeful, and uses school as a means to a short-range vocational end.

    The noncoop student who works, on the other hand, does so for very different reasons. He works for the money and the independence and feelings of worth that this extra money brings. Working appears to satisfy many of his social needs; e.g., the fact that he is more likely to socialize with his fellow employees than the coop student. He is not yet career oriented, and if he is, he is willing to defer for some time the most important career decisions. In the meantime, he is more concerned with the social milieu of the school than the coop student. School activities such as sports and social events mean more to him. Indeed, the social rewards offered by the school are more salient for him than his coop counterpart; e.g., grades and attendance records appear more important to the noncoop student than to the coop student. In short, the noncoop student is willing to defer career decisions and works for reasons largely unrelated to his ultimate vocational goals. He is likely to rely on postsecondary education or training if he needs vocational training to attain his career goals.

77. Harry Silberman, "A Proposal for Educational Work Experience," in Seymour Wolfbein (ed.), *op. cit.;* Willard Wirtz, *The Boundless Resource*, the New Republic Book Co., Washington, D.C., 1975; Maurice Gibbons, "Walkabout: Searching for the Right Passage From Childhood and School," *Phi Delta Kappan*, May 1974, pp. 596–602; Dabney Park et al., "A Taxonomy of Basic Competencies in the World of Work," working paper of Cooperative Assessment of Experimental Learning, Princeton, N.J., 1975.

78. A recent effort to classify and evaluate Federal work experience programs was prepared for the Interagency Panel for Research and Development on Adolescence: *Work Experience as Preparation for Adulthood*, George Washington University, Social Research Group, Washington, D.C., 1973.

79. *NIE Education and Work Program Plan Fiscal Year 1977, op. cit.*

80. U.S. Office of Education, *Review of Progress—National Defense Education Act, Title V-A 1969*, U.S. Department of Health, Education, and Welfare, Washington, D.C., 1970; National Center for Education Statistics, "Counselors in the Public Schools" preliminary report, Washington, D.C., spring 1970.

81. Figures which bear precisely on this point do not exist. Nonetheless, the conventional wisdom among counselor educators and the American Personnel and Guidance Association is that most counselors in school today, indeed, were trained between 1958 and 1967.

82. Labor market success, job satisfaction, occupational knowledge, self-concept, preventing or remedying underachievement, reducing dropout rates, promoting better job matches, or any other career-related criterion one could name, are generally unrelated to the kind of guidance process or the extent to which it is used (see Ginzberg, *op. cit.*; Coleman, *op. cit.*). Furthermore, students rarely seek or obtain occupational information from either counselors or teachers and infrequently consult with them in making career or job decisions. Like the rest of the population, students usually get occupational information and advice from friends and relatives (*National Longitudinal Study of the Class of 1972, op. cit.*; *Jobseeking Methods Used by American Workers, op. cit.*; Parnes, *op. cit.*

83. Dale Prediger et al., *Nationwide Study of Student Career Development: Summary of Results*, American College Testing Program, Research Report No. 61, November 1973.

84. "An Evaluation of the Role and Functions of the Guidance Counselors," *op. cit.*

85. Massey, Scott, and Dornbusch, *op. cit.*

86. For a comprehensive review of the use of graduation requirements by schools, see James Clark and Scott Thompson, *Competency Tests and Graduation Requirements*, National Association of Secondary Schools, Reston, Va., 1976; for an inciteful analytic discussion of this issue, see William Spady, "Competency-Based Education: A Bandwagon in Search of a Definition," *Educational Researcher* 6(1), January 1977.

87. "The Adult Performance Level External High Scool Diploma Program Pilot Project," Division of Extension, Industrial and Business Education, University of Texas, Austin, 1974 (mimeographed); Norvell Northcutt et al., "*Adult Functional Competency: A Summary*," Division of Extension, University of Texas, Austin, March 1975 (mimeographed).

88. These are described and evaluated in the *Annual Evaluation Report on Programs Administered by the U.S. Office of Education Fiscal Year 1975, op cit.*, pp. 296–320.

89. Under the recent Family Education and Privacy Act of 1974 (Buckley Amendment), students and parents have the right of access to the school's information about them. They would probably appreciate help to understand and intelligently use this information.

90. Examples of these include numerous career education "decisionmaking" projects, the College Entrance Examination Board's "Deciding" project, and the National Student Education Fund's "Information Gap" project.

91. Rosalind Barnett and Grace Baruch, "Occupational and Educational Aspirations and Expectations: A Review of the Empirical Literature," paper prepared for the National Institute of Education, Washington, D.C., 1973 (mimeographed).

92. Prediger et al., *op. cit.*

93. Several of these activities funded by NIE are described in *Education and Work Program Plan Fiscal Year 1977, op. cit.* (Strategy Package No. 2).

94. *The Condition of Education 1976,* National Center for Education Statistics, U.S. Department of Health, Education, and Welfare, Washington, D.C. Though these enrollments are about the same for men and women, the jobs that are obtained after training are very different. The men are much more likely to get managerial jobs; women are more likely to become sales clerks.

95. Enrollment data provided by Bureau of Occupational and Adult Education, U.S. Office of Education.

96. *Women's Educational Equity Act, First Annual Report,* U.S. Office of Education, Washington, D.C., Sept. 30, 1976.

97. These include the National Institute of Education, the Fund for the Improvement of Postsecondary Education and OE's Bureau of Occupational and Adult Education, Women's Programs Staff and the Office of Career Education.

98. See Sheila Huff, "Credentialling by Test or by Degrees: Title VII of the Civil Rights Act" and *Griggs* v. *Duke Power Company, Harvard Educational Review* 44(2) : 246–269, May 1974.

99. In a later case, *Castro* v. *Beecher,* 1972, a U.S. circuit court of appeals did accept the validity of a high school diploma or its equivalent as a requirement for appointment as a municipal policeman, thus modifying to some extent the impact of the *Griggs* decision. However, the court indicated that the constitutionality of requiring a college degree for such a position was not under consideration.

100. The percentage of the labor force having 8 years or less of schooling is expected to decrease to about 6 percent by 1990, and the estimated proportion of high school dropouts is expected to be less than 13 percent. Persons who have gone through high school but no further are expected to account for 41 percent of the labor force, the same proportion anticipated for the year 1980. By 1985, more than one out of every five workers will have attended college for 4 years or longer; by 1990, nearly one out of every four workers will have attended college for 4 years or longer (see *The Condition of Education 1976, op. cit.*).

101. Educators and students will want to know the occupational utility of certain skills, and employers can tell them this. Employers may need the assistance of educators in developing assessment techniques which truly measure competencies required by the job.

102. Upgrading a credential is accomplished by: (*a*) improving the quality of the educational offerings, or (*b*) being more selective or raising the standards to whom the credential is awarded. A lesser known school might have to resort to this anyway during a slack (or buyer's) labor market where qualified applicants appreciably exceed the number of opportunities.

103. Stephen Dresch, "Demography, Technology and Higher Education: Toward a Formal Model of Educational Adaptation," *Journal of Political Economy* 83(3) :535–569, 1975; Stephen Dresch, "The College, the University and the State," policy research paper prepared for the Assistant Secretary for Education, U.S. Department of Health, Education, and Welfare, Washington, D.C., August 1974 (mimeographed).

104. William Byham, "Assessment Centers for Spotting Future Managers," *Harvard Business Review* July–August, 1970, pp. 150–165.

105. William Byham and Carl Wettengel, "Assessment Center for Identifying and Developing Management Potential in Government Operations, *Public Personnel Management,* 1974.

106. Joseph Froomkin, *The Productivity and Screening Effects of Educational Attainment,* prepared for the Assistant Secretary for Planning and Evalua-

tion, U.S. Department of Health, Education, and Welfare, contract No. 100–76–0012, 1976.

107. Clark and Thompson, *op. cit.*; Spady, *op. cit.*

108. Data showing a gradual increase in the proportion of high school graduates who obtained their degrees through nontraditional means come from *Statistics of State School Systems*, National Center for Education Statistics, U.S. Department of Health, Education, and Welfare (biennial publication until 1971–72), and *Statistics of Elementary and Secondary Day Schools*, National Center for Education Statistics, fall 1973.

109. For a comprehensive treatment of the GED testing program, see Robert Stump and Beatrice Lumpkin, *The General Educational Development Testing Program: An Examination of Issues and Outcomes*, National Institute of Education, Washington, D.C., 1975.

110. In its first year of operation (1975–76), almost 31,000 students attempted to take advantage of the California program to allow early graduation. College-bound students have been much more likely to take the test for early graduation than their noncollege-bound schoolmates. Of this number, 11,560, or 37 percent, passed the test and graduated early. (Unpublished data provided by the California Department of Education.)

111. Wirtz, *op. cit.*, p. 42.

112. Data supplied by the U.S. Employment Service, Employment and Training Administration, U.S. Department of Labor.

113. Wirtz, *op. cit.*, p. 43.

114. Data supplied by the Bureau of Labor Statistics.

115. *Jobseeking Methods Used by American Workers*, *op. cit.*, table C–1.

116. Andrew Kohen and Paul Andrisani, "Labor Market Experience of High School Graduates and Dropouts," *Career Thresholds, Vol. 4: A Longitudinal Study of the Educational and Labor Market Experience of Male Youth*, Manpower Administration, Research Monograph No. 16, 1974, pp. 23–24.

117. David Saunders, "The Company Youth Keep: An Empirical Analysis of Job Finding Among Young Men 14 to 24," Unpublished Ph. D. dissertation, Bryn Mawr College.

118. Parnes et al., *op. cit.*, p. 101.

119. Fetters, A Capsule Description of High School Seniors: *op. cit.*, p. 7.

120. *Ibid.*, p. 9.

121. American Institutes for Research, *Practical Career Guidance, Counseling and Placement for the Noncollege-Bound Student*, Palo Alto, California: report for U.S. Office of Education, contract No. OEC–0–72–4986, 1973.

122. *Job Placement Services Provided by Public School Systems in the United States 1976*, National Center for Education Statistics, Fast Response Survey System Report No. 2, U.S. Department of Health, Education, and Welfare, 1977.

123. Research and exemplary projects in school vocational guidance and placement can be funded under VEA, as well as through NIE.

124. Fetters, *loc. cit.*

125. Of course, there are some exceptions to the rule. Three States (Florida, Michigan, and Virginia) require that job placement services be provided to students. Others, like Wisconsin, are encouraging LEA's to adopt successful placement practices from demonstration programs, many of them funded by OE.

126. Wirtz, *op. cit.*, p. 38.

127. *Job Placement Services Provided by Public School Systems in the United States 1976*, *op. cit.*

128. James O'Toole, "The Reserve Army of the Underemployed: The Role of Education," *Change*, June 1975; Grasso, *op. cit.*

129. Walter Guzzardi, "Education for the World of Work," *Fortune*, October 1975, p. 188.

130. When training provisions in collective bargaining agreements are analyzed by industry, it is clear that employers in high technology industries (communications, transportation equipment, electrical machinery, etc.) provide the most training. See, for example, *Training and Retraining Provisions*, Bureau of Labor Statistics, Bulletin 1425–7, Washington, D.C., 1969.

131. Annegret Harnischfeger and David Wiley. "Achievement Test Scores Drop. So What?" *Educational Researcher*, March 1976, pp. 5–12; Leo Munday, *Declining Admissions Test Scores*, American College Testing Program, Research Report No. 71, Iowa City, Iowa, 1976. Harnischfeger and Wiley, "The Marrow of Achievement Test Scores Declines," *Educational Technology*, June 1976, pp. 5–14.

132. R. Farr et al., *Reading Achievement in the United States: Then and Now*, Indiana University, Bloomington, August 1974; A. Ferris, *Indicators of Trends in American Education*, Russell Sage Foundation, New York, 1969; Iowa and Minnesota Scholastic Aptitude Test data cited in Munday, *op. cit.*, pp. 15–17.

133. Joseph Froomkin, (*Declining Test Scores: Reasons and Impact*, policy research paper prepared for the Assistant Secretary for Education, U.S. Department of Health, Education, and Welfare, Contract No. 300760026, May 1976) cites evidence which refutes the following hypotheses for declining test scores: (1) The retention of more of the less able, less affluent, or dropout prone students, which makes the high school population less able, on the whole, than in previous decades when the dropout rate was substantially more than the current 25 percent; (2) an increased proportion of women taking college admission tests who are less able, on the whole, than the previous generations of college-bound women; (3) systematic drops in the number of adults populating family units, indicating perhaps poorer child care and cognitive stimulation; (4) the increasing proportion of second and third children enrolling in college, because verbal ability of subsequent children is lower than that of the first born; and (5) increased television viewing which possibly results in poorer verbal communication skills (reading and writing).

134. John Flanagan and Steven Jung, *Progress in Education: A Sample Survey* (*1960–70*), American Institutes for Research, Palo Alto, Calif., 1971; *The Condition of Education 1976, op. cit.*, p. 44.

135. John Flanagan, "Changes in School Levels of Achievement: Project TALENT Ten and Fifteen Year Retests," paper presented to annual meeting of American Educational Research Association, San Francisco, Apr. 22, 1976; *The Condition of Education 1976, op. cit.*, p. 45.

136. Flanagan, *op. cit.*

137. A comprehensive study being conducted by the Educational Testing Service no doubt will examine this and other interpretations.

138. For comprehensive discussions of this issue in the United States, see Grasso, *op. cit.*, and Beatrice Reubens, "Vocational Education: Performance and Potential," *Manpower* 6(7):23–90, July 1974. For discussions about vocational education in other countries, see Eugene Staley, *Planning Occupational Education and Training for Development*, Stanford International Development Education Center, Stanford University, prepared for U.S. Office of Education, contract No. OEC–4–7062597–1654, 1968; and Manuel Zymelman et al.,

Economic Evaluation of Vocational Training Programs, World Bank Occasional Staff Paper No. 21, Johns Hopkins University Press, Baltimore Md.

139. M. U. Eninger, *The Process and Product of T. & I. High School Level Vocational Education in the United States,* American Institutes for Research, Pittsburgh, Pa., 1965 (vol. I) and 1968 (vol. II) ; J. J. Kaufman, and M. V. Lewis, *The Potential of Vocational Education: Observations and Conclusions,* Institute for Research of Human Resources. The Pennsylvania State University, University Park, 1978; J. J. Kaufman et al., *A Cost Effectiveness Study of Vocational Education,* Institute for Research of Human Resources, The Pennsylvania State University, 1969; A. J. Crazzini, "The Decision to Invest in Vocational Education: An Analysis of Costs and Benefits," *Journal of Human Resources,* 3:88–120 (supplement), 1968; M. K. Taussig, "An Economic Analysis of Vocational Education in New York City High Schools," *Journal of Human Resources,* 3:59–87 (supplement), 1968; Gerald Somers et al., *The Effectiveness of Vocational and Technical Programs: A National Followup Survey,* Center for Studies in Vocational and Technical Education, University of Wisconsin, Madison, 1971; Ernest Stromsdorffer, *Review and Synthesis of Cost-Effectiveness Studies of Vocational and Technical Education,* Center for Vocational and Technical Education, The Ohio State University, Columbus, 1972, Reubens, *op. cit.,* Grasso, *op. cit.*

140. Grasso, *op. cit.;* John Grasso, "High School Curriculum and Vocational Choice," paper prepared for Center for Human Resource Research, The Ohio State University, Columbus, 1976 (mimeographed).

141. Grasso, *op. cit.*

142. Howard Vincent, "An Analysis of Vocational Education in Our Secondary Schools," staff paper for Office of Planning and Evaluation, U.S. Office of Education, Washington, D.C., July 1969 (mimeographed).

143. Fetters, *A Capsule Description of First Followup Survey Data, op. cit.*

144. Grasso, *op. cit.*

145. *Ibid;* Vincent, *op. cit.*

146. Fetters, *op. cit.*

147. Grasso, *op. cit.*

148. *Ibid.*

149. *Ibid.*

150. Data provided by Bureau of Occupational and Adult Education, U.S. Office of Education.

151. Oddly, no comparable argument is heard in the higher education sector, where a constant tuition policy supports curriculums or majors having widely divergent per capita costs.

152. Between 1966 and 1976, almost one-third of all OE expenditures for secondary education supported vocational education, with a markedly higher proportion devoted to vocational education in the 1970's (34 percent) than in the 1960's (27 percent). This estimate is based on comparisons of actual vocational educational expenditures with very rough estimates of all secondary education expenditures. In addition to vocational education activities, other OE programs supporting (in part) secondary education are ESEA titles I, II, III, V, VII, and VIII, School Assistance in Federally Affected Areas (SAFA or Impact Aid) : Education of the Handicapped Act; NDEA title III; and ESA.

153. The same line of reasoning would hold for higher education. The number of students who attend college is of no particular Federal concern. The Federal Government provides student assistance to assure equity of access—that all qualified students are financially able to attend. The equity

of access argument also holds for public secondary education, but not for any particular curriculum or kind of education.

154. D. W. Drewes and Douglas Katz, *Manpower Data and Vocational Education*, Center Occupational Education, North Carolina State University, research report for National Institute of Education, contract No. NE–C–00–3–0069, 1975.

155. Of course, the education and work budget (which includes vocational education, career education, and adult education) ought to compete with other educational areas for Federal funding.

Adults: Career and Life Redirection and Renewal

1. Retirement, while a blessing to many, is a time of boredom or anxiety to others, especially to those who are forced into "premature" retirement. In 1970 the Social Security Administration found in a survey that one-half of the men who were subject to compulsory retirement said that they did not want to stop working. The same survey found that these men suffered a 60-percent cut in income after retirement (*Reaching Retirement Age: Findings From a Survey of Newly Entitled Workers 1968–70*, U.S. Department of Health, Education, and Welfare, Social Security Administration Research Report No. 47, 1976, p. 60).

2. Smaller firms are much less likely to provide paid vacations than larger firms. Almost 3 out of 4 employees who do not receive vacation pay work in establishments employing less than 500 people. Only 15 percent of workers in establishments having more than 500 people do not receive any paid vacation, while 43 percent of workers who do not receive any paid vacation are employed in establishments having fewer than 100 people. See *Major Collective Bargaining Agreements: Paid Vacation and Holiday Provisions*, Bureau of Labor Statistics, Bulletin No. 1425–9, 1969, p. 12.

3. *Characteristics of Agreements Covering 1000 Workers or More, July 1, 1973*, Bureau of Labor Statistics, Bulletin No. 1822, 1974.

4. Evidence that workers in the technologically progressive industries get the overwhelming share of the opportunities for further education and training comes from two sources. First, and the most empirical, are the Bureau of Labor Statistics' analyses of training and retraining provisions in collective bargaining agreements (*Major Collective Bargaining Agreements: Training and Retraining Provisions, op. cit.*). Second, are the rough estimates of the total amounts of resources devoted by various companies to education and training, such as a current study being undertaken by the Conference Board (Seymour Lusterman, "Education for Work," *Conference Board Record* 13(5): 39–44, May 1976). Though analyses of collective bargaining agreements provide more objective data, they grossly understate the incidence of training, as against training provisions, in private industry. Not included in these agreements are short-term, on-the-job training programs, apprenticeship programs, and a variety of other ad hoc or ongoing training arrangements which companies provide with little urging from organized labor. The new Conference Board study of companies with over 500 employees finds that 80 percent of private industry's education and training costs are for instruction in company-specific skills (not including any costs incurred from employees being away from their jobs). Only 10 percent of the costs are for tuition aid programs in which the employee studies after work hours. The remaining 10 percent pays for outside courses taken during work hours.

5. That women and students want more work is most convincingly demonstrated by their increasing labor force participation rates during the last several years. The labor force participation rate for students 14 to 24 years of age increased from 20.5 percent in 1948 to 25.3 percent in 1960 to 35.0 percent in 1973. For women over 16 years of age the rate increased from 32.7 percent in 1948 to 37.8 percent in 1960 to 45.7 percent in 1974 (*Manpower Report of the President 1975*). Now women represent two out of five members of the labor force; from 1940 to 1970 they accounted for about two-thirds of the increase in the working population. Participation of mothers in the labor force rose even faster, showing a fivefold-increase—from 9 to 42 percent—in that 30-year period. For an increasing number of women, the time out of the labor force for purposes of child rearing is becoming shorter; many stay in the labor force at least part time while their children are young; one out of 3 women with preschool children is now in the labor force; 4½ million women with children under age 6 are working (see Wirtz, *op. cit.*, p. 130).

6. Despite some data which show a modest decline in the average weekly hours of nonagricultural employees (from 40.9 in 1948 to 38.1 in 1975), this drop appears to reflect changes in the composition of the labor force rather than a reduction in the hours of work of the individuals or groups that compose the work force (see John Owen, "Workweeks and Leisure: An Analysis of Trends 1948–75," *Monthly Labor Review*, August 1976). As a result of postwar trends, a larger proportion of the work force are women and students. Women holding nonagricultural jobs made up 29 percent of the work force in 1940 and 40 percent of it today; students made up 1 percent or less in 1940 and 2.5 percent after World War II, but are now at a level of 6 percent. In the same period, the proportion of nonstudent males in the nonagricultural work force dropped to under 57 percent. Because of group differences in hours worked—women average 34 hours per week; male students, 22 hours; and nonstudent males, about 43—the declining proportion of nonstudent males in the labor force has produced a statistical decline in average weekly hours. However, when the number of work hours per week is disaggregated by demographic group, no decline in weekly hours is observed for the nonstudent males. Though the number weekly work hours has remained constant, these workers are experiencing somewhat more free time over the course of a year due to an increase in the average length of full-time workers' annual vacations (increased by about 2 days between 1960 and 1969).

7. Increasing desire for more free time is suggested by: (1) Increases in the maximum number of weeks of paid vacation as well as by (2) surveys of the kinds of benefits that workers want. The proportion of workers in collective bargaining units of 1,000 personnel or more, who were covered by agreements specifying at least 4 weeks of maximum paid vacation, increased from 70 percent in 1966 to 89 percent in 1973 (*Characteristics of Agreements Covering 1,000 Workers or More, July 1, 1973, op. cit.*). It should be noted, however, that seniority workers are the ones who benefit from these maximum vacation periods. Almost half of all workers (in 1972) got less than 2 weeks per year (*Handbook of Labor Statistics 1975*, Government Printing Office, Washington, D.C.). It should be noted, also, that increasing the maximum number of weeks or days of paid vacation is not solely the result of workers' desire for more free time. It might reflect, also, the desire of union leaders to spread employment among more workers or the belief by management that workers will become more productive if they are given more time off with lower pay than if their wages were increased with no increase in

time off. Workers in these cases would merely take free time when it is available to them. Attitudinal studies on the subject, however, suggest that the hypothesis that the "rank and file" want more free time cannot be dismissed. Better vacation benefits are high on the list of workers' desires (*Work: Desires, Discontents, and Satisfaction*). Special Report, the Roper Organization, New York, N.Y., June 1974; Robert Quinn and Linda Shepard, *The 1972–73 Quality of Employment Survey,* University of Michigan Institute for Social Research, Ann Arbor, 1974; "Workers' Preferences Among Time-off Benefits and Pay," Stanley Nealey and James Goodale, *Journal of Applied Psychology,* 5(1) :357–361).

8. Increased participation rates of adults in educational activities and the responsiveness of educational institutions to provide adults with more options for combining work and education indicate the growing desire for education among individuals who are beyond the normal school-going years. Conspicuously on the increase are those opportunities for adults variously described as open university or external degree programs (see, for example, Commission of Non-Traditional Study, *Diversity by Design,* Jossey-Bass, San Francisco, 1973; Theodore Hesburgh, Paul Miller, Clifton Wharton, Jr., *Patterns for Lifelong Learning,* Jossey-Bass, San Francisco, 1973).

9. "Changing Patterns of Occupational Opportunity," *Manpower Report of the President 1974,* U.S. Department of Labor, pp. 104–130.

10. Marcia Freedman, *op. cit.* Harold Wool, "Future Labor Supply for Lower Level Occupations," *Monthly Labor Review* 99(3) :22–31, March 1976; Howard Hayghe, "The New Worker: Implications of Demographic Trends," in Seymour Wolfbein (ed.), *op. cit.,* pp. 59–71.

11. Wool, *op cit.*

12. Quinn and Shepard, *op. cit.; Survey of Working Conditions,* Survey Research Center, University of Michigan, under contract with the Employment Standards Administration, U.S. Department of Labor, 1971.

13. For example, the mere presence of a high average level of schooling among members of the baby-boom cohort might lead to increased demand for even more schooling with which to distinguish themselves from their peers.

14. See, for example, Barry Anderson and Jonathan Mark, (*Attrition, Mobility, and Productivity Among Teachers: The Case of Metropolitan St. Louis,* St. Louis, Mo.: CEMEREL, Inc., 1976) who found that with decreased turnover or migration of teachers, the average age and salary level of teachers increased, resulting in higher salary expense and lower teacher productivity per pupil.

15. Quinn and Shepard, *op. cit; Survey of Working Conditions, op. cit.*

16. Having a greater portion of their lives free of dependents will give adults more freedom to leave their jobs or occupations in order to seek a new start elsewhere. An adult is more likely to be willing to endure sustained periods of unemployment or training with little income if he or she does not have to subject dependents to a reduced standard of living as well.

17. It is difficult to measure "dependency" with a single statistic. One common measure is to look at the ratio of the sum of younger (under 18 years age) and older (65 and over) persons to the number of persons between these ages (18 to 64 years old). Past and future years with their recorded and projected "dependency ratios" are: 1945, (0.59), 1960 (0.82), 1975 (0.71), 1990 (0.65), 2005 (0.59), and 2035 (0.70). See Dennis Johnston, "Aging and the Baby-Boom Cohorts," *Statistical Reporter,* March 1976, table IV (Series II Projections). Another means of measuring "dependency" is the ratio of persons outside the labor force to those inside (nonworkers/workers). Actual and projected figures of this type have been computed. Respective

ratios are: 1950 (1.38), 1955 (1.44), 1960 (1.50), 1965 (1.52), 1970 (1.38), 1975 (1.25), 1980 (1.15), 1985 (1.11), and 1990 (1.11). Calculations derived from data found in Howard Fullerton, "New Labor Force Projections to 1990," *Monthly Labor Review*, December 1976.

18. *Work in America*, Report prepared by Special Task Force for the Secretary of HEW, MIT Press, Cambridge, Mass., 1972; Quinn and Shepard, *op. cit.*, p. 76.

19. Gertrude Bancroft and Stuart Garfinkle, "Job Mobility in 1961," *Monthly Labor Review*, August 1963 (reprint No. 2421); Samuel Saben, "Occupational Mobility of Employed Workers," *Monthly Labor Review*, June 1967 (reprint No. 2531); James Byrne, "Occupational Mobility of Workers," *Monthly Labor Review*, February 1975, pp. 53–59.

20. *Job Changing and Manpower Training*, Manpower Report No. 10, U.S. Department of Labor, 1964.

21. Harold Goldstein and William Delaney, "The Need for Job Related Training Throughout Adult Life," The National Manpower Institute, Washington, D.C., 1974 (mimeographed).

22. Despite widespread reservations about the efficacy and desirability of this lock-step system, negative labeling of people who do not conform to this pattern still obtains. Wirtz (*op. cit.*), for example, says that any 17-year-old not in school is a dropout; any healthy 40-year-old not at work is called a laggard; and a 70-year-old still at work is an anomaly or a "workaholic."

23. K. Patricia Cross, John Valley and Associates, *Planning Non-Traditional Programs*, Jossey-Bass, San Francisco, 1974; National Opinion Research Corporation, "Continuous National Survey, Cycles 5 and 6, fall 1973," conducted for National Institute of Education, Washington, D.C., Peter Botsman, *The Learning Needs and Interests of Adult Blue Collar Factory Workers*, New York State College of Agriculture and Life Sciences, Cornell University, Ithaca, March 1975; Anthony Pascal et al., *An Evaluation of Policy Related Research and Programs for Mid-Life Career Redirection; Volume II: Major Findings*, Rand Corp., Santa Monica, Calif., 1975, pp. 9–16; A. Carp et al., *Learning Interests and Experiences of Adult Americans*, Educational Testing Service, Berkeley, Calif., 1974.

24. Imogene Okes, *Participation in Adult Education, Final Report 1969*, National Center for Education Statistics, Government Printing Office, 1974; Imogene Okes, *Participation in Adult Education 1972*, National Center for Education Statistics, Government Printing Office, 1976; "Triennial Survey of Adult Education 1975," unpublished data, National Center for Education Statistics, U.S. Department of Health, Education, and Welfare.

25. See, for example, J. R. O'Meara, *Combatting Knowledge Obsolescence II: Employee Tuition Aid Plans*, National Industrial Conference Board, New York, 1970; Herbert Levine, "Labor-Management Policies on Educational Opportunity," in Selma Mushkin (ed.) *Recurrent Education*, National Institute of Education, Washington, D.C., 1973, pp. 197–212.

26. When workers are asked to name the additional fringe benefits they most desire, education and training benefits are not even among the top 10. See Quinn and Shepard, *op. cit.*, p. 122, who also found that 43 percent of all workers in 1973 reported that their firm provided "a training program that you can take to improve your skills" (p. 120). See also, *Work: Desires, Discontents, and Satisfaction, op. cit.*

27. Northcutt et al., *op. cit.*, p. 6; Comptroller General, *The Adult Basic Education Program: Progress in Reducing Illiteracy and Improvements Needed*, Congress of the United States, Government Printing Office, June 1975; Virginia Knauer, "The President's Commitments to Consumer Education,"

remarks before Consumer Education "Catch-up" Conference, sponsored by Office of Consumer Affairs, Washington, D.C., November 21, 1975.

28. Quinn and Shepard, *op. cit.*, p. 217; Ivar Berg, *Education and Jobs: The Great Training Robbery*, Praeger Publishers, New York, 1970; Richard Freeman, *The Overeducated American*, Academic Press, New York, 1976; James O'Toole, "The Reserve Army of the Underemployed: The World of Work," *Change*, May 1975, pp. 26–33, 63.

29. According to the Adult Education Survey conducted by the Bureau of the Census, in the year ending May 1975, 3.9 million women took 6.2 courses on a part-time basis to either get a job or improve or maintain their occupational status. There is little evidence to suggest that this number of participants need be increased.

30. Byrne, *op. cit.*

31. Okes, *Participation in Adult Education 1972, op. cit.*

32. James Scoville, *The Job Content of the U.S. Economy, 1940–70*, McGraw-Hill, 1969; Richard Eckaus, "Economic Criteria for Education and Training," *Review of Economics and Statistics*, May 1964; Berg, *op. cit.*; Joseph Froomkin, *Supply and Demand for Persons With Postsecondary Education*, policy research paper prepared for the Assistant Secretary for Education, U.S. Department of Health, Education, and Welfare, Washington, D.C., 1976.

33. The median educational attainment of the U.S. labor force (18 to 64 years old) rose from 8.6 years for men and 11.0 years for women in 1940 to 12.5 years for men and 12.6 years for women in 1974.

34. Berg, *op. cit.*

35. Dresch, *op. cit.*

36. Edward Denison, "The Shift to Services and the Rate of Productivity Change," *Survey of Current Business*, 53:1–37, October 1973.

37. Dave O'Neill and Sue Ross, *Training Under the GI Bill*, prepared for Employment and Training Administration, U.S. Department of Labor, Washington, D.C.

38. Orley Ashenfelter, "Manpower Training and Earnings," *Monthly Labor Review*, April 1975; Robert Smith and Hugh Pitcher, "The Neighborhood Youth Corps: An Impact Evaluation," Technical Analysis Paper No. 10, Office of the Assistant Secretary for Policy Evaluation and Research, U.S. Department of Labor, 1973 (mimeographed).

39. O'Neill and Ross, *op. cit.*

40. Barry Stern, "Desire of U.S. Workers for Education and Training," unpublished staff paper prepared for the Assistant Secretary for Education, U.S. Department of Health, Education, and Welfare, 1976.

41. *Major Collective Bargaining Agreements: Training and Retraining Provisions, op. cit.*

42. *Characteristics of Agreements Covering 1,000 Workers or More*, July 1, 1973, *op. cit.*

43. Quinn and Shepard, *op. cit.*; Robert Quinn and Martha Baldie de Mandilovitch, *Education and Job Satisfaction: A Questionable Payoff*, Survey Research Center, University of Michigan, prepared for National Institute of Education, Contract No. NIE–C–74–0136, Washington, D.C., 1975, pp. 30–31.

44. Many of these studies are summarized in Pascal, *op. cit.*

45. An analysis of training wage provisions in collective bargaining agreements corroborates the notion that there are minor economic disincentives for participating in this job training. In fact, the most prevalent payment practices set scales at the same level as the trainee earned in his former job. This approach accounted for almost one-half of the provisions and

workers in the study which set forth pay practices. Under these arrangements, workers would be paid the "journeyman scale," the "average" on his previous job, his "normal rate of pay," or would work at a higher-related job "without an increase in pay." The workers' previous income level, therefore, was protected during training, but he would be working in many instances at less than the rate for the new job while acquiring the necessary skills (see *Major Collective Bargaining Agreements: Training and Retraining Provisions, op. cit.*).

46. Quinn and Shepard, (*op. cit.*), p. 120.
47. See O'Meara, *op. cit.*, and Levine, *op. cit.* In a 1974 Conference on Paid Educational Leave sponsored by NIE and Rutgers University, union and management personnel responsible for tuition aid programs suggested several reasons for such low participation: (1) Workers are not likely to participate after working hours when they are tired and must attend to family responsibilities; (2) when workers can get time off during workday to attend classes, they usually do not continue to receive income from the employer for this time; (3) the worker is less inclined to take "vocationally relevant" courses than his employer would like; (4) workers frequently are unable to pay tuition when they enroll, even if the expenses will be reimbursed later; and (5) workers are frequently unaware of tuition aid opportunities, or are reticent to apply, distrustful of management, and fearful of rejection.
48. Quinn and Shepard, *op. cit.*, p. 122.
49. *Work: Desires, Discontents, and Satisfaction, op. cit.*, June 1974.
50. Mark Blaug ("Recurrent Education—The New Jerusalem"), policy research paper prepared for the Assistant Secretary for Education, U.S. Department of Health, Education, and Welfare, 1976 (mimeographed) reports that this is exactly what has occurred in the European countries which have recurrent education laws. In the United States, educational attainment is strongly related to the participation rate in the Veterans' education benefits (GI bill) program (*Veterans Benefits Under Current Educational Programs*, Veterans Administration Bulletin No. 20–74–3, April 1974).
51. Experience with the manpower training and work experience programs of the 1960's is instructive here. See Ashenfelter, *op. cit.*; Smith and Pitcher, *op. cit.* Joseph Froomkin (*Adult Education 1972: A Reanalysis*, policy research paper prepared for Assistant Secretary for Education, U.S. Department of Health, Education, and Welfare, Washington, D.C., 1977), moreover, notes that the delivery of adult education in the United States is not as skewed, to the rich as is commonly believed, or as is implied by looking at participation statistics. When the outreach of adult education is measured in terms of "total contracted hours" (the sum of hours in completed, on-going and dropped courses), there is not much of a difference between income groups. In 1972, for example, persons enrolled from households with incomes below $5,000 enrolled in courses which accounted for over 20 percent of the total hours offered that year, while persons from a higher-income group, representing 15 percent of the population took courses amounting to 17 percent of the total. Low-income participants in adult education take courses with more hours than higher-income participants, and they drop out more frequently. High-income persons participate more frequently but they take shorter courses and more frequently complete them successfully than lower-income persons.
52. Calculations derived from unpublished data from the *Triennial Survey on Adult Education*, provided by the National Center for Education Statistics.
53. Dennis Gallagher, "The Present State of Adult Education," National Manpower Institute, Washington, D.C., 1974 (mimeographed).

54. Freeman, *op. cit.*, Berg, *op. cit.;* Froomkin, *op. cit.;* Fred Best and Barry Stern, *Lifetime Distribution of Education, Work, and Leisure: Research, Speculations, and Policy Implications of Changing Life Patterns,* Institute for Educational Leadership, Washington, D.C., December 1976, pp. 36–41.

55. Quinn and Shepard, *op. cit.*, pp. 217–218; Quinn and Baldi de Mandilovitch, *op. cit.*, p. 27.

56. O'Toole, *op. cit.*

57. Freedman, *op. cit.*

58. *Ibid.*, p. 75.

59. *Ibid.*, pp. 25–29.

60. O'Toole, *op. cit.*

61. Berg, *op. cit.*

62. Unpublished projections, Bureau of Labor Statistics, 1976.

63. *Ibid.*

64. Froomkin, *op. cit.* Supply and Demand for persons with Postsecondary Education, *op. cit.*

65. Froomkin states that "during the 1960–70 period, a fortuitous set of circumstances resulted in an equilibrium or slight shortage of persons with college degrees. This equilibrium or shortage was brought about as a result of important shifts in employment in the economy. The sectors which employed a high proportion of professional and managerial workers grew considerably faster than the others, and large numbers of college graduates found jobs in education, the health industry, other social services, and government. During the same decade, the wages of college graduates employed in the nonprofit sector increased more rapidly than those of college graduates in the profit sector. By 1969, the year for which earnings are reported in the 1970 census, average rates of pay in both sectors were equal. Thus political developments which allowed the nonprofit sector to grow, and administrative and political decisions which affected rates of pay, both favored college graduates.

"It appears that little can be learned about the rate of substitution of non-college for college-educated manpower, and vice-versa, from an examination of the differences in their remuneration, either by occupation or for all occupations industry by industry. The market for college manpower was very competitive, and differences in the wages of college-educated personnel in different occupations narrowed substantially between 1959 and 1969.

"By contrast, the experience of person with a partial college education could provide some estimates of what happens when groups with more education substitute for those with a lower educational attainment. This substitution has occurred in a number of white-collar as well as blue-collar occupations. In technical occupations, persons with some postsecondary training were substituted for both college graduates and persons with no postsecondary training. Unfortunately, comparisons for the total United States do not divulge any clear-cut trend, and more detailed econometric examination industry by industry is indicated."

66. Froomkin, *op. cit.*, p. 19.

67. *Ibid.* Individuals with some but less than 4 years of college will also find it necessary to reduce their increasing dependence on the nonprofit sector. In 1970, the proportion of persons with some college in this sector was 17 percent; between 1970 and 1975, roughly half of all the new jobs filled by persons with some college education were outside the profit sector.

68. *Ibid.*, p. 17.

69. Bob Whitmore, "Educational Attainment of Workers, March 1975," *Monthly Labor Review* 99 (2) : 46–48, 1976.

70. U.S. Bureau of the Census, *Current Population Reports*, Series P–60, Nos. 75 and 101, "Money Income of Families and Persons in the United States." Government Printing Office, Washington, D.C., 1970 and 1976. From table 47 in No. 75, and from table 58 in No. 101.

71. Froomkin, *op. cit.*, p. 4.

72. *Ibid.*, p. 5.

73. Stephen Dresch, "Demography, Technology, and Higher Education: Toward Formal Model of Education Adaptation," *Journal of Political Economy* 83 (3) : 535–569, 1975.

74. Froomkin, *op. cit.*, pp. A–14–15.

75. Berg, *op. cit.*

76. Richard Freeman, "Youth Employment Opportunities: Changes in the Relative Position of College and High School Graduates," in Wolfbein (ed.), *op. cit.*, pp. 101–123.

77. *Survey of Working Conditions, op.cit.*

78. Quinn and Shepard, *op. cit.*, p. 217.

79. See summary of several studies on this issue in Robert Quinn, Graham Staines, and Margaret McCullough, *Job Satisfaction: Is There a Trend?* Manpower Research Monograph No. 30, U.S. Department of Labor, Washington, D.C., 1974.

80. It is difficult, nonetheless, to determine whether being overqualified is perceived to be a problem among those who say they are. Extant research does not give sufficient attention to "field of study," which ought to be included as a control variable to determine whether or not individuals taking vocationally relevant courses are as frustrated at not being able to apply their skills in a work setting as individuals who did not expect their studies to be related to their subsequent work experience. For example, it is possible that the labor market is poor for graduates in the humanities, but this is not necessarily relevant for those who select such a field of study. Such persons may appropriately be dissatisfied with many aspects of the state of society, including the availability of nontrivial jobs in the economy in general, and may also be more articulate than the average worker in expressing such dissatisfactions. But unhappiness about these points is still different from unhappiness about being cheated or mislead concerning the expected economic returns to a bachelor's degree in such a field as art history.

81. O'Toole, *op. cit.*

82. Berg, (*op. cit.*, pp. 86–104) cites several studies showing no or a slightly negative relationship between educational attainment among workers in several blue-collar and white-collar occupations and achievements normally prized by managers, such as productivity, attendance, and loyalty (lack of turnover).

83. E. James Maxey et al., "Trends in the Academic Abilities, Background, Characteristics and the Educational and Vocational Plans of College-bound Students 1970–72, to 1974–75," American College Testing Service, Research Report No. 74, Iowa City, Iowa, 1976.

84. Alexander Astin, *The American Freshman: National Norms for Fall 1975*, American Council of Education and University of California in Los Angeles, 1975.

85. *National Longitudinal Study of the High School Class of 1972, op. cit.*

86. *First National Assessment of Career and Occupational Development: An Overview*, National Assessment of Educational Progress, National Center for Education Statistics, U.S. Department of Health, Education, and Welfare, Washington, D.C., 1976.

87. American Council on Education, *Financing Part-time Students: The New Majority in Postsecondary Education*, Report of the Committee on the

Financing of Higher Education for Adult Students to the Office of Governmental Relations, Washintgon, D.C., 1974.

88. The GI bill is not used much to support part-time study, although such use is permitted. In November 1975 approximately 2 percent of college students supported by the GI bill were enrolled less than halftime. Among noncollege participants in the program, who normally constitute about 35 to 40 percent of the total, only 28 percent study part time (i.e., less than 30 clock hours per week) when correspondence students are included, or 11 percent when they are not (*Veterans Benefits Under Current Education Programs*, Information Bulletin, Veterans Administration, Washington, D.C., November 1975).

89. Proponents of financial assistance to low-income adults to continue their education also cite other barriers to participation such as lack of child care, transportation, housekeeping, working hours that conflict with class hours, etc. Overcoming these barriers make sense for many reasons among which additional educational opportunity is only one.

90. Ann Richardson and Laure Sharp, *Feasibility of Vouchered Training in WIN: Report on the First Phase of the Study*, Bureau of Social Science Research, Washington, D.C., December 1974; Ann Richardson and Laure Sharp, *The Early Experience in Vouchering On-the-Job Training*, Bureau of Social Science Research, prepared for Employment and Training Administration, U.S. Department of Labor, December 1975; Ann Richardson, *Summary of Findings on the Administrative Feasibility of Vouchering Skill Training in the WIN Program*, Bureau of Social Science Research, prepared for the Employment and Training Administration, January 1977.

91. George Nolfi and Valerie Nelson, *Strengthening the Alternative Postsecondary Education System: Continuing and Part-time Study in Massachusetts*, University Consultants, Inc., Cambridge, Mass., 1973.

92. Unpublished data from Survey of Adult Education 1972, National Center for Education Statistics.

93. The current structure of the BEOG program is such that by raising the amount of income an independent student could earn, the number of eligibles would enlarge. With limited funding the increased number of higher income independent students would benefit at the expense of lower income independent students. Only at full funding would there be no such effect. To increase the number of eligibles, of course, will increase the cost of the program, if fully funded.

94. O'Neill and Ross, *op. cit.*

95. *Ibid.*, they found that the 10-percent increase in earnings due to vocational training holds only for full-time and continuous participants (GI bill users). Their data indicate that part-time vocational users would not participate at all if full-time participation was made mandatory. Detailed cross tabulations of earnings profiles show that after controlling for personal characteristics, part-time users tend to have higher earnings than full-time users before training. This suggests that the part-time participants already have relatively good jobs and that they would therefore opt not to participate full time.

96. Nealey and Goodale, *op. cit.* A similar survey using a larger and more representative sample was conducted in Alameda County, Calif., in August 1976. Approximately 800 county employees from several occupational groups were surveyed. The study is being readied for publication by Fred Best, Quality of Life Research Associates, Washington, D.C.

97. An interesting "cafeteria plan" for providing workers with time-income tradeoff options has been put into effect by the County of Santa Clara, Calif.

The plan gives employees the choice between keeping their current hours and pay or three additional pay-hour options. As described in a memo to employees dated July 16, 1976, these three options are: (*a*) 5 percent of current income traded for 10½ days off, (*b*) 10 percent of current income traded for 21 days off, and (*c*) 20 percent of current income traded for 2 periods of 21 days off. During the first 6 months of the program, approximately 10 percent of the county employees participated, taking between 5 and 10 percent of their worktime off.

98. See, for example, Pascal, *op. cit.*; Wirtz, *op. cit.*; Nolfi and Nelson, *op. cit.*; Mushkin, *op. cit.*; J. R. Gass, "Education, Work and the Quality of Life," *OECD Observer*, No. 67, December 1973; Gosta Rehn, "For Greater Flexibility of Working Life," *OECD Observer*, No. 62, February 1973; Archibald Evans, *Flexibility in Working Life*, Organization for Economic Cooperation and Development, Paris, 1973; Alan Cartter, "The Need for a New Approach to Financing Recurrent Education," National Institute of Education, Washington, D.C., March 1973; Juanita Kreps, *Lifetime Allocation of Work and Income*, Duke University Press, Durham, N.C., 1970; Norman Kurland, "Financing Lifelong Learning—an Approach to an Age-Neutral Educational Entitlement," Study of Adult Education, Albany, N.Y., February 1975; Henry Levin, *Postsecondary Entitlements: An Exploration*, paper prepared for National Institute of Education, Washington, D.C., March 1975; Charles Benson and Harold Hodgkinson, *Implementing the Learning Society*, Jossey-Bass, San Francisco, 1974.

99. These efforts and related research literature are summarized in Sidney High and Joyce Cook, "Vocational Education and Its Relationship to Career Education." Bureau of Occupational and Adult Education, U.S. Office of Education, 1976 (mimeographed).

100. This project is described by Robert Stump, "Occupational Mobility and Career Planning," Remarks at the Second Annual Career Education Forum, Washington, D.C., February 1976; "Plan for a Study of Transferable Skills," Center for Vocational Education, The Ohio State University, Columbus, Ohio, 1976 (mimeographed).

101. Concern for career ladders and expanding the supply of manpower to meet national needs in critical areas had led to Federal support of occupational and educational analysis in a few fields. For example, the Child Development Associate program, funded by the Office of Child Development—in anticipation of Federal legislation likely to expand child care programs—has studied skills and knowledge transferrable up rungs of a career ladder and identified new skills required for each rung. This program has linked certification and training components so that a person can enter at a low rung (according to tested competencies) and through experience and training designed to develop specific skills move upward after recertification testing at each rung. The program does not, however, concern itself with projecting what competencies individuals certified at various levels could bring to other or new jobs if the child development associate market suddenly dried up, or how horizontal mobility might be increased with the addition of relatively few training activities.

102. This clearinghouse need not be a separate entity. It could be merged with either the Clearinghouse for Adult Education or for Career Education or for Lifelong Learning. The important element is that "flexibility in working life" would be the organizing principle for deciding the content of many of the materials to be collected and produced.

103. The young need basic, general, and comprehensive information about education and occupations, in contrast to most adult jobseekers who require

operational short-run and specific information about the labor market, particularly with respect to the salability or transferability of their skills to other occupations.

104. Many of the precedents for reemployment rights after a leave of absence can be found in the administration of the Veterans' Reemployment Rights law, which has been operative for 30 years.

Glossary of Key Terms
and Abbreviations
and Acronyms

Basic Skills: fundamental reading and computational skills which are the basis of later learning and achievement.

Career Education: planned educational experiences through which one learns about and prepares to engage in work as part of her or his way of living.

Career Information: the sum of: (1) Occupational information, which is needed for vocational choice, and (2) educational information, which is needed by the person who has made at least a tentative vocational choice and desires some formal schooling or training to prepare for entry or reentry into an occupation or group of occupations.

Career-Type Work: work that has advancement potential and access to skill development opportunities. This type of work is more likely to be skilled than unskilled, and it pays better than non-career-related work.

Competency-Based Education: education that results in demonstrable knowledge, abilities, and skills.

Manpower Training: job-oriented or vocational training normally provided outside of formal school settings.

Vocational Education: education in one or more semiskilled, skilled, or technical occupations, provided by a school which is separately organized under the direction of its own administrator.

Acronyms

BEOG=Basic Education Opportunity Grant
BLS=Bureau of Labor Statistics
CPS=Current Population Survey
CETA=Comprehensive Employment and Training Act
DOC=Department of Commerce
DOL=Department of Labor
EBCE=Experience-Based Career Education
ES=U.S. Employment Service
ESEA=Elementary and Secondary Education Act
FIPSE=Fund for the Improvement of Postsecondary Education
GAO=General Accounting Office
HEW=Department of Health, Education, and Welfare
LEA=Local Education Agency
MDTA=Manpower Development and Training Act
NAEP=National Assessment of Educational Progress
NCES=National Center for Education Statistics
NDEA=National Defense Education Act
NIE=National Institute of Education
OE=U.S. Office of Education
OIS=Occupational Information System
R. & D.=Research and Development
VEA=Vocational Education Act
WECEP=Work Experience and Career Exploration Program

146